The Dream of an Acts-like Church

The Dream of an Acts-like Church

Copyright © 2017 by Yong-jo Ha
Translated by Aimee Bak
All rights reserved.

First Edition _ July 26, 2007
Second Revised Edition 1 _ November 6, 2017
Second Revised Edition 3 _ January 12, 2023
Published by Duranno Ministry
Duranno Ministry, 38, 65-gil, Seobinggo-ro, Yongsan-gu, Seoul, Republic of Korea
Publishing Department _ TEL +82-2-2078-3332 FAX: +82-80-749-3705

"사도행전적 교회를 꿈꾼다"
By Yong-jo Ha
Copyright © 2007 by Duranno Ministry
Originally published in Korean by Duranno Ministry

http://www.duranno.com
rights@duranno.com

This edition is published by permission of Yong-jo Ha. No part of this book may be reproduced in any from without permission in writing from the publisher, except in the case of brief quotations embodies in critical articles or reviews.

All Scripture quotations, unless otherwise indicated, are taken from the New International Version.
All footnotes are the translator's comments.

Printed in Republic of Korea

ISBN 978-89-531-3007-4 03230

> Duranno, the Korean transliteration of Tyrannus, was a place in Ephesus where the Apostle Paul discipled Christians with the Word of God who had received the Holy Spirit during his third missionary voyage. With the same spirit of Acts 19:8-20, Duranno Ministry strives to first, assist pastors in their ministry and train lay leaders; second, to provide support for foreign missions through Tyrannus International Ministries (TIM), our publications and resources; and finally, to spread a healthy Christian culture through our All Nation's Praise and Worship and family ministries. Duranno, which was established on December 22, 1980, will continue on this mission until the day of our Lord's return.

The Dream of an Acts-like Church

Onnuri Community Church's Ecclesiology
and Pastoral Philosophy

Yong-jo Ha

Duranno

To my wife, Hyeong-gi Lee,
my son, Sung-seok, and my daughter, Sung-ji,
who waited for me endlessly and loved me dearly.

| TABLE OF CONTENTS |

Prologue   The Dream of an Acts-like Church   8

Part 1 :
Being Led by Grace

My Life and My Faith   27 | Walking in the Way of the Lord   59

Part 2 :
Ecclesiology

The Standard for Ecclesiology Is the Ecclesiology of Jesus   89
Ecclesiology Found in Acts   97

Part 3 :
Pastoral Philosophy

The Standard for Pastoral Philosophy Is the Ecclesiology of Acts   119

Part 4 :

Pastoral Philosophical Methodology

Worship 145 | Ministry 167 | Sermons 195
Nurturing System 215 | Small Groups and Community 233
Evangelism 243 | Missions 265

Part 5 :

Team Ministries and Leadership

Team Ministries: The Driver of Church Revival 289
Leadership That Achieves God's Dream 299

Part 6 :

Singing the Love Sonata

God's Love Story for Japan: Love Sonata 327

Epilogue   When I think about the Church, I feel happy. 360

Prologue

The Dream of an Acts-like Church

The very church of the Book of Acts

When I think about the Church, I get full without eating and excited even when tired. Despite the depth of life's pains and hardships, when I think about the Church, I feel happy. The Church is the key, the way and the spirit that moves the world. So when the Church becomes corrupt, the world becomes corrupt. On the other hand, when the Church is alive, the world is full of hope.

I dreamed of the church described in the Book of Acts when planting Onnuri Church. Before starting Onnuri Church, I served as an assistant pastor at Mapo Church. I had also been trained in a seminary by a pastor from Seoul who was like a strict *seonbi*, a traditional Confucian scholar from olden days. Then, unexpectedly, I came to lead a "celebrity church" where I served for seven years and was able to expand my horizons. There I experienced ministry at the center of pop culture.

After some time, my health deteriorated. I had to give up serving the church and went to England. My plan was to get some rest and study while there. But once again, unexpectedly, I came across Ealing Church, an immigrant church in England, and ministered there. I was able to share in the joys and sorrows of immigrants and Korean expatriates of trading companies who were living lonely lives in an immigrant community.

England, to me, was like a spiritual cradle. It was there where I met a missions organization and spiritual giants who determined the direction of my ministry.

During my first year in England, I received blessings from London Bible College, an evangelical and academic school that planted in me a seed of hope for the Gospel and for academic study.

In the second year, I experienced a year of blessings at a missions organization called WEC, Worldwide Evangelization for Christ. I was trained with Jae-hwan Lee, a missionary, and president of Come Mission. I can say that the foundation of Onnuri Church's mission ministry was established there. Also, the fellowship with All Nations Bible College expanded my view on mission work.

During the third and final year, which was perhaps the most inspiring, I met Rev. John Stott at the London Institute and learned about the problems of modern society and how those issues relate to the ministry. Also, I met Rev. Jim Graham who led a Holy Spirit ministry. I learned about the powerful and beautiful work of the Holy Spirit from him.

Around the time I was about to leave England after receiving such blessings, Soon-young Choi, the former chairman of Shindonga Group in South Korea contacted me. He said that there was a site for a church in Dongbu Ichon-dong and asked me if I would be interested in starting a ministry there.

I didn't have plans to do a ministry in Seoul back then. I started to ponder this with my wife, and this deliberation turned into prayer.

"God, is it your will for me to minister in Seoul?" I prayed. "There are already many churches and pastors in Seoul. Must I serve there? Can't I go to the countryside or the mission field?"

After praying for a long time, I came to understand God's heart. His heart was not to build a church of people who prioritize denominations or institutions but to establish a church He desires. That is, to establish the very church revealed in the Book of Acts.

"The very church revealed in the Book of Acts!"

The moment I realized this, my heart started to race. A burning passion and courage began to fill me, and a wave of inspiration swept over me. I couldn't sleep for a few days after that moment. In fact, that excitement and thrill didn't last for just a few days but has continued to burn within me even today, 20 years later. When I think about the church, I am moved and feel happy like a little child.

After having the vision of "the very church revealed in the Book of Acts," I came to like the expressions, "the very Holy Spirit" and "the very Jesus."

Have you experienced a living church?

Have you experienced a church that is filled with vitality and joy, a church where the power and miracles of God are made manifest, a church where love and grace overflow? I pointed out earlier that the world has become corrupt because churches have died.

Run away from the churches that are empty shells. Expel false churches that operate under the name of "church." In Japan, the Unification Church[1] calls itself a "church" and Aum Shinrikyo, a Japanese cult, also uses the name "church." Real churches are hidden, and the word "church" has been defiled.

Satan is well aware of the weaknesses of people. Because churches are important, Satan makes pseudo-churches or false churches to confuse people. But he doesn't stop there. As salvation in Jesus is a precious truth, Satan devised the Salvation Sect[2] to lead people away from true salvation. And since the Holy Spirit is so important, Satan created impersonal and extreme Holy Spirit followers to make others shun the very Holy Spirit. Furthermore, to water down the amazing doctrine of the Second Coming of Jesus, Satan created Dami Mission[3] to lure people to cults. Finally, knowing that the very Jesus is so important, Satan has often created a false Jesus or pseudo-Jesus, which was why Sun-myung Moon and other cults and heretical denominations have appeared.

The most heartbreaking thing is that churches that belong to our glorious Lord are attacked and treated like prostitutes because of pseudo-churches.

---

1 A cult founded in South Korea by Sun-myung Moon in 1954.
2 This religious movement is criticized by conservative Christian denominations for its salvation doctrine.
3 The Dami Mission was a cult founded in South Korea by Jang-rim Lee. Lee preached that the world would end on October 28, 1992.

The Church is the body of Christ, and Christ is the head of the Church. We meet and experience Jesus and hear His voice in churches. Meeting people in churches is the same as meeting Jesus in them. It is not about meeting with their statuses or positions, such as pastors, elders or deacons, but about encountering Christ who is in them. Through the sermons of a preacher, we hear the words of Jesus. Through other Christians, we feel the heart of Jesus.

When you go to church, despair and suicidal thoughts disappear. You stop thinking about divorce. Churches are holy companions and the ark of salvation in this world.

The model of a biblical, ideal and healthy church is the church revealed in Acts. We call that church the Early Church. The church from the Book of Acts has several characteristics.

The first characteristic:
Ecclesiology and pastoral philosophy

Biblical ecclesiology is the backbone of a healthy church, and as shown in the Book of Acts, pastoral philosophy is like the systematic structure of the Church.

Most churches today lack systems, including biblical ecclesiology or an Acts-like pastoral philosophy. Instead, they minister using traditional or denominational methods. Ministries are often influenced by prejudice or delusion, which is why congregations are often puzzled when their pastors decide to change the way they do their ministry every time they attend a seminar or receive new training.

A blueprint for a five-story building is different from that of a

100-story structure. The design for a building with one hundred floors should be far more sophisticated. A good plan is a must in constructing a sturdy building. Another important consideration is the building's foundation. We cannot see the foundation. All we can see is the external facade. Much like actual skyscrapers, churches that are built with an elaborate blueprint and on a solid foundation will not crumble in the face of an earthquake, typhoon or storm.

Churches are attacked by various philosophies, ideologies, and religions of the world. How then can we build a healthy church? To build a healthy church, we need biblical ecclesiology and pastoral philosophy as shown in Acts. Ecclesiology and pastoral philosophy are the system, frame, and blueprint of a church. So, if the ecclesiology and pastoral philosophy are not strong, the overall health of the church will be unstable as well.

Biblical ecclesiology

First of all, what is "biblical ecclesiology"? Pastoral philosophy differs from pastor to pastor and church to church. However, ecclesiology should be the same across all denominations and churches because all churches belong to Jesus. In this sense, we should guard ourselves against "theological ecclesiology," which is influenced by the ideas and practical problems of the time.

Pastoral philosophy in the Book of Acts

Pastoral philosophy is in the Book of Acts; the church featured in Acts is the church of Jesus realized on earth. Acts is like a textbook that transcends time and teaches how churches should be administered.

Take a look at the church in the Book of Acts! It was not a perfect church. It made many mistakes. The Early Church members sometimes fought and were separated. In these ways, it seems as though the Early Church is no different from the churches we see today.

Yet, the church in Acts is entirely different from churches today because in that church Jesus was Lord, the Holy Spirit manifested, and God received the glory. It prevailed against Rome and transformed the world. That is not all. It turned the world upside down for 2,000 years. Its influence extended to politics, economics, society, and culture. There were no areas not impacted by the church.

The Acts-like church

The church in Acts did not have a building or an institutional system, but it had love and the Holy Spirit. Now, turn your attention to churches today! They have buildings, denominations, institutionalized systems, and people, but they lack the one thing that is truly important: love! Also missing are the glory of God, the lordship of Jesus and the manifestation of the Holy Spirit!

When the ecclesiology of Jesus and the pastoral philosophy shown in Acts are applied to churches today, amazing things will happen, as experienced by the Early Church. If modern-day churches are able to go back to the church in Acts, they will be renewed.

The defining characteristic of the Early Church is that it was built on the ecclesiology of Jesus and the pastoral philosophy of Acts. This is the background with which Onnuri Community

Church was built in 1984.

The second characteristic: Preaching and teaching the Word

The Scripture is a guide from God, given to people. When you live according to the Word, not only will you be saved, but you will also undergo changes in your character and experience miracles in your life. We can learn about the Word through sermons and Bible studies. If ecclesiology and pastoral philosophy are the blueprint and foundation of churches, then sermons and Bible studies are the structure of the building. The structure needs to be strong in order for a building to be safe.

Sermons

Sermons can be categorized into expository sermons and title sermons.[4] Expository sermons explain the Word of God verse by verse (exegesis), while topical sermons quote the Scriptures to deliver a topic (eisegesis). In expository sermons, the Word of God itself is the focus of the preaching, while in topical sermons, the topic makes up the preaching. While the Word of God is at the center in expository sermons, the subject matter or a situation can easily become the focus in topical sermons.

Bible study

There are various approaches to studying the Bible. You can investigate God's Word deductively or inductively, and can explore

---

4 Title sermons can be understood as topical sermons.

the Bible by connecting the entire Bible together or by concentrating on a specific historical era or incident. Of course, you can also study God's Word by focusing on doctrines, topics or Bible characters. While sermons are like proclamations of His Word with the intervention of the Holy Spirit, Bible study is a process of learning that mobilizes both reason and intelligence.

Quiet Time

In our daily lives, it is important to maintain a spiritual habit of meditating, applying, and sharing the Word of God. This is different from simply studying the Bible. Quiet Time is about finding yourself in God. You discover God and find yourself. Quiet Time is about listening to God's voice, recharging spiritually and resting in the Word.

One-to-one discipleship Bible study

One-to-one discipleship Bible study is different from the Bible study that is done in an open and public setting. In this style of Scripture study, people meet one-to-one, have fellowship with one another, and share their lives with each other. The Word and the Holy Spirit are at the center of the fellowship and sharing. It is about creating an open relationship to let Jesus penetrate deeply into their lives.

The third characteristic: Worship and ministry

Worship

When God's Word and the study of His Word work together in harmony, the first thing that will be revived is worship. Worship is the presence of the Holy Spirit and the glory of God. Worship is being spiritually moved. It is about tears shed from deep inside. It is passion and excitement that stir the heart. It is experiencing the glory of God and the anointing of the Holy Spirit. It is witnessing the manifestation of Jesus.

In true worship, evil spirits depart, heaven comes down, and heavenly gifts are revealed. In worship, God's healing and prophecy manifest and people start to speak in tongues. Dead cells in the body come to life again, and they praise God and shout to the heavens.

Worship is like being excited on your way to meet your loved one. It is being lost for words and fainting with a sigh after seeing the glory of God. Are you experiencing such worship, where there are miracles and healings and where evil spirits flee?

Ministry

Worship overflows with dynamic ministries. If worship is the body, the ministry is like the hands and feet. When the body is alive, the hands and feet move actively. Think of water overflowing from a reservoir. Ministry is like that overflowing water. When worship is alive and ministries come into action, the congregations start to truly grow. This is called discipleship. In particular, in such a church, discipleship among church members will thrive, and the anointing of the Holy Spirit will be revealed.

When the Holy Spirit's anointing manifests, a true community will be formed. Amazing gifts such as wisdom, knowledge, healing, speaking in tongues, and interpretation will appear. The world lives by the power of man, but churches live by the power of God. Singing a song with the power of the Holy Spirit and singing for the sake of singing is different. Also, speaking eloquently and preaching well are different. The church is a community of God's people with spiritual gifts, and churches influence the world through such a community of gifts. When ministries are alive, churches will become active.

However, there is one thing of which you must take caution. If you put too much emphasis on ministry, people will quickly burn out and fall into temptation. When you are exhausted from serving in ministries, you should immediately go back to worship. You must stop the ministry, quietly seek God, recharge yourself with His Word, and be healed by the Holy Spirit.

On the other hand, do not just stay in worship. You may become spiritually obese. You must use and release the spiritual energy you receive from worship.

The fourth characteristic: Personal evangelism and world mission

Passionate personal evangelism

When worship is revived and ministries are active as the Holy Spirit anoints the church, the voice of God will be heard and the passion in your heart will blaze. You will have the Father's heart for each soul. That is evangelism. Evangelism is all about having the heart of God. It is the power of the Holy Spirit. It is the tears shed and the deeply felt compassion for dying souls. Evangelism is something you do without being told and something you do even in an impossible situation. We don't evangelize at church, but church itself is evangelism. Personal evangelism is the Great Commission given to everyone whether you are a full-time pastor, part-time pastor or staff member. No one is exempt from personal evangelism.

Mission

Evangelism is the heart of God, and missions is the dream of God. God's dream is to disciple all nations. The Bible can be summarized in two words: "come" (come to the Lord) and "go" (go to the ends of the earth).

The secret behind reviving a church is to send missionaries. Miracles will happen when churches send missionaries no matter how difficult the situation is. Sacrificing and devoting oneself to God brings about spiritual change. Nothing is impossible when you risk your life for God. The church will be revived when you risk your life for the Lord. Man hinders revival, not God. When God comes, men should step aside and make way. We cannot drag God our way. Only God can lead us. Churches on a mission never perish. Churches on a mission cannot help but be revived.

Aspiring to be an Acts-like church

"An Acts-like church" is something that I consistently and constantly think about. It is the very church Jesus intended and showed in Acts. Why does the world today stay the same despite the great number of churches, seminaries, and pastors? It is probably because those churches are not like the Early Church in Acts.

As I lead Onnuri Community Church, I keep these questions in mind: What made up the true church in Acts, which was intended and shown by the Lord to be full of life? What made the church a real church?

The very church!

The very church intended and revealed by Jesus in Acts!

An Acts-like church!

This is my vision, and this is the vision of Onnuri Community Church.

Onnuri Community Church receives the 2,000/10,000 vision

As I ministered at Onnuri Community Church with the "The Acts-like Church" vision, I received another vision - the "2,000/10,000 vision" - which was to send out 2,000 missionaries and raise up 10,000 lay ministers by 2010. When I proclaimed this vision, an elder came to me and said, "Pastor, is that vision really from God?"

He meant that the vision seemed impossible. Later, the elder oversaw the team that dispatches missionaries, and he told me, "It really came true."

If you and I can do something on our own, why would we need God? Wouldn't it be enough for people to just work hard and do their best? God's dream is to make something impossible come true.

Prologue

On Easter Sunday 2007, our church sent our 1,000th missionary. We were surprised ourselves. Wow! Isn't this something only God could have done?

Acts 29, Onnuri Community Church's vision

Vision is important. I mean a vision that is truly for Jesus and a dream that is from Jesus. It is a kind of dream that excites you and causes you to lose sleep.

If an idea is devised by man only, it will weaken or be forgotten with time, no matter how unbelievable or amazing it may seem. However, a dream from God is new every day and does not fade, even after 30 or 40 years. Vision, dreams, and passion will keep you awake at night, make you skip meals, and drive you to pursue them even to the point of risking your life! That is the vision God has given me. A vision cannot be stopped, as much as trouble, hardship, persecution, famine, nakedness, danger, or sword cannot separate us from the love of Christ (Romans 8:35).

A person will go as far as the extent of his vision. You go as far as where a dream from God leads you. About 2,000 years ago, when the Holy Spirit came upon 120 people like wind and fire on Pentecost, the people could no longer sit quietly inside the room. Instead, they stormed out and proclaimed God's power. Similarly, people with God's vision are not afraid of any hardship. They are not afraid of pain or sickness. They are not worried about having no money.

People without vision are the unfortunate ones. People without vision are like animals because animals do not have dreams. However, those who have met God have a vision and a strong desire to share the new heaven, the new earth, and Jesus.

A dream to build a church

Jesus' vision is to establish the kingdom of God on earth. Yes, it is to build a church. Jesus said, "Foxes have dens and birds have nests, but the Son of Man has no place to lay his head" (Matthew 8:20). Jesus didn't have room to get married or go to school. For three years, he met anyone and everyone and worked until he was exhausted.

His dream was to die on the cross. We shouldn't say, "I want to die a painless death." What's wrong with dying painfully? Do you have to die peacefully? It is great if you can die peacefully, but even if you cannot, it doesn't matter. If only Jesus is pleased and if only God is delighted, it doesn't matter!

Jesus said, "Therefore go and make disciples of all nations" (Matthew 28:19). My church's vision is to continue to write Chapter 29 of Acts, following Jesus' command.

The Book of Acts is not finished yet. This part of Scripture is about Christians sharing the Gospel with all nations in obedience to Jesus' command, and it is still ongoing.

Acts 29! This is why Onnuri Community Church exists, and it is a vision that cannot be abandoned.

The Book of Acts is not finished yet. This part of Scripture is about Christians sharing the Gospel with all nations in obedience to Jesus' command, and it is still ongoing.

My Life and My Faith

Walking in the Way of the Lord

PART 1:

BEING LED BY GRACE

The pastoral philosophy of a church is closely related to the experiences of the church's spiritual leader. My faith is shaped by my parents who lived godly lives.

1. My Life and My Faith

Unforgettable stories as we fled

My family fled to South Korea from Jinnampo, North Korea at the "January–Fourth Retreat" during the Korean War. My parents, older brother, sister, and I fled together. I was six years old at the time.

My mother had been a Christian since birth and my father was also a Christian. They met at church, got married, and lived a Church-centered life. Jinnampo Biseong-ri Church was my parents' spiritual home. My father participated in the young adults group, joined the choir, and served as a Sunday school teacher for children. My mother served with him. This is perhaps why they continued to serve in a choir and children's Sunday school all their lives, even after fleeing to South Korea, regardless of age, as long as their health permitted.

Whenever my parents talked about their escape, they would emphasize many times with a resolute look on their faces that they escaped with nothing but a Bible in their hands, trusting God. My father also told us about the cruelty of the communists and the horrible things they committed, such as "people's courts," executions by firing squad, along with plundering and raping women.

This story is about our family before we reached South Korea. In the middle of the night, as our entire family was fleeing along a wide road, we heard soldiers from the North Korean People's Army chasing us with guns. The soldiers were only interested in men and didn't care about young children and women. The moon was shining brightly, so there was nowhere to hide. We sat down at the bottom of a rice paddy, shaking with fear. My father lay flat next to the road, and then an amazing thing happened. When the soldiers were just about to pass my father, they decided to turn the other way and went to the other side. Why did they turn and change direction?

Our family remembers that night deep in our hearts when God protected us safely in his grace. By the way, our family developed an animosity towards communism because of our personal experiences like this.

I remember another story. We were on a boat named "Namyoungho," traveling from Incheon to Mokpo. The boat got damaged, and its engine room started to flood. As people attempted to drain the water from the engine room, they were surprised and said, "This is a miracle. With this much water, the boat should have already sunk. But how can it still be moving?"

The reason why my parents told my siblings and me these stories, again and again, was to make sure we remember that our family did not survive by chance at such trying moments. We survived because God intervened.

Every family has an unforgettable spiritual experience. It could be a story of one rising from the dead, winning over despair, or recovering from a difficult situation that one could never have survived but by the grace of God. My family also has such a story to tell.

Even in my memory, my family escaped with absolutely nothing. We had to start a miserable life, just like other displaced families. We hitched a ride on a boat from Jinnampo to Incheon. From Incheon, we had to move further south to Mokpo.

Mokpo was an extremely unfamiliar city for all of us. My family had no one to rely on, and it was the American missionaries from Southern Presbyterian Church that extended their hands to help. We started our life in South Korea as sojourners in a tent set up in the backyard of American missionaries. I can't express how much I liked it and how happy I was to live under their roof. I will never forget the memories of my family coming together to worship in the morning and evening.

From morning, my father had to work here and there to make a living. My mother would go to more rural areas and do day labor. I sold *pulbbang*[5] bread, *bungeobbang*[6] bread, and traditional

---

5 Pulbbang bread is a kind of street food made with a flour batter.

6 A kind of pulbbang pastry in the shape of a fish. It has a sweet red bean filling.

taffies called *yeot*. I would yell, "Buy *pulbbang*! Buy *yeot*!" These are still fresh in my memory. I remember following my brother with a runny nose, wearing worn-out rubber shoes and tattered underclothing.

I was told that as a little boy I used to smile a lot and liked saying "hi" to people. The only way I could help my brother sell was to stand behind him and say "hi!" to everyone with a big smile. If someone did not respond, I would chase after them and say "hi" again.

Such a habit became my trademark even to this day as I serve a church as a pastor. I am not that good looking. But when you look at it as a whole, I am not that ugly, either. The highlight of my face is my smile.

The impression of missionaries

I admired the American missionaries I met in those days. Although I had never seen an American before, their loving smiles, care, and encouragement are fresh in my memory. To me, it was amazing to see them pray and share the Gospel. The image of American missionaries giving me food and comforting me stayed in my heart for a long time. It was perhaps that beautiful image of American missionaries I encountered when I was young that led me to pursue a mission-focused ministry.

Later, we left our tent in the missionary's backyard and moved to a new place. It was a house of a non-Christian ship owner who was as old as my grandfather. Amazingly, the wife of the ship owner started to go to church after my father shared the Gospel with her. I grew up basking in her love. Later, we honored the couple as our own grandparents. It was the first relationship we established after fleeing the North.

Their house was big and fancy. It was a beautiful, handsome house overlooking the sea. We lived in a room next to its entrance. In front of this wealthy house, many war orphans, especially infants, were abandoned. We looked after those children. We encountered newborn infants wrapped in cloth with little notes on them that said, "We cannot raise our baby anymore since we don't have anything to eat. Please look after our child. We will never forget your goodness."

The number of children grew one after another. Soon, our home became a house of infants. To make a living, my father started a soy sauce factory while my mother looked after the babies.

My siblings and I grew up in this environment, which is probably what motivated me as an adult to have unconditional love for orphans and the poor. Little did I know that it would become a seed that would flourish and lead me to the path of becoming a pastor who looked after abandoned souls.

I was born in Jinnampo, Pyeongannam-do, North Korea, and lived there until I was five years old. From elementary school to middle school after fleeing the North, I resided in Mokpo, Jeollanam-do Province, and finally in Seoul, where I have lived since high school until today. These are my hometowns. If someone were to ask about my hometown, I would have to mention these three areas. The dialect we use in my home is a blend of North Korean, Jeolla province and Seoul dialects. In the end, I am indebted to Korea, which is why I love all the regions and have a responsibility to share the Gospel with them all.

My father fiercely believed in God.

Faith in God was the only vision that protected our family. Early morning prayers, Sunday worship, Wednesday worship, and Friday small group were a must.

My father was a thorough worshipper. He was all in for worshiping God. He knew that worshiping God while we live is the most important thing.

He rarely missed an early morning prayer. Every morning when I woke up, my mother's and father's beds would always be empty. My family worshipped God together twice a day, in the morning and evening. After returning from early morning prayer, my father would wake up the entire family and make sure we didn't skip morning worship, even if that meant we'd be late for school. Also, even if he had already fallen asleep, he would get up, put on proper clothes, gather us, and have evening service with us at 9 p.m.

We sang hymns together and then always read a chapter of Scripture. Even today, I can clearly remember us celebrating and shouting together, "We finished reading the New Testament today!" or "We completed the Old Testament today!" I often fell asleep when my father was praying during the service. My father's prayers were extremely long.

Our family's special Bible passage was Romans 12. We memorized the chapter together at important family events.

> "Therefore, I urge you, brothers and sisters, in view of God's mercy, to offer your bodies as a living sacrifice, holy and pleasing to God - this is your true and proper worship. Do not conform to the pattern of this world, but be transformed by the renewing of your

mind. Then you will be able to test and approve what God's will is - his good, pleasing and perfect will." (Romans 12:1-2)

Our family's hymn was hymn no. 469.

> Far away in the depths of my spirit tonight,
> Rolls a melody sweeter than psalm;
> In celestial-like strains, it unceasingly falls
> O'er my soul like an infinite calm.

My father never spanked or scolded us, but we didn't dare disobey his words. It wasn't just us. Whenever my dad showed up at Sunday school, the children would become quiet. He was quite strict.

Also, my father was a man of prayer. He prayed for four to five hours a day. He always carried a prayer diary and prayed. In his prayer diary, there were more than a hundred names written in tiny letters, including the names of the children in the infant home. He also filled up his notebook with more than 30 names of countries.

My father believed in God very fiercely. I still think that I can't follow God the way my father did. I just try to imitate him.

My mother was loving, humble and gentle.
My mother was a genuinely humble woman. So everyone would bow their heads to my mother. I think I inherited her smile. In her pocket, she always carried candies and instant noodle packets that children liked so she could share them with kids and poor neighbors.

My father was an extremely strict legalist, but my mother was a gentle advocate of grace. She was calm, forgiving, and would easily shed tears. She had a warm heart.

If my father was someone who experienced the Word, my mother was someone who experienced the Holy Spirit. She spoke in tongues, prophesied and cast out evil spirits. I watched how my parents believed in God and realized that experiencing the Holy Spirit makes a significant difference.

There is an image of my mother that I cannot forget even to this day. We were living in Mokpo, and my mom had just returned from a revival assembly. Her palms were all warm and red. Her body was on fire. She hugged me, and it felt hot as if a fiery seal were being stamped on my chest. I think my mother's body was burning like fire for about a week. Since then, she has driven out demons and laid hands on many. She carried her instant noodles or candies and shared the Gospel in mountain villages or impoverished areas behind our house.

Traditional folk religion was strong in Mokpo since it was a seaside village. There were many demon-possessed people because the village was prone to serious tragedies. My mother cast out evil spirits as she evangelized, and people would rush to see her do it. They were like those people in the Old Testament who watched how Elijah contested against the worshippers of Baal. The villagers witnessed demon-possessed people falling and foaming at the mouth in the name of Jesus Christ. Then some of them would accept Jesus saying, "God is strong!"

My mother used to say that she had to die in Mokpo because she said if she ever decided to leave, the entire city would grieve and be very sad. I would reply in jest, telling her, "Mom, you are free to delude yourself!"

I learned an important thing from my mother's life, and that is the joy of sharing the Gospel! I witnessed joy.

My mother who compassionately looked after poor people and my father who thoroughly believed in God became role models for my faith. Prayer, evangelism, faith, and the Holy Spirit! I have never given up such evangelical spirituality while serving in ministry. I do not ever want to lose it. Onnuri Community Church may seem like a cultured church at first sight, but that's not true. At its foundation, there is a dynamic evangelical spirituality. The image of a praying father and evangelizing mother is always inside of me and so, also, inside Onnuri Community Church.

My five siblings and I became a family living for God, probably because of our parents' spiritual influence. My oldest brother is a pastor; my oldest sister, a pastor's wife; my first younger sister, a lawyer's wife; my second younger sister, a wife of a missionary; and my youngest brother, a missionary.

Meeting Christ

Although I am a so-called "Christian from his mother's womb," being born to a Christian family and receiving infant baptism, it was through Campus Crusade for Christ (CCC) that I accepted Jesus Christ and devoted my life to Him. On August 4, 1966, in Ipseok, Gyeonggi-do Province, I accepted Christ as my Savior and experienced His cross and His hands covered with blood. This experience changed my life.

Every Christian has had a moment that led him or her to accept

Jesus Christ as one's Savior, whether the encounter was intellectual, emotional, or experiential. Someone might have experienced that Jesus is alive through the Word of God piercing through the deepest part of his or her spirit, not through a vision or a special experience. Some people have met Jesus while reading the Bible, some met Jesus while listening to a sermon, and some in the midst of intense pain and suffering. Some may meet the Lord by listening to His subtle voice after a sweeping storm.

I don't know how shocked I was when I met Jesus Christ for the first time. It was a shock that was hard to describe with words. This is because faith is not about ideas but experiences. There is the hymn I sang a lot in those days.

> O Jesus, Thou art standing,
> Outside the fast-closed door,
> In lowly patience waiting
> To pass the threshold o'er:
> Shame on us, Christian brothers,
> His name and sign who bear
> O shame, thrice shame upon us,
> To keep Him standing there!
> ("Jesus, Thou art Standing")

This hymn is just like my confession that although my Lord stood outside, knocking on my door, I did not respond. Until then, I believed in Jesus only with my knowledge and ideas. But when Jesus' hands covered in blood appeared to me in a vision, I met the Lord who touched my sins and iniquities. I experienced

1. My Life and My Faith

the Lord who changed me. There is another hymn that I used to sing a lot when I met Jesus.

> When I survey the wondrous cross
> On which the Prince of Glory died;
> My richest gain I count but loss,
> And pour contempt on all my pride.
> Forbid it, Lord, that I should boast,
> Save in the death of Christ, my God;
> All the vain things that charm me most,
> I sacrifice them to his blood.
>
> See, from his head, his hands, his feet,
> Sorrow and love flow mingled down.
> Did e'er such love and sorrow meet,
> Or thorns compose so rich a crown.
> Were the whole realm of nature mine,
> That were an offering far too small;
> Love so amazing, so divine,
> Demands my soul, my life, my all.
> ("When I Survey the Wondrous Cross")

I would sing this hymn in tears. I sang until I lost my voice. Even now, whenever I sing this song, I am deeply moved just as before. I can't tell you how much I love this song. This hymn talks about the blood and power of the cross, which I personally experienced. There was another hymn I sang as I think of Jesus at that time.

> In fancy I stood by the shore, one day,
> Of the beautiful murm'ring sea;
> I saw the great crowds as they thronged the way
> Of the Stranger of Galilee;
> I saw how the man who was blind from birth,
> In a moment was made to see;
> The lame was made whole by the matchless skill
> Of the Stranger of Galilee.
> And I felt I could love Him forever,
> So gracious and tender was He!
> I claimed Him that day as my Savior,
> This Stranger of Galilee.
>
> ("The Stranger of Galilee")

Whenever I sing this song, all trials, doubts, and tribulations melt away. I feel like I can hear the footsteps of the Lord coming towards me. I can sense the risen Lord so real. The thrill of meeting the Lord is coming back to me again.

Since then, I have loved Jesus passionately. When I look back, I cannot believe how I was able to do that. I would sing worship songs until I lost my voice. I prayed in tears. I stood up all night reading the Bible. The Bible verses I remember today are mostly the verses I memorized back then. Also, I named my quiet time journal "My Pensées" and regularly meditated on the Word. I lived like someone deeply in love and someone who is out of his mind. Eating or sleeping did not matter to me. I shared the Gospel day and night. I met death-row convicts in jail. I evangelized in Myeongdong, Namsan Mountain, or Sajik Park. I discipled students from the College of Liberal Arts and Sciences and College of Education of Seoul National University. I would go to Incheon every Sunday to evangelize people.

Among those with whom I was able to share the Gospel, some became elders, deaconesses, and even pastors of Onnuri Community Church. A storm must have stirred my spirit during those years. These days, there are times I feel a heaviness in my heart as I see younger pastors, assistant pastors, or missionaries wondering why they live such complacent lives.

Sharing the Gospel without fear

I underwent training at CCC for about seven years. One of the blessings I received from the missions organization was learning the joy of evangelism. In those days, I would share the Gospel and declare, "Believe in Jesus!" in a crowded bus even at midnight. I shared the Gospel in places like Namsan Mountain, Jangchung Park, Sajik Park and Seoul Station. In fact, there aren't many places I haven't been to evangelize. On my way home after midnight, I would sing praises although I felt exhausted. Back then, I sometimes skipped meals without realizing it because I didn't feel hungry. On days I couldn't evangelize, I felt like weeping and thumping my chest. My heart was heavy.

I used to play sports. I also took violin and calligraphy lessons because I liked them. However, as I started evangelizing people, I forgot about violin and calligraphy. I understand how some people are able to stop drinking alcohol after they believe Jesus. I understand why this is so, because it is more fun to believe in Jesus than to drink alcohol. They will naturally stop drinking because their joy is so intense, and the desire to continue drinking is naturally quenched.

CCC trains university students how to evangelize and sends them out into the world. We would go out and evangelize individually for two hours. Then, we would all come back together and talk about how we shared the Gospel. Every time we shared, there were numerous testimonies.

One day, a sister shared her testimony and told us that since she couldn't dare evangelize, she thought about what to do. Instead of evangelizing, she simply went to a coffee shop and thought she would just sit there drinking tea and listening to music until we gathered again after two hours. Then she noticed a woman sitting in front with her head bowed down. She seemed sad. For more than one hour, the woman sat like that, and so our sister thought, "How about sharing the Gospel with that lady?" The sister finally approached the woman and spoke. "Have you heard of the four spiritual laws?" she asked, as the lady sat still. "I would like to talk to you about God. Would you mind?"

So that's how she came to share the Gospel with the lady. When our sister led the lady in prayer accepting Christ, the woman started to cry uncontrollably.

After crying for a while, the lady took out a little bag from her handbag and confessed, "Actually, I went to 30 pharmacies to collect these pills because I wanted to commit suicide. I sat here after collecting enough medicine, then I heard about God's love from you. I don't need these pills anymore. You can take them."

The sister who shared the Gospel with the lady brought back the bag filled with drugs and said, "If I didn't share the Gospel with her, who knows what kind of choice she would've ended up making?"

We heard so many testimonies like that as we evangelized. This is one of the reasons we couldn't stop sharing the Word.

Also, we did a lot of "beggar evangelism," which is a method of evangelism introduced by the late pastor Joon-gon Kim, aiming to personally experience the events in the Book of Acts. Beggar evangelism means going to places without money for 15 days and sharing the Gospel. When we did this, we experienced many events and miracles similar to what was revealed in Acts. For instance, a brother who couldn't eat because of an ulcer was able to eat really well after evangelizing for 15 days. After spreading the Gospel this way, people's lives were turned upside down because of the living Lord.

I don't think we should have a separate team in church specifically designated to evangelize. I believe the whole church is called to share the Gospel, and all ideas and principles within a church should reflect this. There is nothing more important than sharing the good news.

Nothing apart from Christ should be the center of myself.

It is a fact that we are too obsessed with church, denominations, systems, and groups, and we groan in the midst of these.

I was deeply engaged with CCC for seven years from 1965 to 1972. I thought no other organizations served God better than CCC. It emphasized the Holy Spirit and the Gospel, and held the banner of bringing Korea back to Christ. CCC was also filled with many people who love the Lord. For some time, I deluded myself into thinking that being loyal to CCC was synonymous with being faithful to God, and I can't tell you how strong my conviction was. However, I learned later, no matter how great an organization is, an organization is an organization. It should not become an idol. I still hold fast onto this revelation.

A pastor who preaches eloquently or a pastor who greatly inspires us can easily become our idol since they are great men of God. But no matter how great a pastor is, he cannot be a substitute for Jesus or the Bible. We are just partnering with these groups, organizations or churches until Jesus comes again. These groups absolutely cannot take the place of Jesus.

It took me seven years to let go of CCC. Since I loved it so much, I debated with myself day and night whether I should leave this organization. This is why I understand so well how difficult it is for a Christian to free oneself from an organization or group that he or she has been deeply rooted into. But still, we must be set free. We must not be bound by anything or anyone other than Christ.

Jesus Christ and the Word of God should be at the center of our faith. Think about cult denominations. They appear as churches and claim the name of Jesus, but in reality, they can easily transform into an organization that stands against Christ.

I don't think denominations are wrong. I am part of a denomination and respect the denomination I belong to. However, denominations are not be absolute. The only absolute standard for us is Jesus Christ and his Word. Nothing more.

The experience I had at a missions organization served as a foundation for my ministry. As I ministered in church, I never gave up the spirit of missions organizations. A church is not a missions organization. However, a church can be an influential church when it has the dynamic spirit of a missions organization.

The church is different from missions organizations, but it should never lose the missions organization spirit. Nevertheless, no organization or group should take precedence over the Lord.

Entering into the suffering of illness

When I was a junior in college, I learned at a camp that I had tuberculosis, and so I had to take a break from school. At that time, I was evangelizing until midnight, not eating or sleeping well. I couldn't understand why God would allow me to get sick at such an urgent time. However, what can you do when your body is beginning to hurt? Taking medication and being hospitalized were extremely painful to me. It wasn't the illness so much as it was the fact that I couldn't evangelize.

And so, I started to encourage the patients around me in the hospital and evangelized them. People started calling me by a new nickname, "evangelist."

"Hey, evangelist, come over here," said one of the patients.

Most of the hospitalized patients heard me sharing.

When I was admitted and quarantined at a tuberculosis sanatorium in Incheon, I had nothing to do in the facility, so I started evangelizing, which was my specialty. I shared the Gospel with a patient whose lung was almost completely damaged. Later, the same patient experienced a miracle as his lung completely healed, and he became a pastor. Although I led Bible studies with other patients, I spent most of my time deeply praying to God, and reading and meditating on the Bible. God put me in a hospital and isolated me from others, making me lonely. He made me hopeless. Then, He led me to read just the Bible. He made me think only of Him.

One day when I was reading the Book of Psalms, a vision unfolded before my eyes. It was the second vision I saw.

> The rain was pouring, and I heard someone moaning outside. I opened the window and found a terribly poor beggar standing under the roof. He was carrying a little bag at his side and was shivering. He seemed extremely cold and starving. "What should I do?" I thought. Feeling so sorry for him, I opened the gate and approached him.
>
> "You must be cold and hungry?" I said. "Come inside and warm yourself and have some food."
>
> I let him in and prepared food for him. Then something miraculous happened. At that moment, the miserably poor beggar turned into our glorious Lord! In contrast, I turned into the sickest, most tired, exhausted, and tragic person in the world. Our positions took an 180-degree turn. Then, the Lord approached and hugged me. I was wearing stinky and filthy rags. That was the presence of the Lord. The Lord came to me… I couldn't help but cry when I looked into His eyes. It was at that moment that I realized I was pathetically waiting for the Lord. I thought I loved Him, but after meeting Him, I realized that He loved me and was waiting for me. It was the Lord who was waiting anxiously for me with the gift of love and salvation. Not minding all my shame, condemnation and contempt, He didn't move a step away from the door where I had

pushed him away. He was waiting for me there. He opened his bag and in it was a message: "I love you as much as the cross."

Then, He asked me, "Son, don't you want to be a pastor?"

I saw that vision 40 years ago, but it is still so vivid. Imagine how surprised I was. I lay down and cried my head off. A nurse rushed into my room and asked me what had happened. It was about 1:30 a.m. That night, while my face was still drenched with tears, I wrote in my journal:

> My Lord couldn't just love me or wait for me. He died for me on the cross. Now, He says He needs me. When else should I do but obey Him if not at this very moment? He knew that I would just throw away my life if I followed my own plans, and so He made me sick.

That night, I gave my entire life to Him. My illness became the first stepping stone of my ministry. I am who I am today because of the grace of God, as Paul confessed.

I think God carries fire in one hand and water in the other. I couldn't understand how I could get tuberculosis when I had been serving him passionately, but to Him, it was a fantastic plan.

"Ah! I wanted to serve the Lord with all my life as an influential elder," I told myself. "Why does he want me to go further and become a pastor?"

A more surprising thing happened the following day when my mother came from the countryside to visit me.

Out of nowhere, she told me, "Yong-jo, have you thought about becoming a pastor? I was praying last night and had a strange thought. That's why I rushed to see you."

When the voice of God spoke to me last night, it also spoke to my mother at the same hour while she was praying. But still, I told her, "I will think about it." I didn't give a definite answer. I didn't feel confident about becoming a pastor. Also, I think the natural instinct to escape kicked in. Yet, ultimately, I changed my mind and seriously contemplated becoming a pastor.

Later, I was miraculously released from the hospital and was sent home. Humans are cunning. When God heals people from being sick, they easily forget what He has done for them. This also happened to me, as I totally forgot about my experience with the Lord in the hospital and went on to serve in the military. I was serving for a while when my tuberculosis recurred. This was evidence that God doesn't forget, although a man may forget. As I suffered from tuberculosis again, I encountered God and learned that he will never let us go.

I was sent to a military tuberculosis nursing home in Masan. I wore a patient's gown and started the second round of medical treatment.

What could I do? I started sharing the Gospel again. When all my paths were blocked, I began to share God's Word to people. I started an early morning prayer, targeting patients in military tents. I chased people to evangelize them. Then, an assistant pastor asked me to preach in the barracks, so I did and also conducted Bible studies. I was neither a pastor nor an assistant pastor, but as I preached and evangelized fervently, to my surprise, people listened carefully, and miracles happened - evil spirits were cast out, and the sick were healed.

There was one person I cannot forget. He stayed in the same barracks where I stayed, and he was a staff sergeant, a career soldier. He had been a gangster before. He had gotten into a group fight and ended up killing someone. He was afraid of being caught by the police, so he entered the military and became a career soldier. His father was heartbroken because of him. In the middle of winter, his father came to visit him in our barracks, but a sad thing happened. His father unfortunately slipped on an icy road and died. The staff sergeant, perhaps overwhelmed by the pangs of his conscience and guilt from feeling responsible for his father's death, bullied other privates.

One winter day, he got so drunk that he committed an unspeakably barbaric act in the barracks. He hit his superior. He caused a disturbance for a while, and then he tried to push his own head into the heater's blazing fire, yelling that he deserved to die. I grabbed his head, and as I wrestled with him, I prayed. That very moment, the Holy Spirit manifested and all of a sudden, an oppressive man became gentle like a child. For the first time, I witnessed an evil spirit leaving a person. After that incident, that man changed a lot.

There was another person that I cannot forget. He was a brother who used a bed right next to mine. He had only received an elementary education, but I never met anyone who could swear more than he. Whenever he opened his mouth, he would start his sentence with a curse and then end with another one. I realized how many swear words exist in the world because of him. To evangelize him, I used the Four Spiritual Laws, and honestly, I didn't expect him to become a Christian at all. Since he swore all the time, I thought there would be no space for the Gospel in his heart.

Amazingly, however, he began to believe in Jesus. He never skipped early morning prayer meetings. He was suffering from tuberculosis for the third time and was in bad shape. He may have held onto God more because he was desperate. He clung to the Bible. He read the Bible so eagerly that later on, I would amuse myself watching him read the Word. He said he realized for the first time that reading the Bible could be fascinating. I asked him what was so interesting. He replied that his heart burned like fire when reading the Book of Acts.

He knew Jesus. He believed Jesus as it is written in the Bible. The Holy Spirit changed him, and my heart also went ablaze as I watched him. Yes, one thing I learned clearly is that there are many things that cannot be understood merely with the human mind.

So, that's how I spent my time in the military, and I eventually got discharged due to my illness. Then, God led me to study theology. In fact, although I heard God's voice, I was afraid of becoming a pastor. On the last day to apply for the Presbyterian University and Theological Seminary in Gwangnaru, I hesitated until the last minute. I did rock-scissors-paper with a friend and said that if I won, I wouldn't submit the application, and if I lost, I would.

I lost.

I told myself, "I can submit my application and not take the exam," but I ended up taking the test. As I took the exam, I convinced myself, "I don't have to go even if I pass."

I passed.

Then I thought, "I don't have to go if I don't pay the tuition." Soon after, I had money to pay for college, and this was how I got into the seminary.

The sermon at the first chapel was this.

"Is there someone who has come to the seminary because he has deluded himself that God has called him? It's not too late. You may go back. When a person who should not be a pastor becomes one, God will suffer, that person will suffer, and his congregation will suffer as well. So, please be clear about this and go back."

Strangely enough, most of the freshmen who heard the sermon wavered. I also couldn't stop thinking, "Maybe his message is for me?" Even as I was already studying theology, I thought to myself, "I will attend one more semester to confirm if this is truly my calling." Well, I did, and that's how I became a pastor. When I think about it, it's amazing and also something I can't understand.

Illness to illness, but living in His grace

When I was first diagnosed with tuberculosis, the medicines that were given to me were all primary drugs such as relief patches, isoniazid, and streptomycin. At that time, there weren't any sophisticated drugs like we have nowadays. I had to take a palm full of medication. As a side effect of taking too much medicine for a long time, I suffered from diabetes and hepatitis. Hepatitis developed into hepatocirrhosis, and hepatocirrhosis became liver cancer. Eventually, I would receive surgeries. Later, cancer recurred five times, and I had to undergo surgeries again. What's surprising was that no matter how many tests I took, they showed that there was only a trace of liver cancer but the liver cancer itself was completely gone. God is amazing. He removed it and healed me completely. I suffered from diabetes for more than 30 years. It became my chronic disease, and high blood pressure is a byproduct that naturally follows. Recently, my condition developed into renal insufficiency. I receive a four-hour-long dialysis three times a week.

I have suffered from multiple illnesses since I was in my 20s. When I was a senior in high school, before going to university, I was hospitalized and quarantined for typhoid fever. When I look back, I realize there was not a point in my life when I was not sick during the past 40 years. Illnesses were like the partners of my life. Why did God allow this to happen? Only now do I understand why. The reason was that God wanted to mold me into the "me" that I am today. God put me into a furnace of suffering called illness to train me. It is also the grace of God. God knew that I would become arrogant and so gave me diseases, much like how the Apostle Paul suffered from a thorn in his flesh. Don't fool around. Don't become swollen with pride. When disease flares up, I can't do anything. I go back to the starting point yet again. But not once was I unable to preach for being sick. In my life, sicknesses and sermons always went together. This was God's amazing way of taking hold of me through illnesses. So, sickness for me is like not being sick at all. This may sound strange, but I recover when I preach. When I go up to the podium, I am refreshed. In contrast, when I don't preach, I lose heart and don't have energy. Consequently, I preach so I can live, just like you eat to survive. This is the grace of God, and I will preach until I die.

I also have high blood pressure. I had three stents poked into my heart, I received many laser treatments on my eyes, I was told that my blood vessels are clogged with limestone, I lost all my hair, and no part of me is in good condition. Someone once said,

"Pastor, you're like a moving general hospital." That's true. When I think about it, I can't point to any part of my body from head to toe that is working properly or is in beautiful shape. Despite such a condition, I held on to the church of Christ unceasingly. The Lord also takes hold of me just like that. Is this possible?

When my hepatitis developed into hepatocirrhosis, my doctor recommended that I give up my ministry. But what use do I have if I lay down my ministry? That's why when I left for the UK, I felt as though I were giving up my ministry. At that time, I thought I wouldn't be able to minister ever again. Before we left, I went to say farewell to Pastor Gyung-jik Han, who officiated our wedding. He said, "Pastor Ha, if I hadn't had hepatitis in Princeton and thrown up blood, I probably would not be a pastor today. So don't worry, and just leave." When I look back, I can see that illnesses could not take me down, sufferings could not harm me, and Satan's attacks could not destroy me. Satan's attacks, diseases, and painful situations cannot hurt us. We don't need to be afraid of suffering or the environment. When we fix our eyes on God and move forward, we can unbelievably leap over all suffering and win the victory as though we were jumping over waves or hiking over mountains. I firmly believe this - through my sickness, I met God who heals. Every time I got ill, the church grew. This is odd. Every time I am in pain, I experience spiritual fullness.

People who are sick are always in my heart. Some people struggle to live even for just a day. I feel as if they are my family and my alumni. Through sickness, I understood God's grace and the Lord's heart for people in pain. Onnuri Community Church may seem fancy, but in fact, the church was born when I was battling illnesses day after day. Such experiences are part of the reason why I always try not to forget about taking care of the weak.

Meeting mentors during college

I cannot forget my mentors in Christ who had a crucial impact on me.

First of all, I cannot forget Elder Yong-gi Kim

After entering college, the first group I started was the Farm Research Society (FRS). Of course, I was the president. We entered Canaan Farmers School as the 44th batch. I met Elder Kim there. The moment he saw me, he said, "What happened to your hair? Get a haircut. Wear something nice, and stay neat." From there, he pointed out my bad attitudes one by one. On top of that, I found the Canaan Farmers School's motto and the learning motto to be daunting.

> Canaan Farmers School's motto:
> 1. Learn so you will know
> 2. Work with all your strength
> 3. Serve humbly
>
> Canaan Farmers School learning motto:
> 1. Blessed people, learn as you work, work as you learn.
> 2. Blessed people, know that there will be success when you work together.
> 3. Blessed people, thoroughly learn new processes as you walk along your path.
> 4. Blessed people, find truth with passion and protect it bravely.

5. Blessed people, build your our family, homeland, and country with your hands.

On the first day of the school, I thought I would die. How could I think that I could do such backbreaking farming work my entire life? When I wanted to become lazy, however, I would come to my senses as I saw Elder Kim. He once shared the following:

"I am a man of twelve ugly things. First of all, my face is ugly. Second, I am not tall. Because I am only 156 cm tall, I had to stand on four layers of cushions whenever I preached behind the tall podium of Youngnak Presbyterian Church. Third, I weigh only 53 kg. Fourth, I have never worn a suit or necktie. Fifth, I never wore leather shoes. Sixth, I never drank or smoked. Seventh, I never tried bulgogi. Eighth, I never drank coffee. Ninth, I never slept in until seven o'clock in the morning. Tenth, I've never been to plays or movies. Eleventh, I never held a public post. Twelfth, I never chased around women. I am a man with twelve ugly traits."

Elder Kim started farming following his father's last will and testament. His father told him that when God sent Adam out of Eden to a farming area (Gen 3:23), God spoke to Adam, "By the sweat of your brow, you will eat your food until you return to the ground." (Gen 3:19) His father added that first, farming is partnering with God; second, farming is to make atonement for the sins of *yangban*[7] ancestors who did not sweat but lived idly; and third,

---

[7] *Yangban* was the highest social class of Korea's Joseon Dynasty (1392–1910). The *yangban* were granted many privileges by the state, including land and stipends according to their official grade and status. They were exempt from military duty and corvée labour.

reaping what you sow is a good thing without deceit. Elder Kim's father left him a will and gave him several reasons why he should engage in farming.

From age 23 on, Elder Kim sought God in the soil and shared the light of God to the world through the dirt. He founded the first Canaan Farmers School in 1962. Even former South Korean President Park Chung-hee said that "the way for us to live is to live out the life and spirit of this family."

I learned a great lesson from Elder Kim because he planned and acted according to the Word and the spirit of the Bible in whatever he did. He did not just teach moral and ethical diligence, but also taught us how we could act out the Gospel in detail, together with others in our lives. The inspiration I got from him was incomparably greater than the thrill I felt when reading the novels of Kwang-su Yi that dominated my adolescence. I did not know back then how much impact the elder's life would have on mine. Before he passed away, he called me. I stopped what I was doing right away and went to see him.

When he saw me he asked, "Do you know why some innocent children die early?"

I wasn't sure where he was going with this. His answer was like this: "I know now. Taking the child before he committed any sin was the best that God could do for the child."

Why did Elder Kim call me to tell me this simple message? He was like that. His dream was to die while working. And as his wish, he passed away on a podium while giving a lecture. It became my wish to live like him.

Secondly, I cannot forget Pastor Joon-gon Kim who taught me about salvation and the Holy Spirit.

I took some time off from university due to tuberculosis and was admitted to a sanatorium in Incheon. One day, Pastor Joon-gon Kim visited me. I was so thankful that he came all the way to this shabby place to see me. He went straight to the point and told me, "God must be considering using you. Pastor Gyung-jik Han and Miura Ayako, the author of *Freezing Point*, all suffered from tuberculosis. Mr. Ha, when I was young, I also had tuberculosis. I was little then. When my village was taken over by communists, I saw the communists tying up good, Christ-following villagers the way we would tie up dried fish, and killing them with bamboo spears. It was a horrifying death, and their faces were beyond recognition. The village stunk with the smell of their blood. From that massacre, among 52 people, only one person survived. Do you know who that person was? It was me."

Jesus said, "In this world, you will have trouble. But take heart!" (John 16:33). Mr. Ha, do not be hard on yourself. Jesus loves you. Do not stifle and abuse yourself and your conscience but embrace them like the warm sun and the spring breeze. I hope you don't reject the Lord's calling and mission. Don't make decisions based on your thoughts. I want you to seek His grace quietly and wait for His calling."

Back then, I inwardly resented God who took me down with tuberculosis. Pastor Kim must have clearly seen how I blamed God. I quietly confessed inside.

"You're right, Pastor Kim. Only after I had this deadly disease did I realize that I was full of pride, thinking no one could believe

God more passionately than I. But I did not really believe in God. I believed in my own strength. I may have only realized now that faith, the power to evangelize and pray, and all things are from the Lord. So, even if I die now, it is the grace of God. I will not make a decision based on what I want. I will wait for my Lord in silence"

Pastor Kim is a person who took time out of his busy schedule to visit a young man like me who was suffering from tuberculosis. He forgave those who killed his father and his beloved wife. That incident led him to meet Bill Bright and create a missions organization called CCC. He carried out evangelical movements with many young people. He only thinks about the cross of Jesus Christ and evangelizing the nation. Even after Pastor Kim left, I pondered on the message he shared with me for a long time.

Thirdly, I cannot forget my seminary professor, Sun-ae Joo.

Professor Sun-ae Joo is the one who prayed for me and encouraged me to study theology. When I was an assistant pastor, I went to meet her because the celebrity Bible study meeting I was leading suddenly got big, and I was overwhelmed. I told her, "When I think about the future, I sometimes doubt if I'm doing it right. There are so many things to do, but I'm so far away from accomplishing them."

I talked on and on. She looked at me with sparkly eyes and gave me a simple answer. She said, "It's good to serve as a student ministry pastor. It's also good to prepare for your studies abroad. But if famous celebrities are coming to know Christ and are getting passionately involved with Bible study, that is an opportunity given by God. I think you shouldn't let it go. To hold on to that chance, I think it would be good for you to quit the student ministry pastor position and dedicate yourself to handling a Bible study for famous people. You will surely bear fruit."

She came all the way to where we met for celebrity Bible study, and we served together in worship. She encouraged me by saying this: "This is truly a miracle. God will do great wonders." From that time on, she accompanied me when I visited celebrities, saying that a young pastor like me should not go alone. She came with me whenever I went to visit celebrities no matter what time of day it was. I clearly remember the loving, motherly encouragement I received from her, as she would sit at the back and worship with us at the beginning of our celebrity church. She is now over 80 but remains by my side as always.

Such experience is deeply related to the pastoral philosophy of Onnuri Community Church. Onnuri Community Church always strives for five kinds of spirituality: A spirituality that is focused on the Word, the Holy Spirit, community, social participation, and missions. Community is like the foundation laid at the bottom. The church is the center of it all and the center of the universe as well. On the other hand, the Word, Holy Spirit, social participation, and missions serve as the four pillars of the Church; the Word and Holy Spirit face inward, while social participation and missions face outward.

2. Walking in the Way of the Lord

Planting a celebrity church

When I was an assistant pastor at Mapo Church, an elder who worked at a broadcasting station asked me for a favor.

He said, "Can you do a Bible study for Fly Boy, Gyu-seok Kwak? His faith is still weak. It's a bit hard for him to study with other people because he's so famous. That's why I'm asking you for a favor."

I'd never thought about it before. But if it was sharing the Gospel, there was no reason for me to say no. Since then, God has sent celebrities to me constantly, even today.

It was 1974. At first, I shed a lot of tears and faced many difficulties. I went to the broadcasting station to meet celebrities. Whenever I met a celebrity, I would drag the person to a café in front of the television station, pray for him or her, and then share the Gospel. Whenever I got there, however, many would sneak away so I wouldn't see them. Celebrities have always been extremely busy. Why would busy people like them want to waste their time listening to a stranger tell a story about something they're not interested in? As a result, I had to endure many insults. Whenever I entered the broadcasting station, I could hear people jeering, "Pastor Ha alert!" Yet, I would say "hi" and greet everyone with a smile, and some of them would listen to me out of sympathy. Then someone would say, "Oh, no, you're busted!" and giggle behind our backs. I also heard people whispering, "I heard he's a seminary student. Why does he come here every day instead of studying? Doesn't he have any self-respect?" Nevertheless, I continued to talk with a smile. I told myself, "If the suffering is for Christ, I will rejoice and be happy whatever hardships come my way." Perhaps if the celebrities knew my heart, it would have startled them even more.

Maybe because Gyu-seok Kwak and I passionately shared the Gospel, people started to join the Bible study one by one, according to God's plan. Gradually, many celebrities joined our group. It was interesting to see famous people I saw on television listening to God's Word and coming to our Bible study.

Then, the entertainment industry was hit by a massive storm. Massive scandals broke out that rocked the country, and drug and bribery scandals erupted one after another. TV personalities who were kicked out of the television station had no place to go, so they came to our Bible study. It was strange. The moment they stepped into the room, they wept. Then, they knelt down before God and came back to Him. I thought, "The storm must have been created by God." With them, we did our best to evangelize celebrity entertainers, and eventually we were about to build a church. It is not an exaggeration to say that most of the famous celebrities at that time were at our church. God is truly amazing. As these people worship Him, God must have laughed with joy!

I remember the conversation I had with Gyu-seok Kwak on a grass field at Asia United Theological University when I was planning to build a church for celebrities. He grabbed me and said, "You don't understand us, entertainers. I can't ask you to plant a church for us. Because we're so famous and have been taken advantage of many times, we also take advantage of others as well. We swallow something when we need it, but when we don't like it anymore, we spit it out. The future is uncertain. When you become sick, we'll ignore you. Also, it will interrupt your studies."

In short, he was saying, let's not do it. At that moment, I replied, "Don't ask me if it's difficult or easy. But answer me whether it's God's will or not. Is it God's will to minister in a church for entertainers or not?" With that, he replied and told me that I must plant the church. So I did.

Pastors have no freedom to stay or leave.

I worked hard without fear. I slept for four hours a day, preached seven times, prayed until late in the night, and fasted. I lived like that for ten years. During those times, miracles happened, demons fled, and sick people got healed. If it were not for such visible manifestations of the Holy Spirit, entertainers who are the so-called "flowers of humanism" would have had a hard time believing Jesus.

When we worshipped God, famous female celebrities shed black tears as their tears melted the mascara. For the first time, I saw celebrities crying for real, and not just faking it for the camera. Also, I couldn't help but cry when they come back to God and repent before the Lord, and when they innocently had fellowship with one another after receiving the Holy Spirit. I couldn't help but confess, "Lord, this is the Church. This is the Church. Your Church is incredibly beautiful."

They were a group of people with strong personalities. Imagine how fun our worship with them was! No one was confined within the traditional framework of a service.

The choir's praise was magnificent. It was exciting to see and hear famous singers, such as Bok-hee Yoon, Eun-mi Bang, and the Cool Sisters, as well as actors, voice actors, and comedians freely singing together in a choir. Their choir, although in discord, was always on fire. Some sang passionately, some cried in the middle of their singing, and some sang their hearts out without knowing they were out of tune. The choir was total chaos, but it was one of holy harmony. I don't think I could ever find such a moving choir anywhere else.

Celebrities who have never been to a church before would react to sermons in different and peculiar ways. When agreeing to the preaching, some would give a standing ovation, shouting, "That's right!" A famous singer from Jeolla Province would reply, "Oh, how good...!" with a Jeolla accent.

The giving of announcements was also quite interesting. It didn't start with the usual "We have some announcements for you," but instead with "I'm sure there was an announcement..." Famous emcee Gyu-seok Kwak (who later became a pastor) and the elder Bong-suh Gu, who was a popular comedian, made the announcements according to their own unique styles. They made everyone laugh until they cried. People got confused whether those two were doing announcements or performing standup comedy. I can't express how happy we were worshipping and evangelizing together.

When I ministered at the celebrity church, I once visited a place called "World Cup." It was a bar. Why did I go there? Because our celebrity members were there! When I visited the place during the day, the members would say, "Oh, pastor, you didn't need to come here." I still had to go, however, because my beloved people were there! Although I served the church passionately, ministering in a celebrity church was very difficult. These people were not easy. They were used to getting the spotlight, so no one would bring me a cup of water when I preached. No one would clean the church, so I did it by myself. After the service, as these famous people were going home, I even had to catch taxis for them. No servant was as servant-like as I was, but doing the ministry with these people was exciting and fun.

After three years, however, I started to complain, "This is just too much!" Honestly, I tried to escape and leave this church several times, but there was no way out. The most rational way to flee was to study, and what an excellent excuse it was! Without letting the congregation know, I applied for schools and was accepted by one and even given a scholarship.

Then, I went to a prayer mountain to fast and pray, "God, I will leave." My heavenly Father answered, "No! You can't." I asked Him, "God why not? Please send me," and God would just tell me that I could not. I implored Him, "But, God, the people are treating me unfairly." At that point, the Lord gave me an answer in my heart: "Was there ever a time they weren't?"

That struck me. It wasn't they who had changed, it was I. Was there a time when they hadn't had any faults? The problem was that when you don't have love, you see people's shortcomings. Their imperfections had always been there; I just hadn't seen them before because I loved them. It was important for me to restore that love. Then I wouldn't be able to see just their flaws.

When I think about it now, there aren't people who are as pure, honest, and beautiful as those celebrities. I still miss them each day. There wasn't a point in my life that was happier and more fun than those days.

When the ministry became too difficult, my wife and I went to Namhansanseong Fortress to meet my mentor, Pastor Gyung-jik Han. I told him, "Pastor, I am now going to leave the church. I will leave."

He seemed to know everything when he saw me. Then he replied, "Pastor Ha, sit over here. Ministry is about patience. When I escaped North Korea, I was planning to stay here for only three months. If I had known that I would live here for good, I would not have left. God did not command me to leave. Pastor Ha, if there is no sign from God, don't you ever leave. You may only leave for these two reasons: first, if you can no longer continue ministry because of illness, and secondly, when 100 percent of the congregation agrees and asks you to leave."

At that moment, I felt as though a big hammer had struck my head. These words impressed me strongly: "You should never leave the ministry. Never leave because you want to. Move when God makes you move. Don't leave because there are troubles and sufferings. Don't leave until God directly gives you a sign to leave."

I learned a very good lesson. Ministers don't have freedom. We ministers cannot leave even when we want to, and we cannot go even when we want to. I also realized that God plants us in the right place and moves us when it's time to move.

But if God asks us to leave, then we must leave.

After planting the celebrity church in 1974, I went through hardships, but with joy. After a while, we started constructing a church building. We purchased a piece of land and began the work. Then I began to feel sick again. My liver deteriorated further worse. One day, my wife gave me a note and explained that when she was praying, the Holy Spirit prompted her and spoke to her. She then wrote down the Holy Spirit's words on a note. I read it. It was simple:

"My son! Build this house faithfully, but you won't be able to stand on the pulpit and preach. Then leave."

It was a prophecy. A letter that started with "My son!" could not have come from a man. If that's the plan of God, I thought, it would come true. After all, God made David prepare the temple, but it was Solomon who built it! Also, God gave me another message. He said, "I will lead your way." So before the building was completed, we gave up the church and let it go.

During that time, I got more and more sick. I suffered from cirrhosis of the liver and had no choice but to resign from the celebrity church. As God had said earlier, I couldn't stand in the pulpit of that church even during the church dedication after the new building was completed. When I resigned from the church and left for the UK with my family, I thought, "Oh Lord, what should I do from now on?" I had no clue how my future would unfold. Back then my condition was so bad that if I rode in a car for two hours, I would become so exhausted that I would collapse. How could I plan for my future in such a condition? Nonetheless, as I looked to God at every moment of my life, God led me as He promised. It was at this moment that I stopped thinking that I have to do all the work whenever I do God's work. If it is my role, I will do it. If it is not, I will leave. That is so obvious. If you don't leave when you should, you will be kicked out, and it is much better to leave than to be expelled. If it's God's command, we should obey and leave quietly at any time.

When we were building Onnuri Community Church, I told my wife, "Honey, what shall we do if God asks us to leave again after the church is completed?"

You never know what God might ask you to do. I may want to do something with all my might, but I don't know His plans. I always remind myself that I should not force my plan on God, whether I minister in a church or do His work.

While I served at the celebrity church, I learned how to approach the general public, and that kind of culture is important when sharing the Gospel. But the most important lesson I learned from ministering in the celebrity church is that I am a servant of God. If God asks us, the ministers, to leave, there is nothing else we can do.

2. Walking in the Way of the Lord

Pastor Dennis Lane opened my eyes to preaching.

I stopped serving the celebrity church and took a rest due to my deteriorating health. During that time, I started Duranno[8] and through it, met Pastor Dennis Lane. He said something that I cannot forget even today:

"God doesn't come early and never arrives late. God comes at the right and most appropriate time. So never be impatient. Never doubt Him. Even if a knife is held to your throat or even if it has cut you already, do not doubt Him. He comes at the most accurate time."

I can never forget his message. When Abraham grabbed a knife to sacrifice his son, Isaac, God came at the perfect time. God did not tell Abraham beforehand that everything he had gone through was "just to test your faith." There was no sign from God even at the very moment Abraham was about to stab the heart of Isaac with a knife. God came with the most accurate timing.

We shouldn't become like Saul, who became impatient because he couldn't endure for even one moment. We must be patient one more time. We must wait once more. We should turn a blind eye one more time. Elijah praying seven times, Joshua marching around the walls of Jericho seven times, and Naaman dipping himself in the river seven times are perfect examples. Christ came when the time was full. Everything happened according to God's timing. In saying these things, Pastor Danis Lane helped me to understand the power of the Word. And then, I realized that the power of the Word was so great. When I understood the power of the Word, my

---

8 Duranno is a Christian publishing company founded by Pastor Ha.

eyes were opened to preaching. And so Pastor Dennis Lane opened my eyes to preaching.

I was also drawn to preaching after I encountered the UK's expository sermons. I like and respect Charles Spurgeon, Campbell Morgan, Martyn Lloyd-Jones, and John Stott as preachers. I was once immersed in modern theological sermons. I was attracted to Bonhoeffer, Karl Barth, and Paul Tillich, but once I experienced the sermons of great expository preachers, human ideas no longer attracted me.

Dennis Lane was an ordinary missionary from OMF (Overseas Missionary Fellowship), and there weren't many people who could move hearts through preaching as he did. There is no greater message than life. There is no bigger sacrifice than giving one's life. Dennis Lane had "life" that could not be found in theologians. He preached in the mission field all his life, outside the spotlight. I don't preach the way Pastor Lane does, but I've learned the framework and structure of sermons from him. I learned exegetical preaching by teaching the Bible with the Bible.

Beyond academic study, from Bible to Bible

In the UK, I discovered something new academically. Before studying theology, I knew and believed in Jesus as He was revealed in the Bible. After entering the seminary, however, I started to have some internal conflicts. Theology seemed to propose so many methodologies and ideas that all seemed great. Just as the Theory of Evolution seems reasonable, such methodologies made me think that if one reasons logically, one would reach such a conclusion. Although I knew that such thinking was not right, I didn't have the power to reject it academically. I struggled a lot over this.

When I studied the work of well-known theologians such as Bultmann, Barth, or Tillich, I found that their ideas seemed reasonable. The problem, however, was that I couldn't experience Jesus in their theological theories. After learning many other things, I became dry and powerless. Among many reasonable theories, Jesus seemed like a mummy. With such thinking, the Jesus I met with such joy seemed to be fading away. Fortunately, a great number of Bible studies I did at CCC during college and the overwhelming experience of meeting and sharing the living Christ sustained me. I almost lost Jesus, the Savior and Lord whom I had met and experienced in 1966.

During those three years in England, I learned that there was more to theology than the kind of theology I'd learned up to then. There was another type of theology - Evangelical Theology, and this represents what we believe. I was able to overcome my academic inferiority complex as I met a number of scholars and faithful people who witnessed the Gospel in the sphere of academics. Through this process, I realized that the Bible is truly the Word of God and that we can meet and have fellowship daily with Jesus through the Scriptures.

Such experience plucked up the courage in me to pursue expository sermons. When I preach, I don't quote other philosophers or theologians. I just move from one Bible passage to another. I do it this way because I am convinced that only the Bible is the Word of God that is complete. I preach and teach the Bible this way, and I am certain that Jesus Christ is alive, not dead.

Risking my life for mission

While I was in the UK, I received missionary training at WEC, a missions organization. While there, my wife and I experienced two shocking incidents.

I remember when a leader took us, trainees, down to the dark basement of the WEC building, where there were piles of abandoned clothes. We passed by that dark place and reached a very spacious basement storage area. It was an eerie place, and the moldy smell made me cringe.

The storage was filled with a number of closets, and every shelf had luggage covered with layers of dust. Each luggage had a tag with its owner's name and the year it was left there. Some bags were only a year old while others were 10 to 20 years old.

The WEC leader who brought us there explained, "The missionaries who have gone to their mission fields left their belongings in this storage basement."

Their luggage silenced me.

I quietly asked myself, "Why did these people choose this kind of life for themselves? Why did they leave when there was no one to blame them if they didn't go in the first place?"

From there, the leader led us to a small hall that could hold about a hundred people. The leader pointed to the 20 picture frames on the wall and said, "These are the portraits of young missionaries who were martyred in their 20s and 30s in the mission field since the foundation of WEC."

Doctors, nurses, pilots... I stared at the brief profiles written under the pictures. My heart started to beat faster.

"Why did they sacrifice their youth in the mission fields?" I thought. "Who drove them to go in the first place?"

Our Lord shed His own blood and died for us, and it is because of overwhelming gratitude that these missionaries followed the Lord's command. They knew the things they had to do in this world. Neither health nor physical limitations, nor anything else, can be a stumbling block to following the Lord's command. Shouldn't I also run towards the one and only command that my Lord gave all men, as these men had done?

These two incredible experiences - seeing their luggage and their pictures - captivated me throughout my training at WEC.

Learning team ministries

I lived with trainees during the six months I received training at WEC. We, the Korean trainees, couldn't speak English well, so we gathered around people we knew and talked together and ate instant noodles and *kimchi* together. One day, someone came to us and said, "Go over there and talk." The message was that if we wanted to form a self-enclosed group of people, we should go somewhere else and do it. WEC did not encourage us to make best friends. The logic behind it was that if you become best friends with one person, other people will lose the opportunity to get to know you and they will feel hurt. When evaluating people, WEC valued "partnership" the most. Establishing partnerships is only possible when you, your individual self, "dies." If you put yourself first, the partnership won't work.

I cannot emphasize enough how important partnership is in missionary work. It is important for faith to be manifested personally, but it must also be expressed as a community. When our faith is shown personally, we could feel proud of ourselves because it's the "me" that stands out. But, if our faith is expressed as a community, it ceases to be exciting because the "me" becomes hidden. Faith that is manifested as a community, therefore, is real faith. When that is the case, then I shall be hidden and only Christ will be revealed. I won't be the only person involved but will become one of many other people. That's why WEC greatly emphasizes partnership training. It's not just WEC. All missions organizations highlight teamwork in ministry as if it was a matter of life or death. There is no one you are closer to or less close to. There should be no one else besides Jesus Christ.

At my age, you need a good partner in order to do God's work well, and of course, the best partner for a pastor is his wife. A pastor, however, must exhibit good teamwork with everyone he gets to work with, in addition to his wife.

I witnessed one church that had great teamwork in ministry. It was the All Souls Church where Pastor John Stott used to minister.

The following occurred when I attended All Souls Church. When Pastor Stott was the senior pastor of this church, he used to do all the preaching. After he retired, however, he worked with a team. All ministry programs, sermon Scriptures, and sermon themes came out in advance in three-month, or 12-week, plans. Pastors rotated in delivering the sermons. For example, to cover 12 Sundays, the first sermon was delivered by the senior pastor, the second by the junior pastor, the third by an education pastor, and the fourth by an evangelism pastor. The senior pastor would give about three sermons in 12 weeks. Then, in the last week, Pastor Stott himself would conclude. That's how they handled the

12-week series of sermons.

The amazing thing was that when it was the turn of a young pastor (someone in his 30s) to preach, Pastor Stott or the senior pastor would preside over the service or serve as an usher during the offering.

It was a beautiful sight. The church emphasized the Bible passage and the message, not the preacher. If we ministered like that in South Korea, the number of the congregation would vary every week depending on who was preaching on Sunday. However, this church was different. One thousand, five hundred Christians would gather in the mornings and evenings because of the Word of God, not because of who the preacher was that week.

I witnessed the same phenomenon at All Date Church, located in front of Oxford University, led by Pastor Michael Green. Here, the senior pastor mainly preached, but the church had set a beautiful model of teamwork, in which the senior pastor and junior pastors helped each other. I thought I would create such beautiful partnerships as well. Junior pastors should still be respectful of their seniors even when their seniors treat them well, just as senior pastors should not rebuke their juniors for their shortcomings. Seniors and juniors should trust and have faith in each other. If ministry ethics are observed well, such things will become possible!

Having the vision of Duranno

I studied at London Insitute, founded by Pastor Stott in England. Located in the heart of the city, London Insitute offers to many experts a Christian perspective on various social issues such as abortion, pornography, crime, psychology, and counseling. We studied the harmony and balance between the Gospel and social responsibility, which follows the Gospel.

When I saw London Institute, I thought, "Ah! I will create something better than this when I return to Seoul." Before leaving Seoul, I established Duranno, but it barely had any substance. It only offered counseling, discipleship training, Bible studies, and expository preaching. The moment I saw London Insitute, however, I had a vision of how to lead Duranno once I returned to South Korea.

The Church is a church, and Duranno is a parachurch. I am still experimenting and trying to understand how churches and parachurches can coexist in Korean society. The first attempt to make that happen occurred with Onnuri Community Church and Duranno.

A missions organization is a missions organization, and a church is a church. I wondered, "How can a church publish books?" Such tasks may be difficult for churches, but they are possible to achieve through organizations like Duranno. On the other hand, there are things that Duranno can't do, but churches can. I wanted to create a model where these two entities worked in perfect harmony.

In the past, the elders of our church would tell me that they would like me to give up Duranno or appoint someone else to take care of it so I could focus on the church. However, I couldn't give up either of the two, because the church and Duranno were both my beloved children.

Learning how to love

At London Insitute, everyone would gather around a table for

2. Walking in the Way of the Lord

a meal after Pastor Stott's morning lecture.

One day, my wife and my son were also invited to join them for lunch. Pastor Stott sat right next to me that day. While we ate, he asked me questions and talked slowly in simple English because my English was not that good. It was a pleasant and enjoyable time. All of a sudden, my wife kicked my foot under the table. I was puzzled and tried to understand what was going on. I realized that I was making noises while I slurped my soup. My wife was embarrassed and wanted me to stop. Then came a pleasant surprise: Pastor Stott started to slurp his soup, making a louder noise than I. Further, he picked up his bowl to his mouth and drank his soup. "I think it is tastier when you make a noise," he said. Then he took some rice from his plate and placed it on mine. "Please eat a lot. This is the Eastern style of love." To save the face of a pastor from the East who was not used to Western culture, Pastor Stott observed table manners that a Western man would never do.

It was my turn to wash the dishes that day, so I went to the dining room downstairs and washed the bowls, spoons, and forks with the other students. While I was busy doing the dishes, I noticed someone taller than me washing the bowls and humming a song. I glanced over and realized that it was Pastor Stott. I was deeply moved to see him washing the dishes.

One day, I was looking at the books displayed in the lobby after a lecture. All of a sudden Pastor Stott showed up and said, "Love letter!" and gave me a clean envelope. It didn't seem like a report since it had my name, "Brother Ha" written on the front. I opened the envelope immediately and found a short letter with 50 pounds. At first, I thought it might be a mistake, but the letter said, "It's hard studying, isn't it? This money is part of the royalty I received for the book I wrote. Please use it to buy books."

Pastor Stott left, and for a moment there I couldn't move from the spot where I stood. I thought, "Ah, you can also use money like this!" I don't know how many times I read the letter and touched the fifty-pound bill (£ 50) over and over.

Getting rid of unnecessary pretense

Also in England, I learned that unnecessary pretense in our faith lives needs to be removed.

In another instance, my family was invited to dinner at Pastor Stott's house. That night he served take-out hamburgers for dinner, and I couldn't understand why. How can you invite someone over for dinner and serve one hamburger? Yet, the conversation we shared over the burgers was priceless! Although it was a simple dinner with burgers, the talk we had that night became an unforgettable experience of love, encouragement, and comfort.

On another occasion, my wife and I were invited yet again by Pastor Dennis Lane and his wife while we were in England. We met at the OMF office. He said we would have lunch together. There were crackers, cheese, and a half apple. At first, I thought those were just appetizers, but no matter how long I waited, the main dish didn't come. That was it. A similar thing happened when several people were invited by John Willis, who was the director of OMF UK. The only dish that was served that day was stew that looked like porridge. Rice and stew, that was it!

If Koreans were to have guests, they would even go so far as to borrow money to prepare food. Back then, I didn't understand why our hosts served very little food, but as time went by, there were many things that struck my heart. First, I learned that even if you eat such simple meals, you won't really get hungry and second, you can enjoy the evening better by talking with each other rather than just eating. A long time ago, Jesus said something similar to Martha: "You are busy preparing many dishes. Nothing's wrong with just snacks or burgers." Through these experiences, I realized that I needed to get rid of a lot of window-dressing in my walk of faith. This is because faith is not a theory or form, but life. Also, love is not words, but action.

Shocked by worship that was full of life

Another thing that struck me in the UK was the worship. In the UK, I realized how much we limited worship because of the forms and stereotypes with which we are obsessed.

I was used to attending traditional Korean churches, and as I learned the language, participated in churches, studied at a seminary, and saw the worship services in England, I thought many times to myself, "Wow, they're so different from us."

One day, I went to attend worship service at All Date Church. In the middle of the chapel that was more than a century old, an old gray-haired man was playing the drums. There was a pipe organ, but the worship team played a synthesizer instead. People who were worshipping seemed free. In the middle of the worship, people would freely stand up, raise their hands, close their eyes, and sing praises. I thought I was in heaven. To be fair, it was the 1980s, and in South Korea, we had just started listening to worship songs. No wonder such worship surprised me.

I was also quite startled when I went to All Souls Church, ministered by Pastor Stott. During the service, women would dance in strange clothes. I wasn't used to it, so I thought, "Is it okay to do that? Aren't people supposed to dance outside the church, not inside?" When I think about it now, this was worship dance.

I went to Pastor John Graham's church for almost a year because I loved the worship there. The church building was not big, only about half the size of Onnuri Community Church's Seobinggo main hall now, but the chapel was filled with people even before the worship started. Inside a jam-packed hall, people raised their hands and worshipped God. The people sitting in front got up and played tambourines as they sang worship songs until the roof blew off the chapel. They were not in their 20s or 30s; they were old ladies with gray hair! The entire hall was full of joy.

Surprisingly, there wasn't a limit to how long the service should be. During the service, the presider would first proclaim a passage from the Book of Psalms. He didn't say, "Let's pray silently together," like Korean churches do. The pastor started preaching as soon as he stood behind the pulpit, and the sermon lasted more than 30 minutes, sometimes over one hour. Since the preaching was good, I mean very good, people would get sucked into the sermon in complete silence. I thought to myself, "Who said sermons have to be just 30 minutes! Who said sermons have to be short!"

After the preaching, people would dance again. They clapped and danced in joy. Evil spirits would depart in the middle of the service. I told myself, "Wow! This is worship! This is worship!" It was a shocking experience for me. Until then, I didn't know the joy and the holiness of worshipping God in beautiful freedom. I only knew services that started with, "Let's pray in silence." Indeed, because I was so moved, the service may have been ten times better than it really was.

From that point on, I had a dream about a church. I started to have a vision for a church. Experiencing the Holy Spirit's moving presence that filled the worship laid the spiritual foundation of All Nations Worship & Praise Ministries. Also, such experience formed the basis for Onnuri Community Church's service.

Along with the preaching and praise, each ceremony was an amazing experience. In particular, the Holy Communion I participated in at an Anglican church in the southern part of the UK was quite impressive. It was a charismatic church, and around 600 people gathered for worship. During the service, the pastor offered the Holy Communion to the elders first. Then, five to six leaders embraced and blessed each other and shared bread and wine. Then the leaders brought the bread to the congregation. As I watched and listened to a hymn, the Holy Spirit came upon me in a powerful way. My heart was filled with inspiration, and I couldn't control my tears. I wasn't crying because I was sad. I couldn't express what I felt with words. My spirit wept just like that. The presence of God was upon me, and tears trickled down my cheeks. It was the anointing of the Holy Spirit!

As I meditated on the blood and the bread of Jesus Christ, I started to repent before I knew it. I never cried so much during a Holy Communion. That day as I cried, I thought, "When I plant a church in South Korea, I want to do the Holy Communion like this." Also, I observed infant baptism taking place in the International Presbyterian Church of England. During the ceremony, the parents were asked questions before making a vow. The questions were mind-blowing.

The first question was: "Do you admit that this child is the child of God?" All parents have no problem answering "Yes" to this question. The next question was: "Then when this child grows up and says that he wants to become a servant of God or wants to work for God, will you not discourage him?" Parents started to hesitate before answering. The third question: "If this child dies along the way, will you not blame God?" With this question, the parents become serious. Infants are given baptism after their parents vowed to these three promises. As I watched, I learned that baptism is not just a ceremony but should be like this. All that I experienced in England was true worship. I truly encountered the passage, "For the glory of the LORD filled the temple of God" (2 Chronicles 5:14).

I still think about these experiences even today. I ponder, "In the worship that I offer God or lead, does the glory of God fill the sanctuary, do cherubims sing, does a great company of the heavenly hosts blow trumpets, and does God reveal Himself? Can our Sunday service become an experience where tears and joy overflow? Whenever we come to church, can we have a service where the glory of God fills the temple and where His honor and glory manifest?"

Our faith life is dry because we don't have true worship. Although we must worship the Father in spirit and truth, we rarely experience true worship. It's exhausting when heartless people look at each other's faces and think, "Let's see how well you preach," "Aw, today was a bit bad," or "Oh, he did pretty well today." This is how we often think. If this is so, how different is going to church from going to a good lecture? How can we experience the glory and presence of God?

We need to experience a kind of worship where there is a confession, tears, gratitude, and praise. We need to experience a worship that washes our spirit.

In fact, one should not be sane anymore by the end of the service. You should be in shock, wearing your shoes backward and not knowing what to do. When we worship God, our spirits should be struck hard. Through singing, praying, preaching, and offering, we should meet the living God and experience the presence of the Holy Spirit.

"Do the Holy Spirit ministry."

It was the sixth year since Onnuri Community Church started, and from the outside, everything seemed to be going well. Several thousands of Christians gathered, and we had many wise church workers. We saved a lot of the offerings people made and had a grand vision. However, I started to see the problems of our church.

At that time, the church had the appearance of an airplane, but it was nothing more than a car that could not fly. Planes must take off at a particular time. If it misses that critical point, it can't fly anymore. Once it has missed the time to depart, it will feel frustrated, trapped, and be unable to rise above ground level. I felt such a crisis in our church.

Around that time, God finally slammed on the brakes. In the spring of 1989, less than three years after we built our church building, I was diagnosed with hepatocirrhosis. I had no choice but to take my sabbatical a year early.

In 1991, I went to Hawaii for my sabbatical, and as soon as I got off the plane, God spoke to me powerfully. He said, "Do the Holy Spirit ministry." During that one year in Hawaii, God spoke one thing to me over and over again: "Go back to the Holy Spirit. Do the Holy Spirit ministry."

Honestly, such a message made me feel uncomfortable. Ever since I was a young child, I had always been distressed by seeing a group of people who followed the Holy Spirit in an extreme manner. Many of them spoke about the Holy Spirit one-sidedly or too radically, often ending up losing balance. For that reason, although I sought the presence of the Holy Spirit all the time, I was reluctant to approach the Holy Spirit ministry. Instead, I would go back to discipleship or Bible ministries. Eventually, however, God dragged me to the Holy Spirit ministry. I finally surrendered to Him and prayed to the Lord like this:

> Lord! I do not have power. My voice sounds hollow. My voice may be high, but the spirit is empty. God, my Father, come at this hour. My ministry seems splendid on the outside, but there are many hurts and conflicts on the inside. There are many secret sins in my life. There are unconfessed sins.
>
> God, the problems in the church are entirely my responsibility. They're not the elders.' They're not the congregation's. They are mine. Please forgive me. Please have mercy on me. Aren't there many Christians who are hurt because of me? Haven't I wrongly exercised the authority of a pastor many times?
>
> Oh, God, my Father, please release me from all the powers of

2. Walking in the Way of the Lord

evil - Satan, who kills, destroys and binds me, and makes me powerless. Please reveal the evil spirit. May all the evil spirits depart from my heart. I want to be transformed. The Holy Spirit! May the spirit of repentance arise.

Oh, Father God, I cannot continue to minister to the church like this! Let me experience the works of the Holy Spirit on Pentecost before going back. Give me a pure spirit. Create in me an honest spirit.

I've become ill, and my mind is confused. I want you to heal my sickness. I want my body and mind to be restored. I want to be strengthened.

God, open the door of heaven and may the Holy Spirit come upon my head as the Spirit descended on Jesus like a dove, and may I hear your voice that I am your beloved son and your delighted one. Restore the first heart I had when I believed Jesus for the first time and when I first became a pastor. Please save my ministry. I pray in the name of Jesus. Amen.

As soon as I came back from my sabbatical, I gathered the elders and made an announcement. I said, "From now on, we will do the Holy Spirit ministry."

I was thankful that not one of our elders rejected or stopped me. I suspect that they perhaps did not know what the Holy Spirit ministry was.

Anyway, our church held a Holy Spirit rally for two days on May 22 and 23 in 1992. Then something amazing happened. A great number of people, the biggest since our church began, gathered not only on our stage but also in the cafeteria, the first-floor lobby, and the stairs. Our entire church was filled with people. I had no idea that the congregation would seek the Holy Spirit so much.

I learned that members are faster and more eager than pastors. They all had been thinking of and feeling the Holy Spirit before, but simply didn't say anything out of respect for their pastor.

When we open our hearts toward the Holy Spirit, miracles happen. From the following year, people started to flock to our church. They came in like a swarm of grasshoppers. After the rally, Onnuri Community Church took a huge leap forward.

Some people ask what the programs of the Holy Spirit ministry are, since our church emphasizes this ministry a lot. The Holy Spirit ministry is not a program. It is a ministry led by the Holy Spirit. It is to let the presence of the Holy Spirit enter all the things a church does. If I had been making the decisions up to that point, it was now about letting the Holy Spirit decide what our church would do. To do the Holy Spirit ministry is to invite the Holy Spirit and offer our hearts and praises to Him. The Holy Spirit ministry is about changing our attitudes. It's about changing our mindset. The change may seem trivial, but it is fundamental and radical.

The spirituality of Onnuri Community Church is related to my experience.

The experiences I have just described are deeply related to the pastoral philosophy of Onnuri Community Church. Onnuri Community Church always strives for five kinds of spirituality: A spirituality that is focused on the Word, the Holy Spirit, community, social participation, and missions.

Community is like the foundation laid at the bottom. The Word, the Holy Spirit, social participation, and missions serve as the four pillars of a church; the Word and Holy Spirit face inward, while social participation and missions face outward. The motto of the church is the combination of these five spiritualities.

Onnuri Community Church's core values - the Bible, the Gospel, missions, mercy and Christ's culture - are also based on my life experiences. Onnuri Community Church emphasizes the Word, but at the same time, we value culture as well. We highlight missions, but at the same time, we don't neglect mercy. Although we believe that personal spirituality is the basis, we don't ignore spirituality as a whole. We strive towards achieving the culture of Christ and actively participate in society to change the world.

Onnuri Community Church does not neglect any of these aspects, because the Gospel includes all of these. God has made me realize the importance of all of these through the various experiences of my life.

The Standard of Ecclesiology Is the Ecclesiology of Jesus
Ecclesiology Found in Acts

PART 2:

ECCLESIOLOGY

The root of a church's ecclesiology should be the same for every church. The most critical illustration of a church can be found in Jesus.

1. The Standard for Ecclesiology Is the Ecclesiology of Jesus

Churches are Jesus' churches. No denominational or theological ideas can come before Jesus' ideas. In Matthew 16:13-20, Jesus used the word "Church" for the first time, and in this passage, we can find four characteristics of the Church that Jesus dreams of.

First, the community of people who confessed their faith clearly

When Jesus asked his disciples, "Who do people say I am?" Peter replied, "You are the Messiah, the Son of the living God." His view was different from that of religious experts and secular people. They thought Jesus was John the Baptist or Elijah, but Peter made a profound confession with the help of the Holy Spirit. Then,

Jesus told him that He would build His church based on Peter's confession. Jesus said, "Blessed are you, Simon son of Jonah, for this was not revealed to you by flesh and blood, but by my Father in heaven. And I tell you that you are Peter, and on this rock, I will build my church."

Here, you can find the secret of the Church. The Church is not a worldly organization or a group. It is created by people who have thoroughly confessed their faith. It is a group of individuals who are saved. It is not a building. It is not a denomination. Hanging a cross high doesn't make something a church. For it to be a true church, each member should have confessed his salvation and experienced the joy of salvation. What is a confession? It is confessing that Jesus is the Messiah whom God had promised, the Son of the living God.

The reason why some churches are not like the Church that Jesus built and end in failure is that they give important positions to people who haven't confessed their faith clearly, in the hope that their church grows quickly. Some churches may have unbelievers or believers who are weak in faith operating the church, and when churchs do this, they will face a great crisis.

Throughout my ministry, I have reached one conclusion, which is that when the wrong people are involved with church operations, it is like having a pathogen in our body. In particular, we should not rashly appoint elders and deacons. If we appoint someone that we aren't supposed to appoint, it will cause calamities. When people who are not mature spiritually or do not have leadership characteristics become elders or deacons of a church, the church will suffer because thoes leaders will maneuver the church at their level.

Too many churches do not teach the conviction of sin as part of salvation and simply accept members without checking their faith. Many churches register members hastily and baptize people thoughtlessly. This corrupts churches and tarnishes their purity. Even if there are just two or three people who are strong in faith, miracles can happen when they gather in the name of Jesus. There is no room for arguments or unnecessary debates to squeeze in.

"You are the Messiah, the Son of the living God" (Matthew 16:16). Jesus said he would build the Church on this confession. The secret of church growth is simple. It is to lead each member to confess his or her faith clearly.

Second, a community where Jesus is its Master

Who is the owner of the church? It is Jesus. But what is it like in reality? In some churches, denominations are the owners, while for others, senior pastors are the owners, which is why some pastors sell the church and leave with the money they amass. They say that they are entitled to receive financial compensation since they have invested so much in the church. Also, in some churches, the elders of the church are the owners. They fill the church with their friends and relatives, and operate the church to suit their palates.

All these are far removed from the essence of the true Church. It is hard to see the characteristics of the true Church in these churches. In fact, it is the new believers who can best recognize what is real and unreal about a church. Some Christians who have been attending church for years may not be able to notice the real nature of a church, but new believers can sense it more distinctly.

The owner of a church should be Jesus. In such a church, new believers feel Jesus inside the church, as they obey and live out the words of Jesus. In this regard, therefore, the way a church can be revived is simple. When people can come to a church, sense the presence of Christ and meet Jesus in that church, whether it be through a pastor's sermon or fellowship with other Christians, and whether it be in a parking lot or a restroom, their hearts will be moved.

Conducting campaigns on proper ethics or shouting slogans such as "Don't drink" or "Don't smoke" or "Ban nepotism" are not necessary. People are doing these things not because they aren't aware of ethical behavior but because they don't have Jesus in their hearts. It is enough for churches to just talk about Jesus. When people experience Jesus and have faith in Him, then they will quit drinking and smoking. This will happen naturally because the church is a community of Jesus.

Can you see spider webs in the wall corners of a church building? Doesn't this reveal how little its members love the church? Do you find a piece of trash scattered on the church floor? This again shows the people's lack of love for their church. Is the church beautiful in front but looks like a junkyard from the rear? Then, it cannot be considered a church. How can someone foul up a space they love?

One of my pastoral philosophies is to make all areas of our church clean and in top condition. Why is that? It's because it is Jesus' church! So, I strive to bring out the best design and maximum efficiency in every corner of our church. We need to have this level of passion as Jesus described in Scripture: "Zeal for your house will consume me."[9]

God's people come, worship, and praise in the church. Doesn't the church need to be at least better than the house we live in? Our church should be better than my house, the sanctuary should be better than our bedroom, and its restroom should be better than the one at home. It is like wanting to give the best gift to someone you sincerely love. The love and passion for the Lord should be shown and revealed in the church, which is the body of Christ.

The head pastors, senior pastors, and chief elders of the church are the servants of the Lord. A church is the true Church if it strictly follows these principles. Ministers are the servants and workers of Jesus Christ and the gatekeepers of His house. They are called to serve the Lord's church, and ministers should therefore ceaselessly contemplate how they can serve the Lord's church well.

Thirdly, a community that the gates of Hades cannot overcome

The Church where Jesus is the Lord has power. What kind of power is this? It is the power that cannot be overcome by the gates of Hades. No secular organizations or powers, nor anything in this world, can overcome the Church. I believe in this and am confident about this. "For I am convinced that neither death nor life, neither angels nor demons, neither the present nor the future, nor any powers, neither height nor depth, nor anything else in all creation, will be able to separate us from the love of God that is in Christ Jesus our Lord" (Romans 8:38-39).

---

[9] John 2:17

That's right. The church where two or three people gather in the name of Jesus can be victorious over the world. There are three kinds of power in this world. First is the power of Satan; second is the power of the world; and third is the power of lust.

The Church is like a ship sailing in the middle of the ocean called the world. This ship does not rest safely on a mountaintop but is found in the midst of the world's rough waves. Sometimes, a storm can shake or throw it off course. But as long as seawater doesn't seep inside the ship, it is fine. The gates of Hades are things that can shipwreck or sink a church, but rest assured. The Bible says that the gates of Hades cannot defeat the churches of Jesus.

Churches have holy power, and this power is from Jesus. All authority in heaven and on earth is given to Jesus. Churches have the power of prayer. They have the power of the cross and the power of the Holy Spirit. Their greatest power comes from love and forgiveness. The gates of Hades have no authority against the power of the Church. Indeed, the power of the Church is magnificent.

Fourth, the community that owns the key to Heaven

Churches have the key to Heaven. "I will give you the keys of the kingdom of heaven; whatever you bind on earth will be bound in heaven, and whatever you loose on earth will be loosed in heaven" (Matthew 16:19). How incredible is this privilege? It's a privilege that no other worldly power can imagine.

Why then are Christians exhausted and lacking joy? It is because they fail to use this gift. The same goes for pastors, missionaries, and congregations. When you take advantage of this privilege, you

1. The Standard for Ecclesiology Is the Ecclesiology of Jesus

will receive the joy and fullness described in Acts. Churches are to be apostles of reconciliation, forgiveness, and peace. This is the secret of evangelism. When you share the Gospel, new souls will come to the Lord, and when new people enter a church, the church will be moved. Even if only a few people evangelize in a church, the church will be filled with excitement. It will be full of energy. It will be revived. Whatever we bind on earth will be bound in heaven, and whatever we loose on earth will be loosed in heaven. What a wonderful privilege this is! We should live in the church with such pride.

What kind of church is an ideal church and a biblical church? We can find the characteristics of such a church in the Bible. First, it is a church led by the laity; second, a church led by the Holy Spirit; and third, a church led by a vision.

2. Ecclesiology Found in Acts

First, the church that is led by the Holy Spirit

Churches should be led by the Holy Spirit.

One of the truths that I've learned in my ministry is that churches must be headed by the Holy Spirit. The church steered by the Holy Spirit is biblical. A church is where the Holy Spirit is placed at the highest priority.

Then, changes, miracles, and histories will unfold in a variety of shapes. It's not knowledge or technology that changes people. Eloquent preaching cannot transform people, but if the Holy Spirit is present in the words preached, people will change. Without the Holy Spirit, people won't change. That's the difference between lectures and sermons.

When we preach, we must put the Holy Spirit in the forefront. When visiting a church member's home, we should let Jesus go before us. If the Holy Spirit doesn't become manifest, that family won't change even if you visit them a hundred times. However, if the Holy Spirit intervenes, the family can instantly change on that very day. How can we explain this mystery? I won't say that many ministers do not know this secret at all, but it is true that many pastors are insensitive about the Holy Spirit. In fact, they are very insensitive. They don't understand the Holy Spirit. Who among pastors would say they don't believe in the Holy Spirit? But the problem is that they do not invite the Holy Spirit into their ministry. Even if they do, they limit the Holy Spirit as they wish.

How can a man limit God? By confining God and limiting Him down to one's own limitations. People think that if they can't do something, God won't be able to do it either. They believe that nothing will happen if they themselves don't believe. This is the common weakness of people.

"Is our church led by the Holy Spirit?" "Have I received the Holy Spirit?" Finding an answer to these questions is easy. You don't need to ask other people to answer for you. All you need to do is think about them quietly, and then you will know. Ask yourself right now. If you think about the Holy Spirit now, you have the Holy Spirit in you. If you have forgotten about the Holy Spirit, you don't have or haven't received the Holy Spirit.

When a church is filled with the Holy Spirit, its members meditate on Him every day. They think about Him early in the morning, reflect on Him while singing and worshipping, remember Him even when they walk along a road, think about Him in their dreams, and feel Him while doing their work. The same is true with pastors. Pastors think about Him when preaching, are led by Him when counseling and praying. They are not forcing themselves to remember Him, and are always in the presence of the Holy Spirit. These are the churches where the Holy Spirit works together with them.

The amazing works of the Holy Spirit change me, mature my heart, and mold me into the image of Christ.

The Holy Spirit manifests differently in each person, depending on one's nature and personality. His work is like the wind. When the wind blows, pieces of paper on the street are blown away, and leaves on the branches flutter, but the concrete wall doesn't budge a bit. Likewise, when the wind of the Holy Spirit blows, some people will speak in tongues and sing praises, while others remain calm and unmoved. The Holy Spirit works in people differently, depending on their personalities and cultures. Those who are hotheaded will speak hastily in tongues, while those who are naturally cool are calm after they receive the Holy Spirit. So, we should not misunderstand Him because of what we see from one's outward appearance.

The essence of the Church is the Holy Spirit. During Pentecost, the Holy Spirit came to people, and the Church was born. This is the nature of the Church. It means that the Church is the Holy Spirit. The Holy Spirit gave birth to the Church. The Church starts from the Holy Spirit. In other words, the Church should be bound by the Holy Spirit from beginning to end. Then it will become a church led by the Holy Spirit. The Holy Spirit ministry is not a program, but is about putting Him first.

Second, a church where members actively participate in ministries

The Church is a community of Christians.

The leading actors of this changing world are the believers (the laity) who have received the Holy Spirit. Biblical churches are places where members can actively lead the people. We need to build this type of structure and system in churches today.

When I planted Onnuri Community Church, one of my visions was to implement ministries that were led by ordinary believers. I would like to boast about the ordinary believers who led ministries and were trained in our church and baptized by the Holy Spirit.

I think the most beautiful churches in the world are in North Korea and China. I once received several letters from the Christians in North Korea. They had heard my sermons on Far East Broadcasting Corporation and wrote about how much they were touched. Upon reading their letters, I understood that there are churches in North Korea, even though there are no seminaries, pastors, or buildings there, not even Bibles.

Because they didn't have Bibles, believers in North Korea copied from the Bibles their parents had used before the Korean War and read those instead. They also copied hymns. They sent me some of these handwritten hymns, and I felt like I was witnessing the Early Church. In another letter, someone wrote that many people call themselves Jesus in North Korea. This man wrote that since North Korean society is chaotic, people would sometimes claim that Jesus had appeared here or there, and he wasn't sure which one was the

2. Ecclesiology Found in Acts

real Jesus.

Still, in another letter, someone asked Far East Broadcasting Corporation to play old hymns instead of new Praise and Worship songs. He even wrote the titles of the songs he wanted to hear, including "I Have Found a Friend in Jesus." He said that they also liked new worship songs but because those songs were not familiar, the songs did not touch them as much. They wrote "Oneurui Church" instead of Onnuri Church and "Yong-ju Hwa" instead of Yong-jo Ha because they couldn't pronounce them correctly.

These believers were incredibly pure. Their walk in faith centered around Jesus. They were ready to risk their lives for their faith. Although they did not have seminaries, pastors, buildings, or leaders, believers of Christ spread like leaven or wildflower. Churches existed and flourished even under the dictatorial regimes of Kim Il Sung and Kim Jong Il in North Korea and Mao Zedong in China. This is the Church. It is self-sustainable, reproducible, and full of life. It has the voice of God and miracles. How could those Christians survive in such unbelievable situations? They survived not just for a day or two but for decades, leading up to today.

During a church conference in Pohang, an intellectual who escaped North Korea shared his testimony with me. I was so surprised to hear his story. He said that since North Koreans had dug so many underground tunnels, the ground could not absorb rainwater during floods. As a result, rainwater would flood entire buildings. For this reason, once during a big flood in Pyongyang, the military had to remove wet weapons and wet tanks from a building. South Korea had to issue an alert because it thought North Korea was about to attack the South because of the tanks.

But what was more startling was that Christians who lived underground for 20 years also had to resurface due to the floods. They were therefore caught and executed. The communist North Koreans saw the resilience of Christians and said, "There are people in the world (pertaining to Christians) who are more tenacious than communists." That's right. Who supplied food for the underground Christians for 20 years? There must have been people who helped them survive. This is the Church. When you think this way, there is nothing the Church cannot do.

When I went to Turkey, I saw an underground city in Cappadocia. It was 10 to 20 times larger than the catacombs. According to traditional literature, the Apostle Peter and believers of the Early Church fled from the persecutions of Rome and lived in this underground city for three years. They couldn't see the sun and waited for the Lord to come. There were seminaries, places for baptism, and dormitories. This is the Christian community.

The more biblical term for "laity" is "saints." Although churches use the term "laity" to distinguish people who are not part of the clergy, churches are, in fact, a community of saints. Aren't those who are saved and have the Holy Spirit in them saints? Then who are ministers? Ministers are those who nurture and help others, teach the Bible, and coach the people of God; those who are moved, saved, and baptized. Even though ministers and the laity have different roles, they are all saints. In the Early Church, there were three groups of people. There were apostles, the elders (a group made up of dedicated deacons who led the church), and many saints. The people needed order and a set of rules to operate the church. That's why they needed an assembly. However, the rules were never more

2. Ecclesiology Found in Acts

important than Jesus or the Bible.

Means and ends should not get mixed up. Means are means, and ends are ends. For example, circumcision is a means, not an end. Sadly, because Jews saw circumcision as an end, they suppressed many people's faith and put a heavy yoke on believers who were not circumcised. Ordinary believers should think, "I am not doing something because my pastor asked me to do it, but because it is what I must do!" Pastors should encourage believers to have such a mindset. When members think this way, pastors don't have to push them to work all the time. This is called an active church. The more active members are, the more important teamwork becomes between the pastors and members.

When claiming that "a church is led by the laity," there is one thing that we should be careful about. If you oversimplify and define a church as a layman-led church, there is a high probability that it will lead to temptation or cause troubles. "Laity" here means ordinary believers who are dedicated and baptized in the Holy Spirit. A church moved by saints is a church led by committed Christians who are filled with the Holy Spirit. However, when people with humanistic values dominate a church, they tend to try to steer their church into a movement. This will cause members to fight with their pastor, and churches will experience troubles. Anti-clericalism began in opposition to false clericalism, but such anti-clericalism is as dangerous as clericalism. In fact, it is detrimental because this puts the laity up against the clergy, the pastors. In Acts, chapter 6, when conflicts arose in the Early Church, Peter told the believers, "Brothers and sisters, choose seven men from among you who are known to be full of the Spirit and wisdom. We will turn this responsibility over to them and will give our attention to prayer and the ministry of the word" (Acts 6:3-4).

Conflicts are a natural phenomenon that occur when a church grows. To overcome conflict well, each member must understand his or her role. Dos and don'ts must be clear. The things that pastors and the laity should and should not do must be defined. Pastors should not do what the laity should be doing, and likewise, the laity should not attempt to do what pastors should be doing. Pastors should protect and respect the realm of the laity.

If pastors fail to set healthy boundaries between roles, the church may fall into the trap of "laity-centrism." Members will say that they will take over all the work in the church. People will entertain extreme ideas and ask, "What's so special about pastors? They're just salaried men," and such thinking will weaken the church. In the end, both "clergy-centrism" and "laity-centrism" are two extremes that can kill the vitality of churches.

Pastors and members of the church are not in a conflicting relationship, but rather, they are to cooperate with each other and promote teamwork. This is similar to the relationship between a coach and an athlete. The two trust, respect, and love each other, but they have different roles to play. No matter how talented an athlete is, if he ignores his coach or supervisor, he will fail in the game. On the other hand, even if the coach understands the flow of the game well, he cannot jump in and play the game himself.

Pastors are like coaches, and the members of the churches, like athletes. Just as every coach needs a player to compete in a game regardless of how competent the coach is, the most talented pastors need laymen in their ministries. Just as people running on the race

2. Ecclesiology Found in Acts

track are the athletes, the people who will change the world are ordinary Christians. Pastors coach, encourage, give directions, and inspire members of the church behind the scenes so that they can go and transform the world.

A church enters a crisis when a pastor steps into the spotlight. When everything centers around the pastor, the members will remain as helpers. Pastors should make their laymen the main characters and the stars of their ministries. Pastors should make ordinary members pastor-like laymen or shepherd-like laymen who have a vision to change the world.

Whether you are a pastor or a layman, you should have the mindset that you are serving God together. The next important thing is how pastors and the members of the church can create a fantastic team. It's more important to have team members who share the same vision than to have many people on your team. If you are not on the same page, it doesn't help. The fact that you have many people can make things more uncomfortable and complicated. That's why it is easier for small churches to create good teamwork.

You need to think about these aspects if you want to create harmonious teamwork.

First, your team needs to share the same ecclesiology and must guard against theological ecclesiology.

Second, you should share the same vision, pastoral philosophy, and spiritual experience. If pastors think one way and the elders think another, the church is bound to break apart. The most difficult thing is when church members experience the Holy Spirit while the pastor hasn't. It is also hard when the laity hasn't experienced the Holy Spirit when the pastor has. It's not easy when their spiritual experiences are different.

Third, people should respect and recognize each other's gifts. When they do, the church will be able to unite as one. Here, training and discipleship need to be carried out together, and from the beginning, churches need to emphasize the Word of God and the Holy Spirit. When the church is based on the Word and anointed by the Holy Spirit, it will be able to acknowledge everyone's value. Before a member is appointed to a position, make sure that he or she has spiritually experienced God's anointing. If everyone in the church, whether it be the pastor or members, has had such a spiritual experience, the church will grow and mature with active and powerful strength.

A few years ago, our church took a huge gamble and invested a hundred million won (around $100,000 USD) in allowing our pastors and elders to visit about ten churches and missions organizations in the US, including Willow Creek Church and Saddleback Church.

Since then, there has been a remarkable change in our church. In the past, whenever I had passionately talked about the ministry of the Holy Spirit and inspiring worship services, our members would interpret my words based on the limitations of their experiences. They had never experienced such ministries or services. They used to say things like, "Our pastor is very unpredictable." or "He is just full of too many ideas." They could not share the idea that this was from God. However, when we visited the churches in the US together, they shed tears and were moved because they realized that such beautiful churches exist. After the visit, the elders spearheaded and started an "Open Worship" for new believers and unbelievers. The hundred million won had not gone to waste after all.

To be honest, it is challenging for elders and pastors to see other churches. They serve during Sunday services, buried in their churches, and cannot see anything else. If they spend three years like that, they become blind. They cannot see what's around them, and they believe that only they are right.

In some ways, people live their lives as a result of their experiences, which is why they tend to resist when they hear about something that is beyond their experience. Also, they feel uncomfortable around unfamiliar things since people like familiarity. That is why people are greatly influenced by culture.

That is also why there aren't many young people in churches. Churches lack the culture the youth want; churches are decorated in colors and ways that old people like, and young people feel reluctant to come in. When churches create an atmosphere that unbelievers and young people like, wouldn't they want to come in? Churches should be able to boldly transform themselves for the sake of reaching people.

One of the characteristics of most old people is that they believe they don't make mistakes. They made all the mistakes when they were young, and when they are over 60, they just follow a fixed path. When someone tries to do something, the elderly will often stop them and say, "Don't do that. I've tried all of that when I was young." However, young people are different. As adults experienced their own failures in the past, young people should be given a chance to make mistakes as well.

Likewise, churches should entertain mistakes and adventures. To grow, we must continue to take on challenges and venture into new things. If this is discouraged, the path for church growth will be obstructed.

One of the adventures I engaged in was to try to raise male lay leaders. In Korean churches, women's evangelistic societies play an enormous role. However, we were skeptical and asked ourselves, "Can women's evangelistic societies change the world?" Men in their 40s and 50s have nothing to do in churches, yet they are the CEOs, professors, and experts in the world. Although they have leadership gifts and the ability to lead people, they have nothing to do in churches except participate in services. This is because pastors don't give them work to do. They may take part in visiting members or charity bazaars. If they are active, they will join a presbytery, an assembly, or Christian associations. They build walls against the world and focus only on the church. That's why the lay leadership in churches is stagnant.

I believed that the men of the church should participate in ministries so that the church leadership can also become the world's leadership. Pastors should encourage the men to take on spiritual leadership in their offices, homes, and workplaces. Pastors should help them when they face difficulties, be their friend when they are lonely, and give them consistent counseling so that they can bring heaven down to this world.

If our church had been complacent with the women's evangelistic society, like traditional churches have been and did not attempt to establish male leadership, our church wouldn't have been able to spiritually influence the world as we do now. Also, we wouldn't have been able to start a whole new level of women's ministry. We used to think about what women could do for churches. Today, however, women have been developing a new ministry for other women, and the churches are providing ministry opportunities for them as well.

We should account for the gifts of the church.

Which programs are you going to run? How are you going to run programs? When churches are small, there aren't many ministries. Each church has a gift. Onnuri Community Church has a gift of world missions. Some churches are gifted in helping rural churches. Churches with the same budget may spend their funds differently. One may spend more on missions, while another spends more on mercy ministries.

One time, a pastor who was interested in the environment came and asked, "Can Onnuri Church lead a movement in saving the environment?" An environmental campaign is needed, but our church cannot do everything. If we take on the jobs God has given us with all our energy and do the things God has asked us to do, this is good.

Our church has received a lot of cultural gifts. My eyes opened to popular culture when I ministered in a celebrity church. I believe that "the popular culture needs to be saved." So, I initiated various cultural approaches. Also, I am interested in students. I love young people because I was involved with a student movement in college. I get excited when I see young people. When I see them, I want to invest in them without limit.

When we use the gifts that God has given us, people with similar gifts will be drawn closer. Vision attracts people. If someone has a vision to establish a church for laborers, laborers will gather around him. Likewise, students will be drawn closer and will want to work together with those who want to start a student church. Those who want to do theatrical plays or dramas will attract people with similar interests. Churches should be as diverse as the diversity of occupations.

However, no matter how different, all churches have the same root. And that is the Word. In other words, what is truly needed is spiritual training, such as Quiet Time, one-to-one discipleship, Bible studies, and sermons. When a pastor ministers to his church using his gifts, the church will shine, and the members will be moved and empowered.

We should pursue spiritual excellence.

When we specialize in gifts and visions and go out into the world, we can easily move ahead of any other experts in the world. Isn't this the power to lead and change the world?

The same applies to farming or fishing villages. No matter how few have gathered, if the pastor continues to plea, those who have ears will hear and come. Why don't people come to church? It is because the words being spoken do not attract them. They think, "Whether I go to this or that church, they all say the same thing. Also, the beginning and end of what pastors say is very predictable. I thought they'd share something different after a month, but as expected, it's just the same old thing." If people think this way, they will no longer come to church. Who wants to hear the sermons that lack insight into the Bible? Who wants to listen to pastors

2. Ecclesiology Found in Acts

when they simply talk about stories in newspapers or on television?

Churches don't need to repeat the stories that people already know. Instead, churches need to speak about God, His vision, and His dream. Even if only a few people are gathered, when there is spiritual excellence and vision, people will listen to the preaching. They hear and relate to the Word, give their time and materials with faith, and create history together. We should become people who pursue spiritual excellence, not worldly success.

Third, a church led by vision

What kind of church is an ideal church and a biblical church? First, it is a church led by the laity; second, a church led by the Holy Spirit; and third, a church led by a vision.

You need vision.

A nation without vision will perish. It cannot exist. Animals eat food to survive, but people need vision to live. If a man lacks vision, how is he any different from an animal? A society without vision is no different from a society of animals. Churches should continue to move, steered by the dream and vision from God. One pastor cannot minister in a church forever. Pastors will constantly change. If a church changes every time it gets a new pastor, how confused will its members be? However, if it is a vision that leads the church, it is a different story. Churches led by vision, not personality, will become more diversified, deepened, and enriched every time their leaders change. The Church is eternal. It's because the dream of God is at the center of the Church.

Think of God's vision, not yours.

The first thing we must consider when talking about a church that is led by vision is that the vision has to be God's vision, not yours. Our vision and God's vision should be the same. Only then will the vision be a true vision.

What is God's vision? It is to realize the kingdom of God and the dream of Jesus Christ's cross. God's dream is to save humanity, which is doomed to receive eternal judgment, due to Adam's original sin. When we look into the Bible from Genesis to Revelation, the one expectation, one dream, one hope, and one focus is to save humanity. God never lost or abandoned this goal, which is why the Bible is about creation history and salvation history at the same time. When you see the Bible from the perspective of God's creation or salvation, you will understand it all.

What did God do to save humankind? God sent his one and only son, Jesus Christ to this world, and God allowed him to take his cross and shed his cleansing blood to save our sins. Then, God resurrected him, completed salvation, and offered salvation to every human being. This is the dream of God, and it should become ours, too. His purpose should become mine.

Consider the three visions of Jesus.

What is the dream of Jesus Christ which is also the dream of God? If God's dream is to save all humanity, then what is Jesus' dream?

Jesus' vision is to take up the cross to fulfill God's dream. Thirty-three years of Jesus' earthly life focused entirely on the cross. He came to die. There were a lot of temptations, but he resisted all of

2. Ecclesiology Found in Acts

them and walked toward the cross. He agonized with each step he took until his sweat turned to blood and he carried the cross. Bearing the cross wasn't an easy or comfortable task. It was a painful ordeal that he had hoped to avoid.

Jesus asked God, "If you are willing, please take this cup of suffering away from me."[10] However, Jesus did not walk away. The climax of all four Gospels is the cross.

Another dream of Jesus was to raise up the Church. When Jesus was living on earth, there was not a single church anywhere in the world. After He had carried the cross, the Church was not yet born, but for the cross to bring salvation to all humankind, he needed churches. That's why Jesus said, "And I tell you that you are Peter, and on this rock, I will build my church, and the gates of Hades will not overcome it. I will give you the keys of the kingdom of heaven; whatever you bind on earth will be bound in heaven, and whatever you loose on earth will be loosed in heaven" (Matthew 16:18-19).

The Church was built on the cross. A church that does not have the cross is not a church. So Jesus told His disciples not to tell anyone about this until He had taken up the cross. After Jesus shed His precious blood, died on the cross, was resurrected, and ascended to heaven, the Holy Spirit came. Only then was the Church born.

Jesus' third vision was to send the Holy Spirit to us. It was as Jesus said earlier: "…and he will give you another advocate to help you and be with you forever (John 14:16)."

But what is the vision of the Holy Spirit? It is to evangelize and

---

10 Luke 22:42.

build the Church. These are the efforts on which the Holy Spirit focuses, and shouldn't try to misuse Him. The Holy Spirit gives gifts, power, and fullness. However, at the core of His vision, He wants to save all souls through the cross, and to build, lead, and complete churches.

The vision of the Church is ultimately to save souls.

Then what is the vision of the Church? Why did Jesus build the Church? Why does the Holy Spirit give birth to churches and nurture and complete them? The vision of the Church is obvious and clear - it is to save all humanity.

Our job is also apparent and certain, as the focus of our churches should be on God's vision, which is to save a lost soul. The vision of the Church should reflect the reason that Jesus built His Church, and that is to find a lost soul. It is to accept a dying, lost, and abandoned soul to become a member of the Body of Jesus. This is evident in the Scripture stories of the Lost Sheep and the Prodigal Son.

To this end, the Church must have the vision of becoming the gatekeeper of God that transforms the world. Here is why Jesus told us to be salt and light in the world. He talked about personal salvation, but he also said, "Love your neighbor as yourself" (Matthew 22:39). He added that "you will be my witnesses in Jerusalem, and in all Judea and Samaria, and to the ends of the earth" (Acts 1:8). God didn't want to forsake the world, nor did he want to ignore it. God gave us the vision of completing his kingdom in this world. Churches exist to establish God's kingdom by becoming the salt and light of the world, driving out the darkness, and blocking rotten and corrupted things. Ultimately, the core nature of the Church is to save souls.

Churches should be communities whose ultimate goal is to save souls and whose work is to share the Gospel until the end. Evangelism is not just one of the things a church must do, but is what the church should be all about. The focus of ministry is on evangelism. Mission work is about evangelizing people after moving to a different place. But whether it is doing evangelism or missions, the nature of the Church's work is to share salvation.

We don't think about such a simple truth in our daily lives, so we waste time, energy, and resources. We wander around here and there and finally come to our senses only when we are about to die. In the end, we fail to use many of our resources to accomplish God's vision. The same is true for pastors and churches.

The vision God gave us is the same vision that led Jesus to bear the cross, shed His blood, and build the Church - to save all humankind. It is also the vision that the Holy Spirit embraces - again to save a soul! We must clearly define God's vision, Jesus' vision, the Holy Spirit's vision, and the Church's vision, and we must embrace those as our own personal vision. Our vision should be to save humanity, spread the cross, and build churches.

Onnuri Community Church exists for this vision - no more, no less. I hope all churches can focus on saving souls.

The Standard of Pastoral Philosophy Is the Ecclesiology of Acts

PART 3:

PASTORAL PHILOSOPHY

The ecclesiology of a church should be the same across churches. However, the pastoral philosophy could differ between churches. Onnuri Community Church bases its pastoral philosophy on the characteristics shown in Acts. The churches in Acts were tangible, while the ecclesiology of Jesus was intangible. The Church of Christ is like a baby hidden in a mother's womb. But the churches in Acts are like a newborn baby. We cannot see the Church Jesus preached about with our eyes, but we can see, touch, and hear the churches in Acts.

1. The Standard for Pastoral Philosophy Is the Ecclesiology of Acts

The Church in Acts was a community of worship and the Holy Spirit, as well as a missions community. The pastoral philosophy of Onnuri Community Church is derived from the pastoral philosophy in Acts. The Church in the Book of Acts demonstrated ten characteristics.

First: A community filled with the Holy Spirit (Acts 2)
An Acts-like church is a church where the Holy Spirit is at work.
If a church has neither experience nor understanding of the Holy Spirit, it cannot be called an Acts-like church. How was the Early Church born? It was born of the Holy Spirit.

The Bible says that on the day of Pentecost, the sound of a violently blowing wind suddenly came down from heaven and filled the whole house where the disciples were sitting, and they saw what seemed to be tongues of fire that separated and came to rest on each of them. The Holy Spirit came upon those who were praying, igniting their spirits just as we might open our car's fuel door and begin filling up at a gas station. People began to be filled with the Holy Spirit, and at that moment they were filled (fullness) for the fire came upon them (fire), who is the wind of the Holy Spirit (wind) and the breath of life. They started to speak in tongues, following the Holy Spirit (speaking in tongues), and burst out the door from a small upper room (dedication). Without realizing what they were doing, they spoke as the Holy Spirit prompted them and evangelized whoever they came across (evangelism). Their message was always about Jesus.

The people who received the Holy Spirit had nothing to share but Jesus. They proclaimed, "God resurrected Jesus whom you killed." This was kerygma, the essence of the Gospel of the Early Church. Those who were intoxicated by the Holy Spirit shared the message with the people they met. One amazing thing is that everyone who was listening started to hear the message in their own language.

This reminds me of a similar event that happened in our church. A foreigner once came to our church service. At that time, we didn't offer interpretation during our services. He approached me after I finished preaching and said, "I understood all of your preaching." When I asked him if someone interpreted it for him, he replied that there was no one. I asked him if he spoke Korean, and he said that he didn't know any Korean. Then he said that he

1. The Standard for Pastoral Philosophy Is the Ecclesiology of Acts

was just able to understand and told me what the preaching was about. Such things have not happened often in my life, but I have experienced that it can truly happen.

The beginning of the Early Church was similar. People who saw the incredible things that happened during Pentecost said that the Christians were insane. Some said that they were drunk. At that point, Peter got up and said, "These people are not drunk. It's the answer to what was spoken by the prophet Joel." Then he continued to share the Gospel. On that day, 3,000 people repented after listening to Peter's sermon. We should note what the many people gathered did together. There you can see a real picture of the church.

To be filled with the Holy Spirit is simple. It is to receive fire and power, to experience the wind of the Holy Spirit, and to speak according to the guidance of the Holy Spirit. Words are our thoughts. Language does not exist if we don't think. When I am filled with the Holy Spirit, I will speak, assert, and act out the thoughts of the Holy Spirit. If someone lives according to the thoughts of the Holy Spirit, people will gather around that person and will want to listen to him, even if he is not charming. Because the Holy Spirit is in such an individual, people will want to be with him. This is called "revival."

"When the day of Pentecost came, they were all together in one place. Suddenly a sound like the blowing of a violent wind came from heaven and filled the whole house where they were sitting" (Acts 2:1-2). This passage sounds majestic, like a cosmic message as in John 1:1: "In the beginning was the Word, and the Word was with God, and the Word was God." This is the presence of the

Holy Spirit. The presence of the Holy Spirit produces the cosmic creative power of God. It is also Jesus, the Son of God, dwelling in us in spirit. He is the Word revealed in the beginning, filled with grace and truth. No matter how much I try, it is impossible to express the weight, depth, authority, and power of the Holy Spirit. The power of creation, salvation, and love; the power that rules and governs the universe; and, the power that created the heaven and earth all came with the Spirit of God. That same Holy Spirit of God suddenly rested upon 120 people like a rushing wind. This is the baptism of the Holy Spirit.

The members of the Church all received the Holy Spirit without exception. There was no one in the upper room at Pentecost who was not baptized by the Holy Spirit. I hope that all Christians will be filled with and anointed by the Holy Spirit today.

Second: A community that lives the life of Jesus (Acts 2)

The second characteristic of the Early Church in the Book of Acts is that people formed a community that followed the life of Jesus. After the Holy Spirit had baptized them, their lives were transformed. It was something they had never experienced before, as they were caught up by the Spirit. The members of the church in Acts gathered together and were taught by the apostles. They joined Holy Spirit-filled worship, fellowshipped with one another, and shared bread with each other. Every time they met, they shed tears, helped each other, and forgave one another. Where else can one experience something like this?

The Church is not a movie theater, nor a playground, nor a social gathering. Some treat a church offering as an admission

1. The Standard for Pastoral Philosophy Is the Ecclesiology of Acts

ticket, but that isn't true. The Church is where we pray together, learn the Word, worship the Lord, and help the poor. You are used to gathering at home and in your workplaces, but now you gather around the church. The Church is a unique community that you cannot experience anywhere else in modern society. It is a place where hurts are healed, hope and vision are generated, and comfort and encouragement are shared. This is the community of Jesus. The world we live in is fundamentally different from the kingdom of God. The society that Christians seek is the kingdom of God.

A church that is filled with the Holy Spirit can partially experience such an amazing society on earth, but it will always be followed by violent attacks from Satan.

Those who received the Holy Spirit on Pentecost heard the Word and started to share the Gospel. They were baptized and began to study the Bible. This is discipleship. They received the Holy Spirit, shared the Gospel and discipled the new believers. They also shared the food and resources they had with each other according to their needs.

Sharing food is a characteristic of the Early Church. The fact that they shared food means that they were like a family. Enjoying meals with your friends for one year is much better than being friends for ten years and never sharing food together. Try having a meeting with people over a meal, and you will experience how it softens the atmosphere. Haven't you gone on an outreach or worked on a project with people, and then after you talk over meals or fervently pray together, you realize that you've built a close relationship without knowing it? I think that some of the same reasons the Early Church was able to form a beautiful community so suddenly was that the members of the Early Church had meals, broke bread, and prayed together. Teaching, fellowship, and prayer - these brought about spiritual changes in the community!

The first manifestation of spiritual change is sharing. Those who have received grace will share it naturally. A person who does not share reveals that he or she has not received anything. Those who have been forgiven can forgive others, but people who haven't experienced forgiveness cannot forgive others. People who have received love can love others naturally. If someone can't love others, it is because he has never been loved.

As the members of the Early Church experienced the Holy Spirit, shared grace, fellowshipped with one another, prayed, and shared the Word, their love intensified and grew more powerful. And this became a driving force in creating a beautiful community where they shared their resources and possessions. The fact that the Early Church was able to share what they owned shows that they overcame the natural sinfulness and earthly desires of people. People are drawn to a group like this. The Early Church attracted people naturally. Where there is love and the Holy Spirit, people will come together.

An interesting characteristic of churches is that when a church shares, people will come. Christians will come every day to a church that is truly touched by God. They will come to church day and night to pray, meet with others, and break bread. It is evident that a person has received the Holy Spirit when that person devotes himself to and serves in the church. As a result, a community of the Holy Spirit, evangelism, and discipleship will be established.

Third: A community where miracles happen every day (Acts 3)

The third characteristic of the church in Acts is that they experienced miracles and supernatural events every day.

"Then Peter said, 'Silver or gold I do not have, but what I have I give you. In the name of Jesus Christ of Nazareth, walk.' Taking him by the right hand, he helped him up, and instantly the man's feet and ankles became strong. He jumped to his feet and began to walk. Then he went with them into the temple courts, walking and jumping, and praising God. When all the people saw him walking and praising God, they recognized him as the same man who used to sit begging at the temple gate called Beautiful, and they were filled with wonder and amazement at what had happened to him" (Acts 3:6-10).

The man who was crippled since birth had neither hope nor a future. However, he experienced a miracle after encountering Peter and John, who were filled with the Holy Spirit. The man's 40-year-long life as a disabled person ended as he got up right away with the power of the Holy Spirit. His feet and ankles were empowered. He got up, walked, and ran. This miracle did not pertain only to the man's physical problems. Instead, it meant people who were spiritually crippled, blind, and deaf, and who had built a wall against God were revived. They came to church, prayed, sang, and worshipped. Their facial expressions, words, and attitudes changed. It was as if they grew wings on their shoulders. The miracle of spiritually running, listening, and understanding occurred. This was the Early Church in Acts.

The Church was witness to a series of small and large spiritual events. If the things that happen in a church are the same as what is going on in the world, then how is that church different from the world?

During Sunday services, people are set free from the clutches of evil spirits, are healed, speak in tongues, and hear the word of the Holy Spirit. Such testimonies are constantly shared in early morning prayer meetings and small groups, as well as stories of people breaking free from drugs, alcohol, and smoking, and stories of forgiveness and reconciliation with one another. Companies that were dying have been revived, and people who were almost dead came to life again. Such events also took place when Onnuri Community Church began.

Testimonies like these are heard and shared in our congregation even today. I think events like these will continue to happen until the day of Jesus. There have been many stories of people who got up from their wheelchairs, who recovered their sight, whose cancer and incurable diseases have been healed, and so on.

Miraculous events have been endless, but the greatest miracle has not been the healing of a sick person or the parting of the Red Sea. The greatest of all is the miracle of forgiveness and love. These are miracles: enemies becoming friends, divorced families becoming one again, and South and North Korea reuniting as one. Miracles of unification take place in churches that closely follow the Early Church in Acts. Miracles continue in workplaces, families, and societies so that there is no time for the tears of joy to dry. Onnuri Community Church was able to grow quietly because such beautiful testimonies happened regularly.

1. The Standard for Pastoral Philosophy Is the Ecclesiology of Acts

Fourth: A community that shares the Gospel even in times of hardship (Acts 4)

The fourth characteristic of the Church in Acts is that they shared the Gospel in times of suffering.

Then Jesus said to his disciples, "If anyone would come after me, he must deny himself and take up his cross and follow me" (Matthew 16:24). It is also written in Acts that "The priests and the captain of the temple guard and the Sadducees came up to Peter and John while they were speaking to the people. They were greatly disturbed because the apostles were teaching the people and proclaiming in Jesus the resurrection of the dead. They seized Peter and John, and because it was evening, they put them in jail until the next day" (Acts 4:1-4). Trouble did not end here. People captured and jailed those who preached Jesus. Some Christians were stabbed or hurled down from the top of the temple.

Believing in Jesus doesn't mean there will not be suffering. In fact, even greater hardships may follow. The Early Church experienced a series of sufferings. A case in point is the Apostle Paul. How much did Apostle Paul suffer? He said, "We go hungry and thirsty, we are in rags, we are brutally treated, we are homeless" (1 Corinthians 4:11); "Up to this moment, we have become the scum of the earth, the refuse of the world" (1 Corinthians 4:13); and he states that he almost died several times (2 Corinthians 11:23).

However, Jesus gives spiritual power to Christians in hardships so that they can overcome their sufferings. The Church is a spiritual community that does not succumb to sufferings and thus changes the world. When you share the Gospel, difficulties come. Sufferings are the completion of blessings. In fact, a characteristic of the Early Church was that it suffered many persecutions and troubles. The Church is not a place of eternal comfort. A real church goes through difficulties and into the fire. It walks into crises. This is the Church. The church that suffers like the Lord is the Church that was revealed in the Book of Acts.

When we face difficulties, crises, and sufferings when serving the church, we might ask ourselves, "Am I not believing in Jesus correctly? Is this why I don't receive blessings?" That is not true. We tend to think this way because we don't know that suffering is a blessing. The true image of a church is a church that is afflicted. Because we don't see churches suffering, the world is not changing. When I suffer and become afflicted, the world changes. We learn from the Early Church that the true Christian life is not about great position, high status, success, or a fancy life.

One day, an Uzbekistani brother whom we had evangelized was sent to prison. He was released after serving one year and eight months. He had been accused of tax evasion. To be exact, he was wrongly accused of a crime that was actually committed by his boss. However, the Uzbekistani brother asked us to let him stay in prison and not to try to take him out from jail. We were surprised to hear his decision. After being in prison for some time, he realized that there were many souls who were waiting for him to share the Gospel with them. For him, it wasn't important whether he was in jail or not. The fact that he could evangelize was what was most important. For him, going to jail was nothing more than moving to another location.

This is how the Church in Acts behaved. The Christians of the Early Church were not obsessed with their position or status but continued to share the Gospel in the midst of much affliction.

Fifth: A community that pursued holiness, purity, and honesty (Acts 5)

The fifth characteristic of the Church in Acts is that it sought after holiness, purity, and honesty.

It is not God's way to use tricks, even if doing so were convenient, or if there were a plausible reason. Acts chapter 5 records an astounding story about a couple named Ananias and Sapphira. They sold their land as an offering to God, but they hid some of the money they received from the sale. Then they lied about it and said, "We gave all the money as an offering," deceiving God and the people. Because of this sin and their poor judgment, Ananias and Sapphira instantly died. It was a miserable death.

Ananias and Sapphira voluntarily sold their house and gave it as an offering. That was a good thing to do, but what's more important is that they didn't do it to follow God's command. Why did they give an offering in the first place? They did it out of spiritual jealousy. They saw Barnabas, who was respected by the members of the Early Church, give a beautiful offering, and they were envious of him. An offering shouldn't be made because you envy someone. It is not mandatory, and shouldn't be offered out of jealousy. You give an offering because you are overwhelmed by the grace you have received from God. Ananias and Sapphira got jealous of all the praise Barnabas received from the people, and as a result, the couple committed hypocrisy. They chose the way of cheating, not commitment. They believed that they could fool God and the Holy Spirit.

I sometimes wonder why God decided to kill Ananias and Sapphira in such an extreme and cruel way. I believe it was because there are no more significant values for the future of the Church than holiness, honesty, and purity. The problem of today's churches is that people lie, and even churches seem to grow numb to lies. Today's culture is about making not just big lies but also small lies. Churches tend to lie about the number of church members they have by inflating the total figure. Sometimes sermons and testimonies are exaggerated, and there is too much emphasis on the appearance of the church. All these lead people to doubt the authenticity of the Church.

That's not all, however. We are also seeing an increase in the number of sexual crimes committed by pastors in churches. Numerous scandals prove this to be the case. The name of a church doesn't guarantee one's holiness or purity. Churches must be born again. Churches must be the standard of morality and ethics. People should be able to trust pastors and Christians. Elders, deacons, and deaconess should become the conscience of the nation. The essence of the Church does not depend on the size of its building, the number of the congregation, or the number of diverse programs it holds. The essence of the Church is internal and spiritual.

Sixth: A community that raises lay leaders (Acts 6)

The sixth characteristic of the church in Acts is that it raised lay leaders. In the Early Church, apostles did not monopolize leadership but shared it with other people. This teaches us that the main actor of the Church is Jesus Christ alone and that we are all supporting actors. Apostles were not the central figures. When

1. The Standard for Pastoral Philosophy Is the Ecclesiology of Acts

a person is glorified, a church becomes the person's church. So the leadership of a church should be shared among many people, according to their roles.

The Early Church in Acts began to grow into a large church as the Holy Spirit came and revived the congregation. But then, as the number of people grew larger problems began to surface. There arose conflicts and struggles in the Church between groups and gifts. This was inevitable because there were many people. The Apostles saw elders and members clashing with each other because of gifts and elected deacons. This was a critical moment for the Church in Acts. As a result, the Church that used to operate just around pastors introduced a laymen-focused leadership. This meant its members started to serve the church according to their gifts, and three of the most notable lay leaders were Stephen, the martyr, Philip, the evangelist, and Paul, the pioneer and missionary. Theirs was a representative model of lay leadership. The church expanded and grew continuously. A pastor alone cannot move a church. A church is made up of many laypeople.

Pastors are just pastors. They take care of the sheep, present visions, and encourage the members to dream of the kingdom of God. Then who can serve as the hands and feet of the church? Devoted laymen can play that role. Pastors are like directors or coaches. They train athletes, set up strategies, select players, give them roles, and put them in a game. This is the role of a pastor. Pastors are not athletes. A coach should not jump into the stadium just because he is frustrated about how his team is performing. On the other hand, the members of the church are like athletes playing in the field. The players must do their best and play as they were trained by their coaches, and they should follow their coach's instructions. The main actors who will change the world are ordinary members of the church. Day by day they live in the world, and as they change and become better Christians, the world can change as well. But what's more important than delegating roles within a church is fostering fantastic partnerships between pastors and laypeople. In Acts, apostles implemented incredible teamwork with ordinary church members who were filled with the Holy Spirit.

One of the characteristics of Onnuri Community Church is its devoted laypeople. Sometimes they become the big brothers or mentors of young pastors in a way. These leaders who devoted themselves at the beginning of the church still passionately but quietly serve the church, as Barnabas or Caleb did, more than 20 years later. Many ordinary members became pastors or missionaries after studying in seminaries. Some time ago, ten new elders were appointed, eight of whom later became pastors.

Seventh: A community that is willing to die for its faith (Acts 7)

The figures that represent Acts were not just Peter and Paul but also the seven deacons of the Early Church. Among the deacons, Philip and Stephen have unique positions. One of them became the symbol of evangelists, and the other became that of martyrs. What is the heart of Acts? It is evangelism and martyrdom. Martyrdom is the "flower" of Acts. The climax of suffering is martyrdom, and Stephen chose the path of becoming a martyr for Jesus.

When we look into the history of Christian churches, there

have been martyrs who shed their blood in every country. In Korea in 1866, for instance, a missionary from England named Thomas, who was then only in his 20s, was brutally slain by Korean government officials along the Daedonggang River. As he died, he gave a Bible to his tormentors. The one Bible he gave and the blood he shed transformed Korea into a blessed land. Why did he have to die in the land of *Joseon*?[11] It was because of the Gospel of the cross.

He was not the only one. Pastor Ki-chul Joo was inhumanely killed inside a prison because he refused to worship a Japanese shrine. The faith of Pastor Ki-chul Joo became the faith of the Korean churches. Also, Christians in Jeam-ri were burned to death during their worship service. Japanese police locked the church door and set the church on fire with all the worshippers inside. Then they shot to death all those who survived the blaze. The blood shed by the martyrs became the root of Korean churches. Examples like these can be found in any country as the Gospel was first introduced in native lands. Stephen was stoned to death, and his face shone like an angel. This is Acts.

Recently, in 2007, some young adults from Saemmul Church in South Korea went to Afghanistan to perform relief work. Sadly, however, they were kidnapped by the Taliban. Two of them were shot, and 19 of them spent 40 days in horrific conditions, experiencing the "march of death." This is Acts. In 50 or 100 years, the deaths of this pastor and an ordinary layman will bear much fruit for the Gospel in Afghanistan.

---

11 *Joseon* (1392-1897) was the last dynasty of Korea.

The Gospel cannot be shared without suffering, and a church cannot be built without martyrdom. The spirit of martyrdom in the Book of Acts was received not only by Stephen but also by many people. Except for the Apostle John, most of the 12 disciples were martyred. Individuals who risk their own lives, these are the people of Acts.

Eighth: A community that embraces foreigners (Acts 10)

The eighth characteristic of the Church in Acts is that it embraced foreigners. "While Peter was still speaking these words, the Holy Spirit came on all who heard the message. The circumcised believers who had come with Peter were astonished that the gift of the Holy Spirit had been poured out even on the Gentiles. For they heard them speaking in tongues and praising God. Then Peter said, 'Can anyone keep these people from being baptized with water? They have received the Holy Spirit just as we have.' So he ordered that they be baptized in the name of Jesus Christ. Then they asked Peter to stay with them for a few days" (Acts 10:44-48).

Cornelius was a centurion of Rome. Although he was a Gentile, he sought God and was a holy man who helped the poor. God especially remembered Cornelius. God instructed Peter to baptize him, but Peter rejected God, saying that he could not baptize a Gentile. Peter believed Jesus and was born again by understanding the Gospel, but he couldn't overcome the limitations of Judaism and the idea of God's chosen people. For this reason, God sternly scolded him. God will save His chosen people, Israel, but He equally wants to save Gentiles who do not believe in God.

People are dictated by their environment and culture. However,

1. The Standard for Pastoral Philosophy Is the Ecclesiology of Acts

environment and culture are not the content but simply a vessel; they are not the fruit but only a shell. Yet, as much as you need a cup in order to hold water for drinking, we need something to preserve the content. The same is true when it comes to the Gospel and culture. To share the Gospel, we need the formality of culture. Peter thought he already knew God's will very well, but in reality, he did not know God's mind at all. Only after God scolded him for looking at Cornelius from a cultural point of view alone did he accept and baptize the Gentile believer.

Back then, the fact that God gave the Holy Spirit to Gentiles was the most shocking news imaginable for the Jews. What was the main message of the Apostle Paul? The Apostle Paul proclaimed that God saved not just Jews but also all Gentiles who believed in Him.

Later, on his first, second, and third evangelistic trips, the Apostle Paul preached the Gospel to foreigners. Because of that, Paul was persecuted, driven out, and beaten by the Jews. But in the Gospel, white and black, Asians and Caucasians, males and females, and adults and children are all one. God pours the Holy Spirit and showers sunlight and rain on all people equally.

The Church in Acts embraced foreigners. Churches today should do the same. For Korean churches, the secret to being truly blessed is to understand, embrace, love, and accept people from different cultural backgrounds; people who are different from us, who have different personalities, languages, skin colors, and habits. In particular, as Korean churches accept migrant workers and North Korean defectors, the churches will be blessed. Doing missions work in distant countries is important, but if churches fail to love the ones Jesus placed right within their arm's reach, they will not be blessed. We should embrace those who come to our country, seek those who are powerless and weak, and accept those who are marginalized.

Ninth: A community that shares the Gospel to the ends of the earth (Acts 13-28)

The ninth characteristic of the Church in Acts is that it shared the Gospel to the ends of the earth. A church that preaches the Gospel to the ends of the world is an Acts-like church. Look at Acts! It has 28 chapters, and the missions work starts from chapter 13. This means 50 percent of Acts emphasizes missions. The conclusion of Acts is missions.

Acts chapter 6 shows that after the Church was organized and filled with people, persecutions followed. Persecutions like this come for the sake of mission work. When faced with oppression, believers scattered. They had to disperse themselves against their will. They fled to Jerusalem, Judea, and Samaria. What does this scattering mean? It means the Gospel was spread. Christians will scatter and preach the Gospel, so we shouldn't feel disappointed about being separated from each other. Going away is another new challenge and adventure; it is a new beginning in God. This is how the Early Church started from Jerusalem and spread to Samaria and the ends of the earth.

As I mentioned earlier, during this time, one very important event occurred - the encounter between Peter and Cornelius, which created a new paradigm for the Early Church. It was time for the Church, which centered on Jews, to reach out to others.

1. The Standard for Pastoral Philosophy Is the Ecclesiology of Acts

The group of Jews that met in Jewish synagogues experienced the incident with Cornelius and then started to share the Gospel to the Gentiles as well. At first, the Church had two groups of Jews: Orthodox Jews and Greeks, and then Gentiles from different areas joined in.

Just like that, the Church was not a community of similar people anymore. Through Acts, we learn that people of different colors and cultures can come together and create a beautiful church of Christ. Taking a closer look at the Antioch Church in Acts, many names were mentioned, including Barnabas and Paul, as well as various races, and even Africans, who gathered in the church.

In Acts 13, Antioch Church finally sent missionaries. It is important to note that the first missionaries were Paul and Barnabas. If we talk in today's terms, Paul and Barnabas were like the senior pastors who decided to go on a mission trip. Usually, assistant pastors go on missions, but in the Early Church, the chief pastors were sent. This is also an important paradigm.

Paul and Barnabas went on an evangelistic trip. How far did they go? They went to Rome. At that time, Rome was the end of the world. Also, they went to Jerusalem, Judea, Samaria, and tried to go to Central Asia, but the Holy Spirit didn't allow the Apostle Paul to go to Central Asia. Instead, he made him cross the sea and go to Philippi. He went to Philippi, then Thessalonica, Corinth, Aden, and Ephesus, sweeping across the large cities in Europe, the cities of philosophy, economy, and commerce, with the Gospel.

As the Gospel rapidly spread through Europe, the Apostle Paul thought, "I must see Rome." At first, he shared the Gospel within Israel but then went to Asia and Europe to evangelize. His mindset changed.

In reality, however, the Apostle Paul's heart was not really for Rome. He wanted to see Rome only because he wanted to go to Spain after sharing fellowship with Christians in Rome. Apostle Paul had a burning desire for the Gospel. He wanted to go to the ends of the earth, where the Gospel had never been preached. No place is off limits to the Gospel. Wherever people live, we should go - to the ends of the earth and the ends of heaven - to share the Gospel, to build the Church of the Lord, and to share the salvation of the cross, just as Paul did.

Eventually, the Apostle Paul went to Rome. How did he get there? Ironically, he went to Rome as a prisoner. He didn't have to pay a penny for the trip. The guards even protected him. God's providence is beyond human wisdom. The moment Paul arrived in Rome, he was confined in a rented house instead of a prison cell that was guarded by some soldiers. He started a prisoner-like life in Rome. Why didn't God give Paul complete freedom? Yet, even though Paul did not have full freedom, nothing prevented him from preaching the Gospel.

As you can see, the Church in Acts had a vision and passion for going to the ends of the earth to save souls and share the Gospel.

And here is another thing you need to think about: Sharing the Gospel is not all about going to a faraway place to evangelize people as Paul did. Our mission field is also where we live. We are missionaries in our homes and workplaces. We are missionaries in our society. It is mission work when we go to our workplaces, as much as when one goes to mission fields preparing to die as a martyr. If other people work eight hours a day, Christians should be prepared to work 10 hours. It is about working two hours more than what is required of you, volunteering quietly and devoting oneself to your company. We should be able to work with joy and sometimes even go overnight, even if we don't get paid for it. That's the heart of missionaries. That's the heart of Acts.

Onnuri Community Church has sent more than a thousand missionaries over the last 20 years. Already, seven missionaries have lost their lives while performing their mission in the fields.

Tenth: A community that continues to write Acts, chapter 29 (Acts 28 and onwards)

The tenth characteristic of the Church in Acts is that it continues to write chapter 29. In other words, it gives birth to new churches.

"For two whole years, Paul stayed there in his own rented house and welcomed all who came to see him. Boldly and without hindrance, he preached the kingdom of God and taught about the Lord Jesus Christ" (Acts 28:30-31).

It is said that many people came to Paul to learn the Word of God, and no one forbade them from meeting him. Our position doesn't have to be free in order to be truly free.

If someone can share the Gospel in any situation like Paul did, that person is free indeed. The Book of Acts does not end with a period. There is no end to Acts. That's right. The Church of Acts never ends. It is not a period, but a comma. The Acts-like Church continues until Jesus comes again.

Although Acts ends with chapter 28, we can continue to ask questions about what happened to the Early Church. "What happened next? Where did everyone go? What happened to the Church?" The early Christians probably built new churches here and there, while continuing to witness about the Lord and perform supernatural miracles with waves of love.

The people who learned the Bible at that time were scattered and continued to build churches and teach the Bible. Others who learned the Bible went out again and set up new churches and taught the Bible as well. So many churches were born. Churches have given birth to new churches for over 2,000 years. This is Acts chapter 29, which is still being written today.

I want Onnuri Community Church to demonstrate the characteristics of the Church in Acts. I also believe that every single Korean church must participate in God's vision and dream of saving individual souls and transforming the world. I hope that we will see the blessings of churches praying and providing support for missionaries, and going to mission fields as missionaries. This is the real church.

A new church should be pioneers. A church should give birth to a new church, then another and another. Koreans have a zeal for building churches wherever they go. The spirit of building a church wherever you are is the spirit of writing Acts chapter 29.

The Church of God is forever. Until the Lord comes back, churches will be his gatekeeper, called to change the world.

Pastoral philosophy of Onnuri Community Church

Onnuri Community Church's method of creating a community that is closely similar to that of the Early Church in Acts includes

1. The Standard for Pastoral Philosophy Is the Ecclesiology of Acts

services and ministries, sharing and proclaiming the Word. Also, we focus on Quiet Time, one-to-one discipleship, small groups, community ministry, evangelism, missions, services, and relief works. This methodology is all linked together.

When ecclesiology and pastoral philosophy are well established, a worship that is alive and full of the Holy Spirit will begin. When worship is alive, ministries will overflow, and you will witness the sharing and proclamation of the Word. This will lead to the rise of Holy Communion and discipleship, creating a true community. The ultimate purpose of all these is missions.

Worship

Ministry

Sermons

Nurturing System

Small Groups and Community

Evangelism

Missions

PART 4:

PASTORAL PHILOSOPHICAL METHODOLOGY

Worship is building a deep relationship with God. It is about meditating on God and entering into the presence of God. All ministries start from worship. When you worship, you will not be exhausted by serving the ministries. The more you participate in ministries, you will feel more empowered. A church should offer worship that is alive. At the same time, it should also engage in ministries. If a church only worships God without serving in ministries, it is like feeding a body without working out. On the other hand, if a church only has ministries and lacks worship, the church will burn out very soon. A church can be healthy only when both worship and ministries are alive and active.

1. Worship

Worship is man's duty.

The most important duty of Christians is to glorify God. This is because God is worthy to receive worship, glory, honor, and praise. True worship means attributing to Him glory, honor, and praise.

The Bible tells us to worship and praise God in many passages:

"'Return to me,' declares the LORD Almighty, 'and I will return to you.'" (Zechariah 1:3)

"Let us acknowledge the LORD; let us press on to acknowledge him." (Hosea 6:3)

"Ascribe to the LORD the glory due his name. Bring an offering and come before him; worship the LORD in the splendor of his holiness." (1 Chronicles 16: 29)

The Book of Revelation talks about four living creatures with six wings and with eyes all around, even under their wings. They never stop praising God day and night, saying, "Holy, holy, holy is the Lord God Almighty, who was, and is, and is to come" (Revelation 4:8). It wasn't only these creatures who praised God but also the 24 elders who were next to them; they worshipped God as they lay their crowns before His throne. "You are worthy, our Lord and God, to receive glory and honor and power" (Revelation 4:11). Revelation also describes an amazing scene of worship. A great multitude that no one could count, from every nation, tribe, people, and language, stands before the throne and in front of the Lamb. They are wearing white robes and holding palm branches in their hands.

Likewise, the entire Bible points out that man's duty is to serve, worship, and praise God, the Creator. We should ask God to come into our lives and sit in the master's seat. We must recognize and praise his greatness. This is true happiness in life.

True worship is to seek God from the center of the heart.

True worship is seeking God from the center of one's heart, regardless of formality and interests. To find out whether you offered true worship or not, think about how much you devoted, sacrificed, and lost. The worshippers are those who willingly sacrifice or suffer loss for God. Just because you go to church, participate in the Lord's Supper, give an offering, and serve the church doesn't mean that you offered true worship.

God said that worship offered in spirit and in truth is true spiritual worship (John 4:24). God is pleased with those who seek him, and he blesses those who worship him. Also, God is pleased with the nations and people who worship him in spirit and in truth. "Praise the LORD, all you nations; extol him, all you peoples. For great is his love toward us, and the faithfulness of the LORD endures forever. Praise the LORD" (Psalm 117).

The Apostle Paul said in Romans that our relationship with God should be right first, and it is spiritual worship that we must offer. "Therefore, I urge you, brothers, in view of God's mercy, to offer your bodies as living sacrifices, holy and pleasing to God - this is your spiritual act of worship" (Romans 12:1).

This is true worship. God's presence is where we worship. His glory is manifested where He is.

Spiritual worship is offering our body.

Sacrifice requires sacrificial offerings, and worship takes place when there is a sacrifice offered. Sacrifice is defined by what kind of offering you bring. Abel gave the firstborn of his sheep and his oil, and it pleased God. Abraham was ready to sacrifice Isaac, his son who was conceived when he was already 100 years old and who was more precious than his own life.

Jesus Christ gave His body on the cross to atone for humankind. This is worship. If Jesus had given only His heart and not His body on the cross to shed blood, our salvation would not have been completed.

Most people try to replace worship by giving just their heart but not their body because it is easier to give your heart than your body. Once, when Jesus was praying and Peter fell asleep, the Lord said to the Apostle, "Watch and pray so that you will not fall into temptation. The spirit is willing, but the body is weak" (Matthew 26:41). You may have already done relief and mission work, loved your country, and brought unification with your hearts, but the problem is what you have done with your bodies!

What does it mean to offer your body? It is to give your time and finances, and offer all of your hands and feet. It is actually giving yourself, devoting and sacrificing your body, not just with mere words, for some great cause. It is about offering your hands and feet, not just your mouth and lips. It is giving time, resources, and labor. This is the beginning of worship.

There is one more important fact. The body should not be dirty but holy in order to please God. Not all bodies are the true body He desires, and not all worship is true worship. The type of body used for worship determines what kind of worship is given. In the Old Testament, things that were unclean, damaged, or not whole could not be used as sacrifices. Sacrifices have to be complete.

We must become true worshippers.

Revelation chapter 4 is like a treasure box of Scripture on worship. If one word is to be chosen from Revelation chapter 4 about worship, it would be "worthy." "You are worthy, our Lord and God, to receive glory and honor and power, for you created all things, and by your will, they were created and have their being" (Revelations 4:11). Our God is worthy of our praise and worship.

Worship is about giving Him the glory, honor, and power. These elements are very important parts of worship: The blood of Jesus Christ on the cross, the anointing of the Holy Spirit and the power of salvation. These three are the most important elements of worship. Worship that lacks these three elements is false worship. There are many counterfeit types of worship around us. True worship is about meeting Him who is worthy of our worship.

Worship is the best language a man can have. The most basic thing that a man should do in his relationship with God is to worship Him. Worship is not a human event but is of God. When we worship, God becomes active inside us and manifest outside. So, worship is the holy of holies.

A spiritual leader must first become a true worshipper.

I'd like to offer three things for people to become true worshippers.

First, dedicate yourself to worship. There are many ways to be devoted, but the most important and essential one is to devote yourself to worship. To believe in God means to devote yourself to worship.

Second, dedicate yourself as a worshipper. The most important thing for a worshipper is holiness and purity. Being able to play a musical instrument, having a good voice, talent, or appearance are not the essential elements of true worship leaders. We fail to worship because we have lost our sense of holiness and innocence.

Third, dedicate yourself to serve voluntarily. To realize what real worship is like, you have to become a volunteer. Worship is labor. There is no worship that doesn't require sweat, volunteering, and devoted hearts. Those who carry the chairs and clean the restrooms are real worshippers. Whatever you do, do not play around, but sweat it out instead. Help others. Whether it is in a study room, a center for foreign migrant workers from Japan, or wherever you go, throw yourself into helping others. Only our devotion and sacrifice can save the world.

There are three things that true worshippers must watch out for.

First, we should not confuse the Gospel with culture. We drink water, not the cup that holds it. However, we need the cup in order to drink the water. We are "consuming" the Gospel, not culture. Unfortunately, many worshippers are infatuated with culture. Although music is important in worship, it is not the main thing. Music is just a tool. The core of worship is prayer, purity, and innocence. We should never confuse medicine and poison.

Second, we should be sensitive to Satan's attacks. Beware of scandals. Don't be full of conceit. A tool like music can be very dangerous. Don't watch a TV series or listen to music that is based on adultery, because their ideas can obsess our minds whenever we are tired and lonely. In particular, worship leaders face many sexual and sensual temptations. I have seen many leaders fall into scandals because they were tempted. Passion and purity should not be confused. A passionate person isn't automatically pure. We should not confuse gifts and talents with purity.

Third, we must guard against jealousy. Some people get angry when they are given a secondary role at church. Such an attitude is hazardous. An individual who wants to be recognized above others may be smiling on the outside but seething with anger on the inside because of jealousy. Such a person is struggling with insecurity and can easily fall into depression. When people with intense

1. Worship

mood swings lead worship, the worship is doomed to be unstable.

The way to church revival is worship.

When true worship is offered, the Church will become alive like vibrant green leaves covered in raindrops. When a soul gains life, that is worship. The most important thing a church should do is to worship the living God. Worship is about experiencing the presence of God and worshipping and praising the Most High by offering everything we have. When you offer true worship, miracles and transformation will happen. When Moses came down from Mount Sinai after seeing God, his face became radiant. That is worship. But in reality, no matter how many times we worship, we don't see any changes or light in our countenance. Our inner self must be transformed by worship. Now is the time for us to think about worship seriously once again.

Sunday services in unhealthy churches are dead. From a pastoral point of view, when the Sunday service (or main service as it is often called) is alive, all other ministerial activities will gain strength and vitality. When other gifts like healing and prophecy appear a lot in a church whose worship is weak and dead, the church will face troubles. This is because worship is at the center of the Church. On the other hand, when a church's worship is alive, gifts and miracles will appear; even if an amazing ministry suddenly sprouts, it won't cause any trouble. No matter how great the discipleship training program is, if the worship is dead, the training won't last long. Likewise, no matter how awesome missions and relief ministries are, if people are not touched by the Sunday service, those ministries won't last. We aim to restore a service that is free from formality. People should be in tears and run to church, singing praises as they come to church and step into the churchyard on Sundays after spending an entire week at home. As they raise their hands and sing praises, they have already met God before they have even heard the sermon. This is a service that is alive.

Special spiritual experiences, such as meeting God at the church after being brutally beaten and almost left for dead for the sake of God's kingdom, build up Sunday services. If worship is dead, there must be an obstacle. Think about the obstacles that may prevent worship from coming alive. Then, get rid of them. "Yet a time is coming and has now come when the true worshippers will worship the Father in spirit and in truth, for they are the kind of worshippers the Father seeks" (John 4:23).

During the early stages of our church, we put most of our efforts on "service." Our goal was to offer such services to God that a pastor like me could be most deeply moved, similar to the experiences I'd had in England that gave me a holy shock. We looked into the items in our services, and if anything did not match with the essence of the church in Acts, we boldly changed it. These are the goals that Onnuri Community Church has set; we long to experience worship where the Holy Spirit is present.

1. Let's long for the presence of the Holy Spirit so we can experience true worship.

People cannot make the service. The service that lacks the presence of the Holy Spirit is not a service. True service is led by the Holy Spirit. Let's have a desire for the anointing of the Holy Spirit. Let's long for the fullness of the Holy Spirit.

2. Let's remember that a pastor is also a worshipper.

The moderator is a worshipper, and the preacher is also a worshipper. Worship is the top priority. Before preaching, immerse yourself in worship. That is why intercession is important. What truly matters is not moderating a service but leading everyone to worship. When a pastor worships, members can offer true worship as well. Our goal was to restore a service that is free from formality.

3. Let's not be too obsessed with order.

You can recite the Lord's Prayer or the Apostles' Creed when they are needed. No matter how good something is, if it is repeated meaninglessly, it can quickly become a dry habit. If it must be recited, make sure people don't chant it out of habit. In other words, do it sincerely. I wanted to make sure that we did such things as a meaningful part of service instead of doing it by habit.

4. Let's preach sermons that are lively.

I realized that it is important to preach evangelistic sermons, not ethical ones. Sermons should sound like the Word of God, not the words of men. When preaching, pastors should refrain from talking about offerings, events, or secular stories. They should shake off the temptation to grab the people's attention with an intellectual and human-focused sermon. They should rather preach that we should live like the disciples of Christ, even if we suffer losses, sicknesses, and pain.

5. Let's not be stiff-necked when preaching.

What I mean here is that pastors should guard against practiced or hypocritical attitudes or expressions. Pastors are servants of God, which is why they received the authority of God. God is manifested when pastors lower themselves. Pastors simply reflect the love, justice, and greatness of God. Pastors should remember that when members of the church humbly show respect toward them, the members are in fact bowing down their heads to God who is behind the pastors, not them. More than anything, the humility and meekness of pastors are important.

6. Let's offer worship with offerings.

We need to prepare fragrant offerings of devotion and sacrifice. Jesus himself was a living sacrifice for the salvation of men. He completed humankind's salvation by becoming a sacrifice on the cross. The same goes for us. A preacher himself should become an offering of devotion and sacrifice so that our lives will be ones of worship. Have you struggled to live for Jesus? Have you sacrificed and devoted yourself for something? Have you kept your purity? We should ask ourselves these questions. We should offer spiritually valuable offerings that are more important than earthly possessions.

7. Let's offer worship with praise.

The church community is about singing praises. I dream of a service overflowing with praises from beginning to end. Praise opens the door of worship. This is why churches should pay great attention to people leading the services and appoint full-time ministers as praise and worship leaders or church choir conductors. The position of praise and worship ministers is as important as that of the preachers.

8. Lower the pulpit.

It is important to lower man's authority in order to raise God. In our church, I moved the preacher's chair down from the pulpit to where the congregation sits. This is to declare that the preacher is also a worshipper.

9. Let's not pass around offering baskets during service.

Passing around offering baskets is not wrong in itself. The point is that we should be careful that it doesn't distract from the focus of worship. This is why we placed offering boxes at the chapel entrance. People can quietly give their offerings before a service without showing others.

10. Let's observe Holy Communion frequently.

The Lord's Supper is as important as sermons. The climax of preaching is in the Lord's Supper. It is to allow people to experience the presence, power, and healing of the Holy Spirit through Holy Communion. People will be able to remind themselves of the meaning of salvation, restoration, and being sent as they participate in the Lord's Supper. Today, the crisis of Protestantism is the crisis of the Lord's Supper.

11. Let's not limit the time for the service.

There is no reason to end services in an hour. Moreover, sermons don't need to be shorter than 30 minutes. The leader of a service is the Holy Spirit. We must watch out for repetitively boring services, and we should be more careful not to let our human minds limit the worship that is led by the Holy Spirit.

It was not easy to reform the formality and ideas of worship, which have become habits. Creating our pulpit like a stage, getting rid of the chair for preachers on the pulpit, not passing around offering baskets during the service, not reciting the Lord's Prayer and the Apostles' Creed and offering frequent Holy Communion caused controversy.

Back then, as the widely used term "preparatory praise" (a praise "warm up" before the service) showed, churches had a low awareness of praise. But I was convinced that praise and worship were important in services. That's why I invited Jung-pyo Hong, the choir conductor who was studying in Germany at that time, to join me. He has been the only one partnering with me continuously since I planted Onnuri Community Church to this day. I wanted to make music ministry staff a full-time position. However, church leaders couldn't understand why I would make a praise and worship leader full-time. Appointing full-time assistant pastors or junior pastors was not a problem, but having full-time praise and worship ministers was possible only after a long time.

Later, Stephen Ha, who had studied abroad with me, returned to South Korea and started a worship team called "Praise and Worship" as one of the college students' and young adults' ministries.

The team held worship rallies that were a mix of praise, prayer, and message proclamation. It set a new paradigm. This team introduced praise and worship services in South Korea for the first time and held a "Praise and Worship" service every Thursday. Korean churches went wild over it. Over 4,000 young people gathered at

1. Worship

Praise and Worship services on Thursdays, when around 1,000 people gathered at Onnuri Community Church on Sundays.

Every Thursday by the end of the rally, people from the neighborhood would call the church and pour in complaints. Their claims were understandable because these young people filled with the Holy Spirit would sing and pray as they walked to Seobinggo Station. In order to get there from our church, they had to walk through the Shindonga Apartment complex.

At that time, the new term "praise and worship rally" was coined among South Korean churches. Also, the new culture of setting up music instruments on the pulpit stage or holding worship services rapidly spread among Korean churches. In some churches, people set up musical instruments during the morning youth services, took them away before the adult services, and set them up again for young adults service in the afternoon because their elders would not allow putting instruments on the pulpit. I doubt that there are churches like that nowadays, but at that time, Korean churches were so rigid that changes like this caused such confusion.

The members of Onnuri Church were no different. Young students passionately welcomed the new style of service by devoting themselves to Jesus and by voluntarily getting rid of their tapes of secular rock or pop songs. It was a miracle. However, adults couldn't embrace the new change like the young people.

I wanted adult services to be as passionate as the praise and worship rallies. How happy would God be if our church members would open their hearts, dance, clap, and worship Him like David? However, adults felt extremely uncomfortable singing worship songs. I could not ask them to sing worship songs when they were already too shy to clap their hands during worship, not to mention raise their hands. So I carefully started by singing one worship song after three hymns.

It took almost seven years for the adults in our church to sing worship songs, raise their hands and shed tears during service. They began to learn little by little the spiritual attitudes of raising hands and kneeling down as they worshipped and approached God.

Limiting the service is like limiting the Holy Spirit.

Once, a person who was a good intercessor in the States visited our church. The person shared that he wanted to come to our church and briefly pray for the church in the middle of a service. I declined, worrying that it might disrupt the service. But later, he still came to our church without contacting me. It was five minutes before the Sunday service. We talked, and I realized that he was indeed a man of prayer. So I asked him to introduce himself to the congregation later. After the service had started, I welcomed him to the stage. At that point, the Holy Spirit gave me the impression *allow him to pray*. So I spoke to the congregation: "Those who want to receive prayer, come out!" Then, people lined up in a long line. I had to give up my sermon. On that Sunday, we just prayed until the end of the service.

However, this doesn't mean that we didn't offer "worship" that day. Through several events, God spoke to me that I shouldn't limit God with the formality and stereotypes of worship.

I was once invited to speak at a missions seminar. When I went there, several students led me to a corner. Then, they started to lay their hands on me and prayed for me. Not only when I preached, but also during prayer and testimony, the intercessory team prayed constantly. I can't explain with my words how shocked I was on that day.

When I came back to my church, I pondered about it. *If we have 80 members in the choir, shouldn't we have at least 80 people interceding for services and preachers?*

From that Sunday, I started recruiting people who could intercede for worship. The intercessory team was formed, and they came up on the stage an hour before service and prayed for that service. Surprisingly, our services began to change as if to show how delighted God was and how much he had been waiting for such an intercessory team. Also, the service didn't change its style, but it became a service powerfully ministered by the Holy Spirit.

The formality of worship wasn't important. No matter how good the discipleship training was, if worship was dead, it didn't last long. Even if a church's mercy or mission ministry is great, it won't last long when people are not touched by the Sunday services.

The way toward church revival was in worship. As the word spread that our church service was on fire, people began to flock to the church to the point where we could not handle it.

When Onnuri Community Church was six years into operations, All Nations Worship & Praise Ministries invited Pastor Jim Graham. (He is the pastor of the church in England where I received a holy shock.) I wanted to share with my church the holy shock I experienced from worship. But then, after the service, he told me that "Onnuri Church's service is amazing. I am challenged a lot!" When he shared that with me, I wept inside. How surprised I was to hear from the pastor whose church inspired me that he had also received a holy shock from us. It would be a lie if I said that I didn't weep at that time.

Of course, Onnuri Community Church services continuously evolved after that. One of the changes was that we required the person who would be praying on behalf of the church during service to write the prayer down beforehand. This was to allow the person to have deep fellowship with God while writing the prayer until he was satisfied with it. Also, we got rid of gowns for the preacher and the choir. I don't usually wear a gown. It's because I want to approach God as I am. Even now, the worship style of our church is constantly changing. It changes as much as our life changes. It's because ultimately, worship is completed in our lives.

These days, most of the Christians who register at Onnuri Community Church say that they chose our church because they liked our services. Many Christians have stated that they were restored to their first love for the Lord while worshipping at Onnuri Community Church. In fact, I, the pastor, also love our church service.

I still long for worship where the anointing of the Holy Spirit overflows. Abraham built an altar everywhere he went. I will not just offer an hour of worship on Sundays, but I will continue to long for worship that is offered to God in every area of my life 24 hours a day. I desire to offer the kind of worship that was offered by Enoch as he walked with God for 300 years. And I will pray like this. "Come Holy Spirit. Please anoint us with oil. Please seal us. Be with those who are hurt, sick, and discouraged. Restore them through the Word, praise, and prayers."

1. Worship

Five suggestions to restore Sunday services

The following five things are important to revive Sunday services.

First: the work of the Holy Spirit

It is the core element of worship. When we worship, the fire of the Holy Spirit comes down, the wind of the Holy Spirit blows, and God's presence and holiness are manifested. This is the anointing of the Holy Spirit. When the Holy Spirit anoints a service, God's holiness is revealed, and the souls of worshippers transform completely. Then we are able to offer worship that God will accept with joy.

In the church where the Holy Spirit works richly, people can experience a new dimension of worship. Another word that expresses the richness of the Holy Spirit is to "pour out." He opens the gates of heaven and pours himself out. A service where there is the anointing of the Holy Spirit is the service filled with the Holy Spirit. When we offer such service, we will experience spiritual fullness and power, our human rationality will be shattered, and we will become a church where joy and excitement overflow.

Second: sermons

Worship must have sermons that are alive. In order to offer a living worship, the sermons need to be lively and anointed by the Holy Spirit. Then why do so many sermons sound like lullabies? It's because they are either the words of humans or words that lack life. Congregations want to hear that they should go and change the world despite losses and pains. When the sermon anointed by God is proclaimed from the pulpit, people will experience the power of the resurrection throughout the week. The most important part is the pastor who has experienced the Holy Spirit. Only sermons proclaimed by the Holy Spirit should be spoken from the pulpit.

Third: offerings

There must be a fragrant offering in a powerful worship. Just as the fragrance is spread when the lid of a perfume jar is broken and its fragrant oil is poured, true worship takes place when our self is broken and offered. There must be devotion. Devotion can be expressed through offerings as well as through our lives. God completed the salvation of humankind through the sacrifice of Jesus Christ on the cross, not by his words. When our worship lacks aroma, it is because it does not have the offering of devotion and sacrifice. Only those who have experienced the pain of devotion will have the honor of meeting God, and only those who have mourned in the past will receive the comfort that comes from heaven.

When Jesus came to the house of Simon the Leper at Bethany, Mary quietly brought a jar of ointment that was precious to her. She knelt down next to Jesus without any words, broke the jar, and poured the ointment on his feet. Then, she shed tears and washed his feet with her hair. This is true, fragrant worship.

Those who had not received the Holy Spirit and had no memory of meeting God could not understand such a heart and such worship. Rather, they criticized it. However, her act was "a holy waste." Would you go just anywhere and eat just anything when dining out with your loved one? No, you wouldn't. Even if you have to spend extra money, you will go to a nice and beautiful place to eat. You spend money because you love the person. You "waste" because you love. You don't feel it's been wasted, because you do it out of love.

We should also sometimes "waste for God." You give all of your time even though you don't have to. It would be okay to give just a few hours to him, but you choose to give all 24 hours. Because you love God, you want to give the best of yourself. You give your time, money, pride, and even your job. It is the overwhelming experience only a person who has met God can have.

Fourth: praise and worship

There must be praise in a service. The Church is a community that gives praises to God. When we raise our hands and kneel down as we praise God, God's glorious presence will appear. Singing praise without tears or out of habit is not worship.

How can singing praise without tears give glory to God? How can singing praises with just your voices in harmony honor God? We often experience in our church that the choir sometimes can't continue singing because they are so deeply moved by God. A cellist, so immersed in praising God, had to stop playing his cello. He raised his bow and hands to worship God. When the Holy Spirit comes and anoints us, we burst into tears. It is real praise. It is true worship.

Fifth: true worshippers

There must be true worshippers in worship. God does not seek pastors, elders, or deacons. These are just positions or functions.

God seeks worshippers. In some ways, it is most difficult for pastors to worship God. It is easy for a pastor to remain as a preacher or a moderator. Worship is about falling deeply into God, walking into the presence of God, and staying in the anointing of the Holy Spirit. But pastors who lead a service often think about the order of the service, rather than God.

Abraham was a worshipper who built an altar wherever he went. We do not have true worship because we do not have worshippers. True worship for God's glory exists in the heart of worshippers, not in the outward formality.

When true worship is offered, the Church will become alive like vibrant green leaves covered in raindrops.

Imagine a church where lay people engage in ministries like pastors, yet the authority and leadership of its pastor are respected. Create fantastic teamwork between pastors and members such that pastors do not monopolize ministries and members think of pastors as their partners. When pastors and members form one body, just like Paul and Timothy, Priscilla and Aquila, and Jesus and His twelve disciples, the church of the Lord will be a beautiful community.

2. Ministry

Give ministry to lay people.

There are many things to touch on regarding ministry for the Lord, but I would like to focus on ministries led by laypeople because this is essential for Korean churches. We need ordinary members to participate in ministries like pastors do, without invading the realm of pastoral leadership. We need to foster an environment where the laity can work freely and creatively.

How beautiful would a church be if its pastors and laypeople could form a fantastic team and operate as one body, as Paul and Timothy, Priscilla and Aquila, or Jesus and His 12 disciples did! Such a community would change the world.

Finding such teamwork in the world is difficult. It is hard to find a workplace where its owner and employees operate as a fantastic team. People in the world today are busy competing with each other, constantly engaging in jealousy and hostility, and taking advantage of each other. The Church, on the other hand, offers itself to be used. The world avenges, but the Church forgives. The world competes, but the Church protects one another. The world is a place of division, while the church is a place of unification.

So even when only 12 people gather, they can create a miracle, and with just 120 people coming together, they can change the world. Church communities like this can bring miracles to and influence their neighborhoods. Churches fail to make an impact on society not because the number of their members is small, but because their quality, substance, and love are not conveyed.

When someone loves his or her church, he or she can gladly spare time for the church. Think how much time and money people devote to things that are not worthy of such investment. Offering your time to God also means that you are spending less time on secular things. When an individual who used to meet and chase worldly friends and events begins to devote himself to the Lord, he can be transformed into a person who spends his resources and time for God and the Church.

Plant the vision.

Before we talk about lay leadership, we need to think about what a true leader is like. A true leader is a person with a vision. A person without a vision cannot be a leader.

The first thing we need to do when starting a ministry led by laymen is to share the vision with our members. They must under-

2. Ministry

stand, "Why do I do this?" and "Why do I have to do this?" They should work because of their own vision, not because their pastor has asked them to. When someone works because his pastor has asked him to or because he simply wants to save his own face, he will become quickly exhausted and cannot last long. If a person, however, does the ministry because he has received a vision from God and believes that it is the vision that he must accomplish, he will be able to complete the task even when he is challenged, hurt, or exhausted. He will devote himself to the ministry because it is God who has entrusted him with the task. God wants to bear fruit through the beautiful devotions of ordinary people.

The power to carry out a ministry comes from a vision. Noah had the vision to build an ark. God told him to build one, despite the fact that the sun was shining bright and there was no sign of rain at all. Although everyone pointed fingers at him, mocked him, and tried to disrupt him, Noah was able to complete the ark because of God's word and promise and vision. Although the rain did not come even a day just before the ark was about to be completed, Noah did not stop building it.

Abraham had a dream of leaving Ur of the Chaldeans and becoming the father of faith in the land God had promised. Although he fell, was shattered and tested, and gave birth to Ishmael, there was one thing that led his life. It was not a small goal that carried him through but a strong current. Just as with Abraham, this is what must lead our lives as well.

Likewise, Moses had a vision of an exodus from Egypt. The prophet of the Old Testament had a vision to save his people after hearing God's voice. And finally, Jesus Himself had a vision to establish the kingdom of God on earth.

Such burning and lingering vision must first be planted in laypeople if we want to raise them well. In fact, praying and dreaming together and having a vision for the Church is more important than working with the laity. In order for people to find their vision, pastors should ask members questions: "Why did we plant this church?" "Why do we serve the church?" "Where is this church headed?" Just asking members to work does not help much.

When members of a church dream, feel joy, and are moved, they will develop a vision. When they have the vision, they will have leadership. People with vision can hear the voice of God. When a person hears the voice of God, even a passive and shy individual can become bold, lead people in front, and persuade others. He will begin to show leadership to the people around him. The passion to accomplish a vision will foster leadership in him.

There are three overall frameworks in a ministry led by laypeople, and these are the Holy Spirit, vision, and leadership. The source of all power is the Holy Spirit. When a person is empowered after being filled with the Holy Spirit, he needs two wings to soar, and these are vision and leadership. A bird can fly high in the sky with its two wings. You shouldn't have just vision or just leadership, but both of these at the same time. Pastors should encourage members to look to the glory of the Lord by fostering leadership in them. Vision and leadership are important components that Korean churches must develop.

At the beginning of Onnuri Community Church, I tried my best to share the vision with the members. First, I started a leadership Bible study, and to promote this gathering, I held an

2. Ministry

opening ceremony. Then, we met at church and attended a seminar-style Bible study. During the Bible studies, I quietly listened while members gave presentations and discussed them with one another. I ended the sessions by wrapping up and presenting ministry directions. There were even some enthusiastic members who would come to Seoul for a few hours just to attend the Bible study in the middle of a business trip.

Through this, the leaders of our church were able to share a clearer picture of our church's vision. We constantly talked about what kind of church we wanted to be, which included a church that plants churches, a church that raises churches, a church that creates Christian culture, and a church that is frequently used by people. As we talked, ideas would come up.

Sharing a vision with the laity is the first step towards transforming the world. It is no exaggeration to say that the ministry of Jesus was to share his vision with his disciples. After the death of Jesus and the anointing of the Holy Spirit, the disciples were able to carry the vision and share it with others to the ends of the earth. If we are gathered to fulfill the vision of Jesus, we should think about various issues, including what kind of church Jesus would want and how we can build a church that is truly the body of the Lord.

One thing we should be careful about regarding lay leadership is that we should encourage these people not to look to church organizations or people. Rather, we should encourage them to look to Christ, who leads the organization and the people.

The reason why many people stumble in church, is that they look to the pastor. If church members rely on and look only to

Jesus and the Holy Spirit who lead the church, instead of relying on the pastor, they will never be disappointed.

Let members work according to their gifts.

An interesting fact is that many people who are called by God and have vision and purpose overlook the fact that they have gifts hidden in them like gems. It is important that one knows what gifts he or she has or does not have.

In many churches, elders and pastors do not serve according to their gifts. Ministries are divided and delegated to leaders. When a layperson has more passion, expertise, and leadership in one area than an elder does but the elder is in the leadership position, the overall organization becomes shaky. The atmosphere around the organization will become icy, and people will become frustrated and lethargic.

To bear fruit, therefore, one must serve according to one's gifts. When a person ministers at church using his talents, he will be extra-creative, work voluntarily, and accomplish 10 to 20 times more work.

For this reason, it would be great if ministry training in the church could become gift specialization training. Those who are doing ministries should do "gift networking" well. Gift networking can be carried out by assigning people to serve in certain ministries according to a "gift checklist" and doing a follow-up after one year.

In sports, some players like to defend while others like to attack, both according to their gifts. As the roles of the guard and the forward are different in basketball, each church member has different roles to play. Indeed, some people are good in all the areas, but this is not true for most of us. If the church is not fun and does not bear fruit, it is because the members are not serving according to their talents.

To discover your own gifts, you need to check yourself against these three points.

First, see if you are happy doing the ministry.

If you are irritated and tired, performing your ministry becomes a duty, not a gift. I've seen someone who left church because of his love for golf. We spend a lot of money on our hobbies and are even willing to stay up late just so we can enjoy doing our leisure pursuits. Gamblers never get tired, even though they play throughout the night. The more they concentrate on gambling, the more their eyes sparkle. Likewise, anglers effortlessly wake up at 4:00 a.m. to go fishing. When people do what they like, they do not feel exhausted even if they skip sleep. No matter how much money you spend and how tired you get, you enjoy doing what you like to do.

But then, some people get exhausted just by thinking of going to early morning prayer. It is a gift when you do it voluntarily because you want to do it and you enjoy doing it. If a task feels light, it is a gift. If something feels burdensome, it may not be your gift.

Second, see if you bear fruit.

Gifts should bear fruit. No matter how hard you try something, if you do not bear fruit, think twice about doing it. If you see fruit in your ministry and others who are involved with the ministry also are bearing fruit, then that would mean that this is your gift. Let's say that a person has a gift of preaching. He loves to preach and is moved whenever he delivers a message, but if those who are listening to his sermons have a hard time, then he should think again about his gifting. If it is your gift, it has to be something you enjoy and at the same time something that helps others to grow and bear fruit as well.

A hobby is something you like to do. It is a personal matter. However, a gift is something that benefits others and does good for others.

Third, see if your gift is continuously developing.

A gift develops when it is used over and over. You might not be good at it at first, but as you use your gift continuously, it will improve, be enhanced, and develop. When we choose a career, we should choose one according to our gifts, not our hobbies. If it is your gift, it will definitely develop. A spiritual person will see and undergo great changes in five or ten years. If you are the same person you were five or ten years ago, you should think over your gifts again.

If what you think is your gift meets all three requirements above, develop that gift actively. When you do that, God will be glorified, and you will be able to give many people joy.

Our church ministries are active because many members have given their gifts to the Lord. Pastor Jae-yoon Jang, who is pastoring Tokyo Onnuri Community Church in Japan, is one example. He started to think about spreading the Gospel in Japan as he visited the country frequently in 1980 for business reasons. In early 1990, he started a children's Japanese ministry, and since then, he has helped establish our church's own Japanese ministry. This was the beginning of multilingual worship services in our church. Later, Pastor Jang studied theology. When we planted a church in Tokyo in response to a request made by a Japanese businessman in 2001, I sent Pastor Jang without hesitation.

Another example is Pastor Hoon Lee, who is now serving at our church after working with the Mennonite Church in Canada. He had a vision for a mercy ministry. I organized a community missions team so Pastor Lee could freely do mercy ministry in our church. He laid the foundations for the mercy ministry teams in our church, including the Hanaro Gunpo Study Club.[12] He also started the Fragrance of Jesus Society, whose members provided lunch to the elderly in Hyochang Park. When the Society heard the breaking news of the collapse of the Sampoong Department Store in 1995, they were the first ones to reach out a helping hand. The Society became the basis in later establishing the Onnuri Welfare Foundation.

Provide an opportunity to exercise one's gifts.

There is a man whose name is Peter Wagner. He became a Christian because of Billy Graham. He loved what Billy Graham did so much that he went to seminary and eventually became a preacher. However, he failed miserably. He thought he failed because he didn't pray enough, so he focused more on fasting and praying. He preached again, but again it was a failure.

After seeking counsel from a friend, he thought maybe a hidden sin was causing his failure. He read through ten years worth of journals to look for any hidden sin he may have committed. It wasn't that he was sinless, but there weren't any that were serious.

---

12 This is part of Onnuri's shelter ministry for troubled youth.

He confessed those sins and preached again, but still, the congregation was not responsive. He was troubled because although he devoted himself in the belief that God had appointed him as a preacher like Billy Graham, he was always struggling.

Through the failures, he realized that he could preach more enthusiastically when in a lecture room of 50 to 60 people, rather than a huge group of several thousands of people. Later, he finally discovered that his gift was in creating strategies, not preaching. He learned that he was more suited to lecturing in schools, meeting people on a one-to-one basis, counseling people, and establishing strategies for missions and churches than to preaching publicly. Today, he shares that he is much happier lecturing as a professor and exercising his gift, although he couldn't achieve his first dream of becoming a public preacher. It's been 30 years since I heard this story directly from Peter, yet I am still impressed.

The moment you discover your talents, the world will be different. Pastors should also remind all members of the church that different people have different gifts. Ministry is about helping members find their gifts. Some people always give to others although they're not rich. They just enjoy giving. On the other hand, some people are stingy and will not spend a penny even though they have a lot of money. As you can see, people have different gifts. As God made us all differently, God gave everyone different gifts. If one uses his gifts well, he will be moved and filled with joy.

When someone is moved and happy, passion will follow. There is nothing more beautiful than a man working hard. At this point, the most important task of a pastor is to provide opportunities for the people. Pastors should offer opportunities to his members where they can sing praises at the top of their lungs or serve happily late at night, pouring their gifts unsparingly into ministries.

When pastors visit their members, pastors shouldn't try to impart and talk about what they think, but should listen to what their members are thinking about. Pastors should listen and try to know what their members are experts in. Even the most reserved person will have a lot to talk about when it comes to his or her specialty. After listening to peoples' stories, pastors should ask, "How are you serving God through your career?" In addition, pastors should provide jobs for him to do in church. Instead of trying to force a person into a position, pastors should create a position to fit a person's expertise. Then, each member's gifts will continue to be developed.

When you create an opportunity, people will come. Usually, at first, people say that they don't have time to serve even if they have gifts and desire to serve. But when we create an event and hold a feast, someone will come and dance, sing, devote themselves, and serve for Jesus. They celebrate, rejoice, and are moved. Throughout my ministry, I have witnessed this many times.

Onnuri Newspaper is an apt example. We decided to publish *Onnuri Newspaper* every three months when our weekly bulletin got so thick with ministry news. When we published the first issue, I wondered if someone could help create the newspaper. Soon, the editorial team was formed, as if the members had been just waiting for such an opportunity. As our church and ministries expanded, the frequency of producing new editions and the number of copies was adjusted from quarterly to monthly, then from monthly to bi-weekly, and ultimately to weekly. Amazingly, every time we needed more help, more people with gifts came and served.

The same thing happened when we were developing our Jesus Discipleship School program. A great number of people participated and exercised their gifts. A former high school principal, who was already 70 years old, used his talents by serving at Jesus Discipleship School after retirement.

Also, our church's Silver Choir is another case in point. Silver Choir is made up of retirees with various experiences, including former ministers. Although they have retired from their respective careers, they decided to use their gifts in the Silver Choir. One time, one of the choir members said he kept forgetting the lyrics of a song. He was too embarrassed to look at the score while singing, so he practiced the song 200 to 300 times until he finally memorized the words. His story touched my heart. They gather once a week and sing, and in doing so, it helps them overcome dementia, a disease often developed among seniors. Also, they seem happy as they wear makeup, hanbok,[13] and beautifully arrange their hair. All of this is fun.

The true picture of a church is to create more fun and rewarding opportunities within the church, not in the world.

Develop a gift.

To develop one's gift, people should try various ministries.

The first is the worship leading ministry. One of the most important ministries that is handled by the laity is the leading of

---

13 Korean traditional dress.

worship. Worship leaders need the anointing of the Holy Spirit above all else. Such a leader needs to be humble and musically talented. Also, worship leaders should not push or pick on others even when they make mistakes, unless it is entirely necessary. A person who is able to do this is able to serve as a worship leader.

The second is workplace ministry. Personally, I think the workplace ministry is the most important ministry for churches in the 21st century. Since we cannot ask everyone in the world to come to church, let us make our workplaces like a church. Workplace ministers help colleagues to work and perform their jobs in the presence of the Holy Spirit. The important thing to note when engaging in workplace ministry is that you first need to be recognized and loved by colleagues. Workplace ministers should possess qualities such as spirituality and excellence. The workplace ministry is an area of unlimited potential. If you are hiding the fact that you are a Christian at work, you need to take time and think about this fact.

The third is day-to-day evangelism ministry. We live in the world. We spend our lives in our offices and workplaces. We should evangelize to people through our lives, not through special evangelistic activities. There are many ways to do evangelism. We can evangelize through revival meetings, Bible classes, group evangelism, and personal evangelism. Also, we can evangelize through radio, television, and printed materials. Most of our evangelism efforts target an unspecified majority. It is like throwing the message in the air, and there is no way to verify whether such an act will yield fruit.

On the other hand, day-to-day evangelism is to help an individual change by constantly interacting with that person for several years. It is about evangelizing friends, colleagues, and neighbors with your life. It is a more concrete, active, and responsible way of doing evangelism. People who do day-to-day evangelism go to work, but their priority is evangelism, not work. Such people change workplaces, homes, and schools for evangelism.

The fourth is a marriage ministry. Nowadays, there is a great need for people serving in marriage ministry. People today face marriage dilemmas. However, there are not many people who can help solve the problems, and even churches are struggling in offering appropriate solutions.

When Christians encounter problems in their marriages, they find it hard to open up with others. Often when it comes to issues like these, couples pray with their pastor and come up with solutions to the problems, but once the problem is solved, it becomes hard for the couple to face their pastor again because their personal lives have become so exposed to the pastor. To prevent such a situation, it is better to encourage Christians to seek help from a professional counselor. This is why we need Biblical professional counselors.

Another program a church must offer is a program for unmarried men and women to help them prepare for marriage. Also, a separate program for newlyweds is necessary because this can help new couples cope wisely with various struggles they may face as they begin to spend their lives together. In addition, considering the growing divorce rate, a program and professional staff that deal with families in crisis are essential as well.

The fifth program is society reforming ministry. We need people who can monitor social issues such as abortion, economic justice, and social systems.

I would like to share a story written by Pastor John MacArthur because it is about an interesting intervention that could be carried out by districts or small groups. In a neighborhood where Pastor MacArthur lived, there was an uncovered manhole. No matter how many times neighbors reported the issue to the regional office, it wasn't fixed. To address the problem, church members who lived in the area wrote a letter to the head of the office. The letter said, "The manhole lid is open but no one has come to fix it. Please let us know if you have decided not to fix it. If that is not the case, please let us know when you intend to fix it. We are a group of people who believe in Jesus." Each member of the church filed civil complaints and the issue was completely resolved. Just like with this example, we can improve local communities little by little. No matter how small an issue is, it can reform society. Most churches are insensitive about how people should live in this world, and some even fear public institutions such as county or district offices. However, interacting with these organizations won't be a problem if churches have people who have gifts in these areas. I hope that more people with gifts in social reform will step up.

The sixth important ministry type is culture ministry. Leaders in culture ministry teach young people in ways that are appropriate within line with today's culture. We desperately need such leaders. We should not approach and educate the youth using old methods, because they are used to modern culture. It is important for churches to understand the culture of the youth. Youth are interested in videos, music, drama, dance, and sound effects that represent today's culture. I once thought, "How about putting up a computer game room in the church?" My reasoning was that if teenagers were going to play computer games anyway, it would be better for them to do it within the church rather than outside.

Some adults complain about students wearing baseball caps during service, but there is no need to scold them for being rude. When a fish is moved from its home to a new place, it will have a hard time breathing at first, and eventually, it will die. It is more important to lead young people consistently to discover their spirituality and give glory to God (even if they still focus on the culture) than to pick on them for dyeing their hair.

Grownups are often too preoccupied with lecturing young people about things that are shown outwardly, such as their hairstyle or the way they dress and talk. But when you look closely within the young generation, you will discover good and positive things such as creativity, independent minds, and clear opinions. When adults appreciate the positive things possessed by the youth, they will never leave the church.

Although there are times I feel that the music played during "Power Station" (the worship rally for middle and high school students) is a little overdone, I don't stop them. The amazing thing is that when kids pray and are anointed by the Holy Spirit, they will come back to the original state and never go too far again. Even when it seems that they may go overboard, they will come back at any moment. I hope there will be more who will stand up as culture ministry leaders.

The seventh type of program to explore is mercy ministry. When it comes to mercy ministry, Catholics are ahead of Protestant churches. Today, Protestant churches need well-trained mercy ministry leaders as well. We could operate mercy ministry directly as mission field workers or missionaries, or we could support mercy ministry leaders.

Our church has many mercy ministry targets. For many years, we have run youth shelters and workplaces for the disabled. These days, we are cooperating with the city government and operating an elderly nursing hospital and elderly welfare center. We need many people to serve in these places.

The eighth ministry to explore is next generation ministry. In this world, we need children's ministry leaders. A children's ministry should transform itself from simply teaching weekly lessons to offering a variety of ways for children to learn.

In one of our camps, we offered this type of program. At this camp, leaders grouped children together and handed them scripts. They told the children that they should prepare to perform a play in three days. That was it. That's all they had to do.

Five to six children would then gather around the script and start contemplating it. At first, they fought over different opinions, but soon they picked people to be in charge and delegated responsibilities like lighting and costuming. Typically, the kids would run against each other at first and break into pieces as they attempted to create a play in just three days. On the last day, however, they would showcase the play they created, and all would end up in tears for their accomplishment. The program helps children build relationships and learn to cooperate with each other. Children ministry leaders, youth leaders in particular, and campus leaders are precious.

The ninth important ministry is internet ministry. We desperately need computer and internet ministry leaders for the future. Many ministries will become active on the internet, and these leaders will be needed in many areas.

The tenth type is community ministry. Some people with the gift of community live together and devote themselves to God. It is time for Korean churches to consider the need to recruit community ministry leaders.

There are many gifts other than the ones already mentioned. Some people are gifted in administration. Whatever task may come their way, these people can draw a clear picture of the job in their heads. They get it at first sight without becoming confused. It is a gift. Some people have a special affection for publication. Secretarial work is also a gift. Not everyone can perform the job. Supporting ministry and self-supported ministry are also gifts.

However, churches do not need to do all of these. If a church only has ten members, it only needs ten gifts. Of course, some gifts may overlap. These gifts can form the basis of the pastoral philosophy of the church. I believe that if we create jobs for people whom God has sent to the church, God will anoint the church.

Establish a model.

You need a model if you want to run ministries led by laypeople. The first elder in our church was a former two-star general. He devoted his life to God when he was already 58. After he had retired as a high-ranking general, he received several work offers by the government, but he gave up all such incentives and went to Japan, where he and his wife lived in a small seminary dormitory.

2. Ministry

After graduating from the school, the former general planted a church for Korean Japanese. We call the church "Jabudon Church"; "jabudon" means "futon" in Japanese. It was called this because the church did not have a building, so its members gathered in a living room, sat on futons, and worshipped God. They only had about 10 to 15 members. Although the church was small, the retired general faithfully served there for five to six years. Due to his military experience, he was used to being in command of many soldiers, but for five to six years, he wrestled with a small church in a small province in Japan.

This story moved my heart in two ways. First, the pastor started at an old age, and second, he endured a ministry that was not fruitful for five to six long years. His story is moving and sets an excellent model.

Likewise, one doctor closed his hospital, which was doing great, and moved to a mission field. A businessman gave his life to the mission field as well, and some elders worked for our church without compensation after retirement. These people are setting a good model for the members of our church.

After our church had developed the 2,000/10,000 Vision, 70 percent of the missionaries we sent were ordinary members. This is ministry led by the laity. Churches shouldn't stop sponsoring missionaries but should send regular members to the mission fields after they devote themselves and serve a ministry following God's given vision. It sets a good model.

The reason churches have problems is that people are too concerned with trying to secure certain positions. When someone tries to make and keep a certain position for a long time, problems may arise. However, if someone thinks about leaving, he won't cause problems, because there is no conflict of interest. People who will leave soon focus on answering the question, "How can I build up the church?" They do not become problem makers.

Create teamwork between pastors and the laity.

Pastors are like the captain of an aircraft carrier or a ship. The most important role of a captain is to hold the helm. Captains don't need to go to the engine room or let down the anchor. Likewise, pastors should do what they need to do, and laypeople should do what they need to do. When these roles are switched between one and the other, ships will capsize, and airplanes will crash.

Pastors often wrongly think, "I need to do everything," "Only I can do things right," or "Since members do not like to serve, I have to do everything." This is absurd. Shepherds don't give birth to lambs, but it is the sheep that do. The shepherd's job is to feed and raise sheep so that they will multiply. It isn't right for shepherds to try to give birth to a lamb.

On the other hand, the laity falsely thinks, "Ministries are only for pastors," "Pastors are the ones that can communicate with God the best," or "God gave pastors all the talent." If a pastor thinks of his members as merely the target of his ministry, the church will not grow. If that is the case, classes will be formed in the church, and the church will be divided into two groups, the top and the bottom. Such a church is called "a centralized dictatorship-style church." If the leader gives orders, and the followers simply execute those orders, something is wrong.

There are roles for the laity and roles for pastors. The pastor and ordinary Christians should form a fantastic team. Both a pastor and layman should know their roles and respect their own positions. The most important role of a pastor is to present directions and hold the helm.

Encourage the members.

Most laypeople are passive and lack confidence. Although they have gifts, they can't step up boldly because they have never used them before. An important role of a pastor, therefore, is to recognize laypeople as his partners, encourage them, and discover their talents. Since pastors have been doing God's work professionally for a long time, they can delegate tasks appropriately to each member with spiritual discernment. Overloading a person with various tasks or too much work is nothing more than killing that person. Churches should always evaluate their ministries and prevent their members from getting burned out. It is important to note that the success of lay ministries depends on how much a church encourages its members to serve in the ministry. A church should recognize its members, encourage, and evaluate them, as well as adjust the ministry so that members can constantly grow. On top of assigning jobs to members, we should also educate the members continuously so that they can perform their tasks. Also, we should aim to improve the quality of members. We must let them know that the ministry is good not just for themselves, but also for the community.

Sometimes it is also important for lay leaders to take a break from their ministries. After they take a rest, the church should let them take on a new ministry or adjust the work they do. When a member does a lot of work by him or herself, it is easy to get burned out. That is why we need volunteers who work for volunteers.

A pastor's job is to encourage everyone to entirely give glory to God and Christ, to help everyone to focus on Jesus Christ, to ensure that all ministries benefit and bless the church, and to make sure that all members come together as one body.

Many pastors are inexperienced in practical areas such as training, helping, and encouraging members and finding their gifts because they focus on spiritual tasks such as preaching, Bible studies, and prayers. But we should not forget that when ordinary members and pastors form fantastic teams and perform their roles, beautiful things will happen, regardless of the church's size.

Offer practical training.

Ordinary members need to be trained to serve in church ministries as laity leaders. When training them, a theological curriculum including systematic theology, historical theology, church history, and mission theology is not very helpful, because all these are too academic. I believe that it is better to teach a practical curriculum that can help a layperson to teach the Bible and to help others, rather than a theological program.

Moreover, I hope that churches will teach their members more of the Bible. I wish Christians would learn how to do one-to-one discipleship training, Quiet Time, counseling, visitation to other Christians, inner healing, and family ministry. When ordinary members learn these, they will have great tools to help other members.

Of course, when someone wants to become a pastor, they must

learn theology as part of their professional theological training. In the field, however, spiritual training, life skills training, and character training are more needed than academic training. For example, during training programs such as the Jesus Discipleship School, participants are given a chance to share and confess about their past. Through this process, they can heal and recover from the hurts that are not seen outwardly. Such things can touch the heart more than academic training. Participants become Christians who set aside time twice a week, five to ten hours at a time, to intercede for others and pray for oneself and to serve God. When they are trained like this for eight months, they can take on any task. Above all, through the program, they can confirm what their gifts are.

Operate ministry committees.

I think there should be session meetings for ministry and elders overseeing ministries in the church. So far, existing church session meetings are too preoccupied in dealing with administrative tasks that churches do. As a result, such meetings are not able to cover ministries or spiritual matters much.

Session meetings for each ministry would specifically evaluate ministries and encourage them to revitalize the church and to instill vision in the church. Each ministry should form a ministry team and a ministry committee. This will allow members to operate according to their ministry.

Through this, the church can maximize the power of the laity and utilize them 100 percent in the organization of the church. The church could go one step further and have a vision of transforming the church and the world by encouraging lay leaders to become leaders in society. Then, churches would be able to function properly and create an ideal model for the church.

Our church started the Family Ministry Committee in early 1990 to restore families to the way God designed them originally. At that time, there were only eight families in the committee, and we did not have a special model for the ministry. In fact, there were barely any churches that had a family ministry.

The family ministry committee first started with prayer meetings. They read the Bible, studied the guidebooks, participated in the family ministry programs offered by local and international missions organizations, and shared their lives with each other. After members of the committee felt the need to have a family ministry, the committee members started to contemplate specifically how Christians should nurture their families, as well as how the husband and wife relationship or parent and child relationship should change. Deliberations on how we could encourage openness with regard to our family problems within the church or family led to a clearer picture of how the family ministry program should be implemented, and this gave birth to "Ha-Ga-Hun" (God's Family Training School).

Finally, in March 1993, the first seven-week long Ha-Ga-Hun program was introduced to the congregation. It was not just a seminar. From the moment participants entered the church lobby, sat around the tables for a meal, and listened to the seminars, the committee had served the participants deeply. The committee made sure that each participant would feel as if each item was prepared especially just for him or her. I could feel the strong sense of mission in the committee from the way they served the participants. I was able to feel the heart of our Father who invites us to a feast and waits for us to come. I was deeply touched by the first Ha-Ga-Hun program. A church program can be so beautiful!

If the lives of committee members had not changed, the program would not have been born. The program was a wonderful success and became very influential, as evidenced by the fact that the children would now tell their parents to take the program again whenever parents who had gone through Ha-Ga-Hun were about to quarrel with each other. Couples, then, could live a life of serving others and grow more mature as they accept one another, as it says in Scripture: "Husbands, love your wives, just as Christ loved the church and gave himself up for her" (Ephesians 5:25).

After the completion of the training, the graduates of Ha-Ga-Hun scattered around various ministry teams in Onnuri Community Church. They played leading roles in each ministry committee, becoming the driving force behind Onnuri Community Church's lay ministry. They enabled the Father School Movement to emerge powerfully, and became a model for the Pre-marital School and Moses College. When Onnuri Community Church grew in size, they continued to serve quietly. No matter how successful the elders or deaconesses were in the world, they did not mind wearing aprons and cleaning restrooms at church. Watching them work humbly became a unique scene at Onnuri Church.

The important thing to know is that if I had exerted firm control over the ministry, the ministry would not have borne so much fruit.

As you can see, from the beginning, we got rid of age or gender groups such as the Women's and Men's Evangelistic Societies.

Instead, our church revolved around ministry committees. With more than 100 ministry divisions, we became a dynamic church in which anyone could serve in a ministry if they wanted to.

How beautiful would a church be if its pastors and laypeople could form a fantastic team and operate as one body, as Paul and Timothy, Priscilla and Aquila, or Jesus and His 12 disciples did! Such a community would change the world.

Worship is like the heart of a church, and sermons are like the heart of worship. When worship is offered well, the heart of that church - the body of Christ - beats well. When the heart beats well, the blood will be supplied to capillaries effectively. If so, it is okay even if you get sick, because when blood circulates well, our body will recover soon. You become ill when a particular part of your body cannot function any more because the blood fails to circulate around the body. When a church worships God well, every corner of that church will be revived.

3. Sermons

Sermons are like the heart of worship.

When God's Word is proclaimed through the Holy Spirit, the worship will gain life. Indeed, praise and worship and prayer are important, but the key to worship is God's Word. What is God's Word? It is God Himself. God is invisible because He is Spirit, not a human being, so He is not limited by time and space.

Then, how can we feel His presence? We can sense His presence through the Word, which is God himself. When we read, memorize, listen to, and meditate on the Bible, and when we apply it in our actual day-to-day life, we can experience and feel God.

The Word is not conveyed just by talking about it. Since the Bible is inspired by God, we can feel God's Word and experience the power of the Word only when we are inspired by the Holy Spirit. Therefore, no other ministry is more important than the preaching ministry. Preaching is the heart of worship.

Preaching is proclamation.

Preaching builds a church, while teaching builds a saint. Church ministry should blend the two together well. A church is determined by the sermons preached. In preaching, the church's vision, color, picture, and scope are manifested.

Also, members grow according to the way they are taught. Some pastors combine teaching with preaching, and some pastors are not good at preaching but are good at teaching. What is clear is that these two activities are not the same. Teaching is more focused on transferring information, while preaching is more focused on proclamation. Sometimes preachers say, "I think so and so" during their preaching, but preaching is not about, "I think so and so," but "It is so." Preaching is proclamation. It should be, "We should repent," not "It is good to repent." Whenever I am reminded about the ministry of preaching, the story below always comes to mind.

> In a town in England, a church was built. On the arch of the front door, the following phrase was engraved: "We preach the crucifixion of Christ." The message of Jesus and his crucifixion, the cross, was the message the congregation wanted to hear, and the pastor wanted to preach it because the Bible said that it was the essence of the Gospel.
>
> But as days went by and times changed, people started to feel that the message on the crucifixion of Jesus was outdated. Because

they had heard the sermon so many times, the message sounded unattractive and out-of-date. So instead of saying, "We are saved by the blood of Jesus," they started to say, "We are saved by the life of Jesus" because the word "blood" was unfashionable. Suddenly, an ivy vine that grew next to the church's main gate grew and covered the words "the crucifixion of" that were written on the front door, so that the words on the arch became "We preach … Christ."

Soon after, the church started to preach various social issues such as social participation, political problems, philosophy, and moral issues without hesitation and people paid a lot of attention to such issues. The church started to compromise the essential message of the Bible.

Later, the vine continued to grow and eventually covered the word "Christ," and now the phrase read, "We preach." This meant that the church was preaching without knowing what they preached. In the end, the church became a church that had lost the Gospel.

When I think about it, I realize that the devil is so smart. The devil has devised and established cults, such as Salvation Sect and Dami Mission to make people hostile to the second coming of Christ, as well as extreme Holy Spirit followers, Odaeyang[14] and Shinangchon, which have made people lose hope in the community. Satan has made it difficult for churches to emphasize salvation, the second coming of Christ, the Holy Spirit, and community. But don't these four things form the basis of faith? The devil would like

---

14 A cult sect which committed mass suicide in 1987.

pastors to avoid these four things when preaching, so that their preaching will become empty, left only with formality.

Preaching saves a dead soul.

Remember that preaching saves dead souls. "The Spirit gives life; the flesh counts for nothing" (John 6:63). When I preach, I don't appeal to people's reasoning. Human logic is only needed during the process itself. Indeed, if a sermon is not logical, people will not pay attention. If a pastor says the same thing over and over or jumps around to and from different topics during his sermons without presenting a clear message, people will not listen. However, we should remember that preaching should be directed to the spirit in people, not to rationality. When the Word is preached to the spirit, we can see dead souls coming alive again. This is apparent on the faces of people. When entering the chapel, their faces seem dead, but when they leave, their faces seem alive again.

These changes cannot be forced. Preaching that only pleases the flesh or the mind falls short and ends there. There is nothing to it. Nothing at all. But I believe that if we preach in the spirit and preach to the spirit, the Word of God will come true, as it is said, "For the Word of God is living and active. Sharper than any double-edged sword, it penetrates even to dividing soul and spirit, joints and marrow" (Hebrews 4:12). When the spirit becomes alive, the flesh will also become alive again.

Preaching is incarnation.

We can learn about the basics of preaching in Philippians 2:5-11. Preaching is incarnational. "Who, being in very nature God, did not consider equality with God something to be grasped, but made himself nothing, taking the very nature of a servant, being made in human likeness" (Philippians 2:6-7). God taking the form of man is called "incarnation." It means that the Word became flesh. Preaching is the same thing. The Word of God must be incarnated into my flesh. In other words, the entire Word of God must come into my body and become my flesh.

Then, as a result, the Word of God should be expressed through my reasoning, language, body, and life. When you see someone screaming and crying out of desperation, is he or she simply reading a script when telling their story? Of course not. Those who are deeply hurt, divorced, beaten, and kicked out can vent about themselves for hours, because their story has become their flesh.

This is preaching. How can we not be excited when Jesus was crucified and died on the cross for us? How can we talk about it emotionlessly? How can we make the congregation fall asleep when preaching the Gospel and the commandments? That is unbelievable. People who are soaked with the Gospel of Jesus Christ get excited whenever they talk about the cross. They have so much to say and don't need a script. It is because they are incarnated.

Preaching is identification.

The Word of God needs to be identified with me. God came as a man, and he identified himself with us. Jesus, therefore, knows God well and knows what it is to be human. Pastors should also know both God and people. They must be familiar with God by having the heart of God, and at the same time, they should know people. However, the weakness of pastors is that they only know one part of people.

People hide their inner being from others. Preaching must penetrate deep inside of men and women and bring to light fakeness, hypocrisy, sinfulness, and carnal secrets! Pastors must dig sharply into this enormous world. The Word is like walking around a dark house with a bright lamp. Open the door and see a man's hidden jealousy, two-facedness, greed, lust, and hypocrisy, all beautifully covered up. Preaching unwraps these covers.

Whenever in my preaching I talk about hidden sins and unveil stories of carnal secrets one by one, people are stunned and wonder, "How did the pastor know my life story?" In reality, I do not know my members' secrets. How then did I seem to know their stories? It is because I dug deep and discovered the secrets of a person's inner being. If you look closely into your heart, you can understand other people's hearts. This is because everyone turns on the light to shine on the outside of things, but they keep the light off inside their hearts.

Preaching is a communication process.

Great preachers are excellent communicators. What is true communication? Jesus came to the world in the form of a man and lived like other men. He ate and slept, was tired and thirsty, and cried just like everyone else. Jesus communicated with people. If Jesus put forth his authority and stayed seated, no disciples would have followed him. Instead, Jesus even washed the disciples' feet, which allowed him to genuinely communicate with his followers. Standing in a pulpit and speaking to the congregation is preaching, but real preaching is done with our own life. If one's preaching is not backed up by his life, the pastor could become a fraud. A common mistake committed by most pastors is to think that people do not listen to their sermons because they don't preach well. In reality, however, members don't listen to sermons not because the pastor preaches poorly, but because the sermons and the life of the pastors do not match. When a pastor's sermons are not supported by his life, the better he preaches, the more the members will be troubled and fall into temptation.

Once, a member came to me and said, "I didn't get to even shake hands with you over the year and a half that I've been coming to this church, but I stayed here because of the preaching. I saw you go through tremendous sufferings for the past year. You were attacked severely, but you never made an excuse. You continued to preach with a smile. I heard real sermons."

If I preach about loving one another but fail to love my neighbors, I am not a preacher. Pastors should think about how well they communicate with the members. How much do you share your heart and life with other people? Although I am a pastor and a preacher, the congregation should be able to feel that I am their friend and brother.

People go to fortune-tellers and consult with shamans, but no parent wants their children to become a shaman. People want to get divination services but don't want to become fortune-tellers themselves. However, when it comes to preachers, things should be different. Members should want to become pastors. They should be able to feel and say, "I think pastors are the best" and "I want my child to become a pastor." If members of a church say, "I love everything but pastors," the pastor must have a problem. In this sense, preaching is identification and communication.

Preaching is a product of sacrifice.

Preachers should sacrifice themselves to the point that they die on the cross. Only then can Jesus be seen. People who don't sacrifice cannot talk about sacrifice. When we lower ourselves, we see Jesus. When we suffer loss, we see Jesus. When we sacrifice, we see Jesus. When we stay still even after enduring unreasonable persecution and suffering, we see Jesus. In other words, preaching is about showing Jesus.

One day, a college professor from the United States registered at our church. He explained why he decided to become a member. He said that he wanted to stay in one church, so he visited a number of churches in Seoul and listened to their sermons. Finally, he decided to stay in our church, because he "chose the church that talks about Jesus the most." The professor and his wife set the criteria and listened to sermons. When they came to our church, for the first time, they heard a sermon that started with Jesus.

The beginning and the ending of a sermon is Jesus. Sermons are not the time to show off great eloquence, logic, or intelligence to attract people's attention. Sermons are able to present amazing insight into today's world, but whether Jesus is in it or not is a separate issue. Pastors are not great philosophers. They don't need sharp intellect. Although preaching may seem ordinary, Jesus who forgives, encourages, and saves should always be in the sermons. In the end, preaching delivers Jesus.

This means that preaching is not my story but God's story. The congregation should be able to confess that they heard the voice of

God through the sermons. If a sermon is fancy, the preacher will stand out. It may make us feel great listening to a compliment such as, "Wow, that person is an eloquent speaker," but we can't say that it was a real sermon. The moment we stand in the pulpit, the "I" should disappear; people should be reminded of God, and Jesus should be revealed. This is preaching.

The depth of meditation determines the depth of preaching.

To preach, we must first develop a habit of meditating on the Word of God. Having a habit of meditation is extremely important for all preachers. Preaching is sharing the Word. In other words, it means that a preacher is deeply soaked in Scripture. From Genesis to Revelation, no matter what subject or what book he is teaching, a preacher should have a profound understanding of the book.

For example, the four Gospels look at the life of Jesus from the perspectives of Matthew, Mark, Luke, and John's perspectives. What we see will change depending on our perspective. For instance, those who see something from the front will describe its frontside, and those who see the same object from behind will describe its backside.

When people look at the Bible from various perspectives, therefore, they may seem to see different things, but in fact they all describe the same object. Some may be describing the ears of Jesus, but it is Jesus; others may be describing the eyes of Jesus, but it is also Jesus; and still, others may be describing the back of Jesus, but it is all Jesus.

Likewise, we can read the Bible with a telescope or microscope, looking for the forest or the tree. We may look at it from a historical or chronological perspective or read it according to the characters in the Bible or according to a theme. A pastor should understand the Bible front to back.

The reason that our beautiful sermons fail to touch the hearts of people is that they lack deep meditation. The congregation can tell if the preaching truly comes from deep meditation, just as you can tell right away if clothes are well-made just by looking at the shape, texture, and style. You can tell the depth of a sermon just by listening to it. A sermon may sound simple, but it may have class and penetrating philosophy. We don't need to quote well-known people. Eventually, the depth of a sermon equals the depth of meditation.

How then should we meditate? True meditation cannot be done overnight. As cows eat grass and ruminate, we should meditate daily, going more deeply each day. This is meditation training. I believe the basis of preaching training is meditation training. Pastor Dennis Rein, who has been doing Quiet Time for almost 30 years, preaches the same passage but delivers it differently every time. Pastor Dongwon Lee also perfectly follows expository preaching. He also puts Quiet Time first.

My sermons are Quiet Time-style sermons. I meditate in the early morning and then include and apply in my sermons what I've meditated upon. Now this style has become my habit. So whatever Scripture I preach, I instinctively preach it following the way I do my Quiet Time. When there are too many verses in Scripture, I will narrow them down to discover the message for the congregation. For those who find this method unfamiliar, you can train yourself by identifying application points after meditating on the Scriptures.

I think early morning prayer[15] is the greatest blessing for pastors. After all, early morning prayer is meditation. As you share with the congregation all the messages and spiritual ideas you learned from your early morning prayer, you will be able to train yourself to apply God's Word in your life without even knowing it.

Most of the pastors who have been in ministry for 20 to 30 years will probably have read most of the Bible commentaries available. However, commentaries instill stereotypes and become obstacles. They prevent people from thinking beyond what is written on the pages. Commentaries merely work as a fence to keep us in check. We should look at commentaries or dictionaries only when we encounter Scripture verses that bother us. But we should tackle the main message one-to-one with the Bible.

I used to refer to the commentaries of Campbell Morgan and John MacArthur because I liked them, but I later realized that commentaries are all pretty much similar to each other, and so I started searching for the message in Scriptures myself for my congregation. The best commentary and the best examples are in the Bible. From the Bible to the Bible, from Scripture to Scripture! By doing so, we help members to develop an ear for sermons and to be immersed in the Word.

From meditation to preaching

How then can one prepare a sermon from the portion of Scrip-

---

15 Korean churches typically hold early morning prayers at dawn throughout the week.

ture meditated upon? I would like to share three ideas on how to get this done.

First, analyze the Scripture and build a structure for your sermon.

Some people deliver inspiring sermons, but their sermons lack structure. This means their messages are not organized. To check if your sermon has substance, try making a Bible study resource out of your own sermon. Doing so will also make you realize whether your sermon is backed by Biblical evidence and whether it is logical. Some preachers can inspire people without substance, but one shouldn't be confused. Whatever sermon you preach, it should have structure, with an introduction, a body, and a conclusion that are well-arranged. And to build a structure, you should thoroughly analyze the main ideas of Scripture.

Second, add flesh - the message you meditated on - to the structure you create.

Include necessary illustrations and encourage the congregation to apply the Word of God to their lives. It is wonderful if the congregation responds this way after listening to your sermons: "Today's preaching seemed like it was prepared for me," or "The sermon touched my heart." Sermons prepared with our heads give others a headache, but sermons prepared from the heart move the heart. Knowledge comes from the head, and knowledge cannot change people, but God's Word poured from the heart inspires people.

Let's say a man meets a woman for the first time. He learns that the woman's parents are nice and her family background is great. She has a successful job, is healthy and even pretty. Yet, there's something lacking. The man's heart doesn't pound upon meeting the woman. In other words, there is no chemistry. If this is the case, it's very unlikely that this man and woman will marry each other because simply having great qualities is not enough. Even if a person is not good looking and lacks some qualities, you will still marry that person as long as you are drawn to him or her; you dream about him or her, and you feel like you want to live with him or her. Even if you can't logically explain such feelings, if you have it in your heart, you will marry that person. Preaching is just like that. We should be able to share the heart of God with the people through our preaching. Sermons should have the heart of God.

In this sense, I think every preacher should study expository sermons. Expository sermons are a way of preaching that focuses on Bible verses. In expository sermons, you thoroughly interpret the intent of God within a portion of Scripture and accurately apply his intent to today's situation. When you do topical sermons, focus on the Scripture, and be careful when you preach based on systematic theology.

Third, share the meditated message with your spouse.

Although I don't get to do it every time, after preparing the sermons, I usually share them with my wife on Saturdays. After eating dinner, I tell her about the introduction, body, and conclusion without going through the entire sermon script. Then, she will advise me in detail as to whether there are too many points or whether the message is a little biased.

Wives can help the pastors with their sermons because it is hard for others to tell pastors whether their sermons were good or bad. I believe it is a good thing to train wives to verify sermons so they can help their husbands. Even if as a result you end up arguing, it is okay because it is with your spouse. It is also great because spouses can point out weaknesses in sermons. Of course, this may not apply to every couple.

The seven characteristics of desirable preaching

To deliver good sermons, you should remember the following seven characteristics when delivering the message.

First, make sure your preaching is easy to understand. It is great if Grade 9 students can understand your sermon. It may be too difficult if you aim for the college level. Television producers tell their performers over and over, "Your audience is Grade 9 students. Make sure Grade 9 students understand." This is because television shows target the public. You will never hear a pastor of a megachurch preach a difficult message. If one does so, not many people would have gathered to listen. However, many pastors try to sound complicated all the time. We should aim to speak at the public's level when preaching so that everyone, even a 9th grader, can comprehend the sermons. However, the message should be deep enough to inspire intellectuals.

I don't understand why some pastors mention terms in the original language when they preach. Indeed, doing so may be necessary at times, but pastors don't need to add what the Greek words "zoe" or "bios" mean. We just need to present essential information when preaching. There is no need to show off what we know.

A number of new believers struggle to understand sermons. The goal of preaching is to interpret the Bible, and so it doesn't make any sense if believers need someone to explain the preaching because it is too difficult.

The sermons of seminary graduates are often difficult to understand because they usually quote theological terms. In particular, Korean pastors read translated books rather than the original text, often using awkward sentences by literally translating English into Korean. This hinders understanding. When preaching, spoken language is much better than written language. We should use plain, everyday language, real daily experiences, and things that anyone can understand to help infuse our sermons into people's lives.

Second, do practical preaching. What does Napoleon Bonaparte from the 1800s have anything to do with us today? Instead of using him as an example in a sermon, it is a hundred times better to use illustrations about what a neighbor's mom experienced today, something that happened to us that day, or what kept us awake through the night. Sermons should be a story of something that takes place in our lives, not an empty philosophical story. They are about things that happen in our lives and can be applied to us. Jesus is real in our lives. Sermons should have something to do with preparing meals, doing laundry, raising children, and so on. This is preaching.

Third, preach from the Bible to the Bible. We should only deliver the message of the Bible. Preachers are not TV commentators, political reporters, or economy analysts. Pastors should be careful about this. There are topics that may be new to the pastor, but his congregation may already know them, and newspapers will cover such topics even if the pastors don't preach about them. Church members are experts in their own respective areas. Many people know things better than preachers when it comes to their specialties. Of course, you can use such information or general knowledge to help people understand the Word of God, but the only message a pastor should preach is from the Bible.

Fourth, sermons should be applicable. Sermons that cannot be applied in life are like a tree that doesn't bear fruit. A sermon is good when the congregation can listen and apply it in their lives on a daily basis.

Fifth, make sure the introduction of a sermon is not too long. How much content you "cut" is important in preaching. Let's say there is a tree. A seasoned farmer will not hesitate to prune this tree's branches to make it grow better. It hurts to cut something away, but in sharing one powerful message, we need to prune all the unnecessary branches. Only then will the main branches grow stronger because they will be able to better receive nutrients.

Sixth, keep the message short and simple. Some pastors say the same things over and over. When I asked one pastor why he kept repeating himself, he replied that he repeats the message just in case the members didn't understand it the first time. Don't make a sermon sound like a lecture. We should preach like planes land: they shouldn't go round and round, circling the runway, but move straight away to land at once.

Seventh, preach with spiritual authority, conviction, and confidence. While secular knowledge is limited to the world, the Word of God is connected to God and heaven. Therefore, pastors should have spiritual confidence that even the greatest expert in the world should listen to them as they preach God's Word. When you feel confident, it is easier for you to talk. But if you lack confidence, you will be tempted to use complicated terms. However, one thing

I have learned as I have been preaching even to this day is that when I don't prepare well, my vocal tone goes higher. I tend to yell or use difficult terms. But when I am well prepared for a sermon, my preaching has power, and I can feel the spiritual authority without needing to raise my voice.

We must push on with preaching at the risk of our lives.
Some say, "Elders determine the quality of a church," or "The size of a church is affected by its pastor." This is not always the case, but in some ways, it makes sense. Just as not all people in business are successful no matter how diligent and skillful they are, not all pastors are successful in their ministry even if they are diligent and talented. The size of a church should not be used to judge a pastor's character. At the same time, pastors should not worry about the size of their church. A church can be big or small. Size is not what is important.

Once, a missionary in Japan shared his testimony, and I was deeply touched. He said that although his church only has ten members, not abandoning this painful ministry was God's grace and blessing. He endured the same state for six years. Is this not a miracle? Would God have given him a higher "score" had he many members and ministries? Not at all. God will reward those who are faithful.

In a sense, preaching is a gift. Even if people talk about the same story, some can make it sound clearer and more exciting. Preaching is sharing the Word of God, but some sermons are so obvious. After hearing them three or four times, it is easy to guess what the pastor is going to say. In such cases, the pastor has failed to preach a sermon that his members can look forward to. In a sense, preaching is like a TV series. Although the storyline is obvious, you can't help but watch the next episode because the stories are all connected. A TV series has an introduction, development, turn, and conclusion. It also has laughter, excitement, joy, and inspiration. Preaching should be the same. Pastors should make sure that their members look forward to the next sermon as soon as one sermon is over. Also, pastors should make sure that their members are eager even to give up their vacation so that they can come to church because they look forward to the sermon so much. When people hear a sermon, they should clench their fists, their hearts should pound, and tears should roll down their cheeks. As soon as a pastor ends his preaching, the people should respond, "That's right. I should change who I am today." Then people will flock to the church. Sermons are like the heart of worship. So when the preaching is full of life and is anointed by the Holy Spirit, the entire service will be alive. When a sermon touches the congregation, they will come to life.

I have learned one thing in my ministry. I have learned that when a pastor preaches well, the members of his church will forgive him for anything. But, if a pastor can't preach well, people are less forgiving. This is preaching. When a pastor preaches well, the entire church is revived, as if it was showered by a downpour of grace. Pastors should deliver a sermon that is anointed by the Holy Spirit, that is powerful, and that is alive and moving. If God has called you to be a preacher, then you should press on with preaching at the risk of your life.

3. Sermons

A preacher should nurture his sermons within his very being, and not just in his head. Whether he opens or closes his eyes, a pastor should have his message within him, and then the Word that is in him will naturally come out at any time. You won't need a transcript. You should be able to preach when the switch is turned on. You can preach the same message for five minutes, one hour, or a whole day. When preaching is in you, this is possible.

Nurturing Christians is the Church's responsibility. Raising children well is more important than giving birth to a child. Now, the ministry of the Church does not end at evangelizing or bringing a person to a church. Churches should nurture and raise Christians to the fullness of Jesus Christ, to become mighty men and women and leaders of God for our age.

4. Nurturing System

We need a nurturing system that fits the current age.
As a mother gives birth to her child, she becomes responsible as a parent in raising her newborn. For our parent's generation in Korea, after they gave birth to their children, the children had to take care of themselves. Our parents did not have the money to raise us, and the school system was pretty bad during the Japanese colonial era and the Korean War. At that time, the best way to raise children was to pay for tuition by selling rice paddies or cows and doing backbreaking labor. The children who studied during those hard times became the leaders of South Korea today. They did not study in comfortable living conditions but in an unbelievably unbearable environment.

But now that we live comfortably, we cannot raise children the way our parents did in the past. So many young people today are exposed to violence, drugs, and sex, and many have fallen! In the past, parents could let their children discover life on their own, but today, if we leave our children to take care of themselves as our parents did during their generation, our children will most likely become gangsters. Today, lurking in our streets are so many dangers that did not exist in the past, such as AIDS and other modern-day diseases, traffic accidents, and high divorce rates. This is the type of environment we live in today.

The situation is the same for the church as well. In the old days, churches offered Sunday service, small groups, Wednesday service, and home visitations, and people could live faithfully. But in the 21st century, the environment has become so complicated. Now, if churches do not train, nurture, and disciple members appropriately, members will face a dangerous environment that will hinder them from growing righteously. This is an important fact that Christians today should not overlook.

Nurturing Christians is the church's responsibility. Raising children well is more important than giving birth to a child. Now, the ministry of the church does not end at evangelizing or bringing a person to a church. Churches should nurture and raise Christians to the fullness of Jesus Christ, to become mighty men and women and leaders of God for our age. I believe it is the church's responsibility to continually impart leadership and spiritual vision to people, and to mold them into the people who make up God's kingdom. This is why we need a nurturing system.

Pastoral philosophy is about the calling of a pastor, a member, and a church coming together as a trinity. They should fit just right. No matter how good something is, it must match who I am in order for me to benefit from it. As such, students, teachers, and textbooks should form a trinity. Why is our church doing one-to-one discipleship training? Why do we use the Navigators books? On what ground? What is the system or the order? These factors should be all linked together.

The core of nurturing is to have a father's heart.

What is important in nurturing is that you should nurture Christians not as teachers, but with a father's heart. "Even though you have ten thousand guardians in Christ, you do not have many fathers, for in Christ Jesus I became your father through the Gospel" (1 Corinthians 4:15). This is the essential idea of nurturing Christians.

What is nurturing? It is giving birth and then parenting, not teaching. The idea of nurturing is to give birth to a child as a mother does. Teachers give information and teach. However, parents love their children at the risk of their lives. Even if a son committed murder, his parents would never give up on him. This is parenting, or, childrearing. One problem that churches have is that they have a strong concept of teaching but lack the idea of nurturing. One-to-one discipleship and fellowship are merely tools. What's more important is that two people are coming together through one-to-one fellowship and opening their lives. It is like giving birth to a child spiritually. Mothers cannot forsake their own babies. We need such nurturing relationships within the church.

The crisis of the church today is that there is no such relationship in churches. Instead, the relationships in churches are too businesslike. Pastors come and go when their time is up. It is hard to find a vibrant relationship anymore. The relationship between a pastor and an elder is not that of a teacher and a disciple. That's why there are head-on confrontations and conflicts. The same goes for the relationship between one church member and another member.

I would like to encourage churches to adopt the concept of nurturing or giving birth. A church is not an institution but a family. It is a true church when it is like a family, resembling the relationship of a husband and wife. We need real churches today. We need fellowship and trust.

That is why I prefer the term "shepherd" over "pastor," and "raising sheep" over "running a church." Pastors are not cowboys but shepherds. As cowboys drive cattle while riding on a horse with a whip in their hand, a shepherd leads his flock of sheep to green pastures and quiet waters with a rod and staff. A rod protects the sheep from wild beasts, and the staff leads them to the right path. Shepherds are willing to give up their lives for their sheep.

When raising the sheep goes well, the ministry will also go well. When a pastor takes on the basic job of being a shepherd, he is truly doing the work of a pastor. How tragic would it be if we were left only with a shell and no true pastoral substance?

The larger the church is, the harder it is for a pastor to visit each member's home. Indeed, pastors cannot be free from their administrative responsibilities, but above all, they should be shepherds. As a shepherd raises sheep, pastors should personally evangelize a soul and raise him or her over several years. Like the Apostle Paul, pastors should teach a soul the Bible and intercede for him or her.

We need a step-by-step nurturing system.

Colostrum is so rich in proteins and antibodies that if a baby who has never ingested breast milk before drinks it, the baby will have diarrhea. After a few days, however, the mother will produce less rich, but more nutritious breast milk and have it available for her child. So the content of breast milk changes as the baby grows. God designed the composition of breast milk to change at different levels. God created us to drink breast milk first, then soft solid food, such as rice, and then later hard and tough food, such as meat. Do kids just crawl around forever? No. God created our body to first crawl, then walk, and later run, as our body grows.

The same is true with our spirit. Our spirit can grow well when we provide for its needs appropriately.

Nurturing is ultimately giving. The important thing in nurturing is to give according to the level of growth. It is okay to spoon-feed a baby, but how would a mom and her child feel if the mom still spoonfed her grown-up child? People who know the real flavor of a dish will get up, buy the ingredients and make their own meal. They already have a mature taste.

The same is true for the nurturing system of our faith. If someone has been going to church for ten years but is no different from a new believer, he or she is not spiritually healthy. Over time, some people don't mature but only change their appearance. Likewise, people go to church and get used to the habit, but their souls do not mature. Pastors should understand the importance of having a step-by-step nurturing system when leading a church.

We need a specialization process.

When you enlist in the army, you will receive PRI, which is preliminary rifle instruction, and the first step is to learn the low military crawl. For 40 days, you will receive intensive basic training as a soldier. In the army, there is a saying that goes: "A drop of sweat during training is like a drop of blood in war." This means that only soldiers who sweat a lot during training can avoid bullets and danger during a war.

The church is also a spiritual training ground. You don't come to church to have fun. Some describe the church as a hospital. In a way, the church is like a hospital that treats the sick and restores the wounded. But for how long will a church just treat and restore people? When people are healed and restored, the church should then transform itself into a military unit. The church is a hospital and a military unit at the same time. It should train people intensively. It should become a place that is able to win over the world and change the world.

We need hope in the church. We should look forward to observing how the church will change in the next ten years. When a new believer walks into a church, he or she should be able to feel at first sight that "I will be able to learn something at this church." To this end, we need to specialize ministries.

In general, church elders take on a variety of roles in the church, but when they retire, they no longer have much to do. Since they have experienced various roles, they are exposed to various fields, but there isn't a ministry where they are truly experts. Elders need the expertise, for instance, to interact with children well or to educate youth effectively.

In other words, we need to acquire expertise in areas such as making Bible study handbooks, broadcasting, discipling one-to-one, running family ministries, providing internal healing programs, and conducting spiritual programs such as "Shining Glory," which make you want to bet your entire life on them. Having expertise could also mean that those who lack relative expertise in an area may need the help of someone with that expertise. Members need to have expertise in God's ministries in order to help other Christians who lack such expertise.

We don't need to have a major while in high school, but we need one in college. This means that college students give up everything else to become an expert in one area. There are many people, but there aren't many spiritual experts for God's kingdom. We need experts in churches on whom we can call when we have an issue in a certain matter. We need experts who are known in South Korea as experts in children's ministry or in kindergarten ministry.

Just as a hospital may specialize in internal medicine, surgery, pediatrics, dentistry, or dermatology (and even these areas can be even further specialized), we need a systematic nurturing curriculum in the church. A church should at least have introductory, intermediate and advanced courses. Don't worry if your church doesn't have a specialized program. There is nothing you cannot do if you have invested in it for ten years.

Raise up lay leaders.

A nurturing program becomes a success or failure depending on how well the church raises leaders who can nurture others. A pastor alone cannot teach many people. Meeting and helping members on a one-to-one basis should be done by leaders, not pastors.

In a sense, raising leaders who can nurture people is important enough to bet the life and death of a church on. This is because depending on who the nurturing leaders are, the pillars of a nurturing system will be different. Since nurturing is raising a person, the pastor must nurture the leader directly. Then, the person who is well-nurtured can nurture others well. In contrast, if a person is nurtured poorly, does not have a role model to follow, and does not learn much, that person will teach others poorly as well.

While appointing leaders who will nurture others is the church's responsibility, looking for a companion, a person to nurture, is the leader's job. The companion will soon become born again, as the nurturing leader himself. In particular, a leader must do a great job in finding a companion in the church. A companion is like a hidden gem. A leader must find a person whom he can teach for more than six months with all his might. In this sense, regular nurturing and one-to-one nurturing is different. Otherwise, the leader will bear no fruit even if he has worked so hard for it. If the leader or the companion is not consistent in attendance or time, they will lose heart in the end.

The nurturing curriculum should constantly be improved.

A church's curriculum should be improved continually. It should be evaluated every year and move forward step by step. Just as the South Korean army aims to develop a soldier of the Republic of Korea, not just someone who knows how to fight well, it is extremely important to offer basic training and leveled training to

4. Nurturing System

raise workers needed for the church. We should not make a half-hearted nurturing system in the church.

Likewise, broadcasting companies evaluate their programs every three months because no matter how great a TV or radio program is, people may lose interest after three months. As we put on spring clothes in spring and summer clothes in summer, we should consistently make a variety of changes to a program. A new product is not something incredibly new, but something that has been altered little by little from existing products. In other words, it is about consistently creating a new paradigm. The same goes with the church. To safeguard the Gospel, which is an unchanging truth, we need to endlessly improve ourselves.

A ministry is not something you can do half-heartedly. You have to pay the price, put in hard work, and sacrifice doing something that no one else will do. For example, if you want to choose a Bible study guide, you should master at least all the guides available in South Korea. After reviewing them, you should pick the one that fits your need the most. Once you master a guide, it is easier to master other guides.

When you reach the top, everything else seems to be the same. Just like that, once you reach the top of something, you will be able to understand the surrounding areas pretty quickly. Those who reach the top of their field, whether it be music, art, or business, can better understand each other because the principle is the same. If we have made our decision to live for God, how can we be content with living as amateurs? We should risk our lives to become an expert for our Lord.

Make a nurturing system that fits your church.

There are four things you need to keep in mind when creating a nurturing system for your church.

First, you must identify the characteristics of the people who come to your church.

Depending on the location, churches attract lower-class, middle-class, or upper-class people. When making a nurturing system for a church, you must take this factor into account. You need to understand what kind of individuals make up the congregation. It is important to identify whether the church is a church of intellectuals or regular workers and whether it attracts young people or grownups.

In the case of our church, many professionals gather. For this reason, we need to provide a curriculum that is appropriate for professionals. A church with many older people should prepare programs fit for the elderly. For instance, when choosing Bible study guides for older people, the church should take into account whether a handbook has a large font size or not. You need to figure out the characteristics of the congregation, then a location and time that works best for them. Think about whether you should deliver a 30-minute or 50-minute sermon and whether you should follow a six-month or year-long Bible study program. In particular, if you are a missionary, you need to develop a nurturing system that is fit for the mission field. In the mission field, even if your nurturing system fits only 60 percent of the congregation, you are doing great.

Second, you should find out if the nurturing program and the pastor have good chemistry.

Next, it is important to understand the style and characteristics of the church's pastor. Think about whether the pastor is a logical person driven by ideas or a passionate person driven by feelings. After all, a church is operated by the pastor's style, which is why the pastor and the Bible study guides should match well. You shouldn't just bring the nurturing system of a large church to any church. You must find the nurturing style that is most appropriate for the pastor and the members.

Third, the nurturing system must be continuously complemented.

Congregations will change, and of course, the pastor will change as well, and so will the social climate. It is good for the pastor to understand the constantly changing situation of the church and to suggest new alternatives. There is no such thing as an everlasting nurturing system. In the beginning, Onnuri Community Church used the study guides produced by university student missions organizations to nurture members. However, as the church grew, we shifted our nurturing program focus from Bible studies to family ministry, restoration ministry, and inner healing ministry. Also, we later changed the focus from our Praise and Worship ministry to emphasizing the Holy Spirit's presence in all our ministries by introducing the Holy Spirit ministry. What was more surprising was that as the number of young people increased, we were led to develop "Open Worship." Then, we focused on nurturing and mission programs, followed by customized evangelism, and a nurturing program according to the vision of Acts 29.

Fourth, aim for a balanced nurturing system.

Above all, it is important to regularly and steadily offer the right amount of training. This may sound obvious and basic, but the problem is that this principle is often not met. In whatever we do, doing too much causes an adverse effect. If a program makes church members fall into cursory mannerisms, legalism, or dogmatism, the situation becomes worse than not doing any program at all, no matter how good the program is.

Onnuri Community Church's basic nurturing system

Onnuri Community Church has seven basic nurturing programs: new believer registration, Quiet Time, one-to-one discipleship, evangelism training, discipleship in a small group, imparting vision and leadership, and sending members for outreach.

First, we have a newcomer registration program. When our church first introduced the newcomer registration program, we were criticized for raising the threshold of the church. However, based on the ecclesiology of the Bible that the Church is a community of Christians that acknowledges the Lord as their Savior, churches need a process that can at least check the beliefs of a new believer. Also, before anyone would like to register at a church, the church should explain what it is, its faith and its vision to newcomers, giving them enough time to think about their decision before registering. This will help newcomers overcome many challenges they might face in the church and help them settle in the congregation.

Second, we train the newcomers in how to do Quiet Time (QT). Our church members start observing Quiet Time the moment they believe in Jesus. Why do we put so much emphasis on Quiet Time?

Members cannot always stay close to the church or pastors.

Only a tenth of the congregation attends early morning prayer meeting. Then, what happens to the rest of the members? Should their faith die because they are not with their pastors? No, that should not be so. Pastors should make and offer a basic framework with which the members can eat, meditate, apply, and share the daily bread of God on their own every day. As we naturally eat breakfast when we wake up in the morning, we should meditate on God's Word when we open our eyes in the morning.

When I first introduced Quiet Time or QT to our church after coming back from the UK, many people would jokingly ask me, "What is it? Cutie? Is it a diaper brand?" A lot of people do Quiet Time nowadays, but back then, there were not many who did it or knew about it. When we first introduced Quiet Time in our church, we even checked the member's Quiet Time notes. Indeed, since Quiet Time is about meeting God personally, examining their journals was not necessary, but we chose to do it so that Quiet Time could become a habit. As it shows, I believe that Quiet Time is fundamental in nurturing.

At first, we published a Quiet Time magazine as a supplement to the first issue of *Light and Salt*, a Christian magazine produced by Duranno. Later, we published *Living Life*, a separate Quiet Time magazine. Since the late 1980s, I have traveled all over the country to offer seminars on Quiet Time with our members. If a person subscribed to the magazine during the seminar, I would always be excited on my way back to Seoul. I cannot forget those days.

The Far East Broadcasting Company led the spread of Quiet Time in South Korea by broadcasting a Quiet Time show that targeted working adults. There were many testimonies given at that time, and there was one that I cannot forget. It was a letter from Northeast Asia, and it went like this:

"I listen to the Quiet Time radio show at 6:15 a.m. at an underground church. I had never seen a commentary before, but I wrote in my notebook everything I heard from the show, thinking that my notes would be my commentary. Later, my notebook indeed became a commentary that explained Scripture. I live day by day thanks to the show."

As you can see, Quiet Time is like a daily meal. No matter what circumstances you are in, it helps you maintain fellowship with God. Quiet Time should become the basis of nurturing.

Third, after newcomers' completion of Quiet Time training, we offer them One-to-One discipleship. Our church is huge, but when you look inside, members are connected to each other deeply through One-to-One discipleship. This is the power that allows our church to move intimately and dynamically without being divided, despite our size.

At first, our One-to-One discipleship training was an adapted version of a missions organization's Bible study to fit our situation. When I think about it, the program was a wonderful nurturing program that God gave to our church. Quiet Time and One-to-One discipleship programs are the most basic programs for the lay ministry of our church. Quiet Time is about my personal relationship with God, while One-to-One discipleship is about my relationship with 'you.' There is one more thing, the small group, which is about 'us' and me. Today, many Christians in our church are reaching out to the world with Quiet Time and One-to-One discipleship in their hands.

4. Nurturing System

Fourth, discipleship is learned in small groups. Discipleship is not about a program, but about how we live. It is a lifelong process. You learn discipleship by having and maintaining relationships with other people. The focus of discipleship is the message of the Cross, which is about obedience, dedication, and self-surrender. Above all, we learn how to live as Christians through the community called "small groups." Recently, we have begun offering the Jesus Discipleship School (JDS) program, which runs for about nine months. Participants meet twice a week for three-hour training sessions. In the end, they go on a short-term mission trip to experience the life of a disciple firsthand. Of course, you can't learn everything about discipleship through classes or training sessions, but all the leaders or members serving Onnuri Community Church have to take the JDS program. Learning how to live in community and learning how to live as a disciple through small groups is the key to Onnuri Community Church's nurturing system.

The Church is neither a denomination nor an institution. It is a community. Since it is a community of the Holy Spirit, worship, mission, Christ, and sharing, it is critical to learn discipleship.

Fifth, we offer evangelism training. Evangelism training doesn't just mean street evangelism, mass evangelism, or evangelism with printed materials. It is about encouraging Christians to evangelize people in their workplaces and at home through their lives.

We value personal evangelism. Everyone is challenged to live the life of an evangelist, which is why Onnuri Community Church strongly emphasizes Open Worship, customized evangelism, and cultural evangelism. Cultural evangelism through festivals is a new way of evangelism. It creates an atmosphere that stirs a passion for evangelism. However, in the end, evangelism is based fundamentally on personal evangelism.

Sixth, we impart vision and leadership. After evangelism training, we will impart vision and leadership to those who have completed the training.

The vision of the church is to become the very church illustrated in the Book of Acts. The most important thing in achieving this vision is leadership. I dream of church leadership, not an individualistic leadership. First of all, we offer the "Elders Cadet School" to train and produce elders. We also have "Deaconess School" and "Ordained Deacons School."

Seventh, we send members on an outreach. Through outreach work, the church should help members decide whether they will go to the mission field as a missionary or live out the life of a missionary where they are. Going on a short-term mission training is the highlight of the training and nurturing programs at Onnuri Community Church. During school breaks, holidays, and vacations, members will visit other cultural groups or unreached tribes. If possible, they will be encouraged to visit the same area on a more regular basis so that they can reap the fruits of their labor. We send outreach teams to poor communities, marginalized areas, and particularly, to foreign workers in South Korea.

This is the basic framework of Onnuri Community Church's nurturing system. It can change here and there, and the name may change, but such changes are not important. What's important is to have a general framework, and based on this framework, various programs are developed. When a member goes through training according to this framework, it will take about five to seven years.

4. Nurturing System

That much time is needed so that learners can adapt to something until it becomes second nature. Moreover, when a layperson is trained this much, he or she can teach and help others.

Since the beginning of Onnuri Community Church, I have firmly told our members to leave our church seven years after they join our congregation so that they can serve and teach others. In fact, many of our previous members who were doctors moved to Jeju Island or China, leaving their successful hospitals behind, because they were challenged by the message, "Leave in the seventh year."

We should not forget that we learn not to boast of our knowledge, but to make disciples to the ends of the earth. Our church's motto of nurturing, therefore, has always been "Learn or teach" or "Leave or send."

The church is a community and consists of many small groups. Small groups are called "Soohn" in Onnuri Community Church. It means a little sprout in Korean. A number of "Soohn" are grouped together as a "Darakbang" or a circle, a number of circles are gathered together as a "Gongdongchae" or a community, and a number of communities come together as a church. The important point is that a Soohn may be small, but it is a complete community. A church is healthy when each Soohn is alive and active.

5. Small Groups and Community

God dreams of community.

Christianity is about community. Jesus had a community-oriented mindset. The Old Testament begins as a community. If there was something critical that the modern churches have lost, it would be the community that appeared in the Bible. Is it possible to create a community as Jesus had intended? Does such community exist on earth today? Jesus' three-year-long ministry can be summed up as an investment to create and lead a community, not discipleship training. The community is the Church. Jesus had a dream of community, and such a dream did not start on earth but had its beginning in heaven. God exists in the form of community. God is a trinity - the Father, Son, and Holy Spirit. This is called "the community of God." God creates a society. The way God exists is community-like.

God's dream is also to create a community. Since this is how God exists, people should also exist in a community. That is why Jesus handpicked 12 disciples and created an experience of community.

Jesus ensured that God's will was done on earth as it was in heaven. He prayed that "all of them may be one, Father, just as you are in me and I am in you. May they also be in us so that the world may believe that you have sent me" (John 17:21).

Another amazing thing to note is that the Holy Spirit did not come upon individuals. For example, the Holy Spirit did not come to Peter first and let him share the Holy Spirit with others. Instead, the Holy Spirit came to a group of 120 people, not to an individual. The Church was born and started as a community.

The community is God's idea and a picture of heaven. The nature of the devil is to divide people, while that of God is to unite people and become one. If someone was moved because of you, that is fine, but if an individual becomes jealous of you, that means that you stirred up competition. Inspiration brings people together, but competition divides them.

We must become one. There must be a unity at home, in the church, and in society. If we can become one, we can bring heaven to earth. The most important step to forming a family is that a man should leave his parents and become one with his wife. The essence of the Church is also to be one.

5. Small Groups and Community

Pursue a true community.

During Jesus' time, the disciples were interested to know who was higher than whom. The mother of John and James tried to lobby for her sons to gain Jesus' favor. There is always competition, division, and selfishness lurking in the world of men and women. Churches compete even when doing good deeds such as mission work. This is a problem in the community. So there is something we should always keep in mind and pursue, and that is how we can establish a community for Jesus.

The basic unit Jesus talks about is not 12 people but just two to three individuals. "Truly I tell you, whatever you bind on earth will be bound in heaven, and whatever you loose on earth will be loosed in heaven. Again, truly I tell you that if two of you on earth agree about anything they ask for, it will be done for them by my Father in heaven. For where two or three gather in my name, there am I with them." (Matthew 18:18-20).

In some ways, Christianity began with just two to three people. Even the smallest church has 12 people, and even with that few, the church can become a perfect church. With only 12 people, they can turn the world over. We need such a pastoral philosophy for our churches today. In particular, if newly planted churches and churches with fewer than 50 members even after 10 to 20 years firmly believe in such a pastoral philosophy, they will not waver and will not be shaken.

What we ought to pursue is not to build a megachurch, although a large church could indeed accomplish a number of things and provide many blessings. However, a small church can be blessed as its members cooperate with each other. The principle of cooperation is that when weak people join hands together, they can become even better than a strong person. This principle of cooperation is a blessing if it does not lead to political or social groups like a labor union, veering away from its original meaning. The principle was shown in Acts in some ways. If denominations had not fought amongst themselves and churches had been able to overcome the walls of selfishness, small communities could have come together and established God's community on earth. Also, cults such as Moon Sun Myoung of The Unification Church would not have appeared. We must now return to the essence of the Church.

Jesus worked with a church of just 12 people. It is also meaningful that Jesus failed with one of the 12 (Judas Iscariot) in the church. This is the Church. When you closely look at a large church, you can think of it as having groups of smaller churches with 12 members each. Some churches may have 10, 100, or 1,000 small churches of 12 people, but in the end, the original form of a church is always 12 people.

There was a small church in China for Korean Chinese people. The church did not have a pastor or a full-time assistant pastor. Only a woman who was called an evangelist served the church. Although the church did not have Bibles or hymnals, Jesus' name was proclaimed, and the people who called upon God's name gathered. I believe that Jesus anoints and loves the family churches in China, underground churches in North Korea, and churches in communist countries.

All problems arise when ministries become institutionalized and serving at church becomes a mere career. A crisis will arise when people begin to compete among themselves and start to compare who is bigger or smaller.

Meanwhile, the first thing many missionaries do when they go to the mission field is to build a mission center or a seminary. Paul, however, did not build a mission center. The only thing he created was the Hall of Tyrannus. When he was in Ephesus, he taught the Bible for three years in a building that was named after a popular philosopher in the second century; his name was Tyrannus. Paul wasn't able to use the hall during its prime time, but had to use it between 10:00 a.m. and 5:00 p.m., the hottest time of day in the Middle East when people typically took a nap. It was there that Paul taught 12 disciples for two years and was able to raise God's amazing people even in such a situation.

As Paul trained 12 people who were anointed by the Holy Spirit for two years, Asians, Greeks, and Jews believed in Jesus. When aprons that had touched Paul were taken to the people, the evil spirits left them.[16] Also, a number of people were added to the church every day, which was an incredible miracle. The 12 people Paul raised in Tyrannus of Ephesus transformed over Asia, Europe, and the world.

The Church is not about how it looks. We exist to build the kingdom of God on earth. The essence of the Church is to take care of the poor and the oppressed, to give freedom to the captives and those who are bound by sin, and to proclaim the Year of Jubilee to the poor. Because of this purpose, the Church and I exist. Of course, we need denominations, churches, institutions,

---

16 Acts 19:11-12.

and pastors. However, all these cannot come before the essence of the church.

Jesus chose 12 people to build a church. It can be said that the 12 people are the internal characteristic of the Church, while the 120 people who gathered during Pentecost were the outward representation of the Church. Any church can lead 120 people if they do their best. When leaders of a small group establish a beautiful small community of Jesus' disciples, big miracles will happen. But please do not be too sensitive about the numbers.

Characteristics of Onnuri Community Church's small groups

Small groups are not just Bible study gatherings. Below are the characteristics of small groups.

First, small groups are sharing communities. Small groups are where people share their lives and discuss how God has touched them. If you use a small group for the teaching of its members, problems will arise. If you want to teach the Bible systematically, then form a Bible college or a Bible study group, and let people with the gift of teaching the Bible take care of that ministry.

A small group is a place to share what you learned from your Quiet Time. When members of a small group begin to talk about how God has worked in their lives for the past week, that small group will experience revival.

Second, small groups are evangelistic communities. A small group is a not a community of just Christians but also a community for evangelism. The amazing thing is that when a church focuses on evangelism, the church will start to be filled with energy.

5. Small Groups and Community

It is like having a baby in the house where there used to be just adults. When a baby is born, you will become busy, but your home will be filled with vibrancy.

To bring back energy to old believers, you need to accept new believers. When new believers join, they may make mistakes, but the church will be filled with life. If a small group has gotten boring and hasn't been growing, that's because it hasn't had a new believer in the group. When a new believer joins, everyone will focus on the new member, and it will be too busy for old members to fight among themselves.

This is where many churches fail. They long for new believers to come, but at the same time, they block the doors to new believers, because it is easier and more comfortable to work with old members. When old members are not willing to let go of the supposed power they possess, believing that new members might push them out, new members cannot take root in the church. Small groups should become a community for new believers; small groups should welcome them, listen to their stories, and answer whatever questions they may have.

Third, small groups are healing communities. Another characteristic of small groups is that they should aspire to be a community of healing. When a small group becomes a place where people encourage and inspire, where people are understood and loved, and where mistakes are forgiven, the group will be a place that people don't want to miss and a place where love overflows.

Fourth, small groups are service communities. Community, by nature, can easily become selfish. Small groups should, therefore, serve according to the gifts that each of the members of the group possesses. The community will grow when it has work to do. A small group should become a community of healing and restoration, as well as of unity and harmony. Small groups should be Jesus' community of 12 beautiful people, which will be transformed into a community of 120 people anointed by the Holy Spirit, ultimately moving on to becoming a community that changes the world.

Jesus chose 12 people to build a church. It can be said that the 12 people are the internal characteristic of the Church, while the 120 people who gathered during Pentecost were the outward representation of the Church. Any church can lead 120 people if they do their best. When leaders of a small group establish a beautiful small community of Jesus' disciples, big miracles will happen. please do not be too sensitive about the numbers.

Evangelism is about sharing the Gospel within your cultural boundary, while mission work is about sharing the Gospel outside your cultural boundary. Both evangelism and missions must be alive and carried out simultaneously in a church.

6. Evangelism

Jesus came for sinners.

Jesus said, "I have not come to call the righteous, but sinners to repentance" (Luke 5:32). Jesus came to the world for sinners. But do churches keep their doors open for sinners? Haven't churches become congregations for holy people who faithfully follow Jesus? Do the sermons consider the many souls who wander around not knowing Jesus Christ? Are church buildings for people who believe in Jesus? Or are they designed in consideration of those who do not believe in the Savior?

Jesus came to this earth for people with whom other people do not want to deal and who were deemed abandoned sinners. He came for prostitutes, a woman with five husbands, tax collectors, the mentally ill, and sinners. We should evaluate if our church is a true church with this perspective.

There will always be problems in the church because it is a place where sinners come together. Immature people gather, fight, make noise, and cause trouble. This is the Church. A church that welcomes such people is a true church.

Jesus came for sinners. Churches today should exist for sinners. Churches should invite, comfort, and encourage sinners, and preach for sinners to become the people of God. Many churches want to grow, but their sermons don't take new believers into account. This is because when the sermons are targeted at new believers, other members who've been Christians for a long time will no longer be moved by such sermons because they have already heard them before. However, it is important to think about new believers. Messages prepared for old Christians are boring and difficult for new believers.

A healthy church has sinners and new believers. Churches should have many new believers because the church is essentially a church for sinners.

Jesus came to serve.

The church exists to serve, not be served. "For even the Son of Man did not come to be served, but to serve, and to give his life as a ransom for many" (Mark 10:45). Problems arise in churches when the members who have been attending for a long time think the church is their territory. They won't let anyone else "invade" their domain. They won't let people who are better than they are enter the church. In the end, they keep the church at their level.

6. Evangelism

When people with high positions or social status lower themselves and take on unpleasant tasks, a beautiful model is set in place. What the world wants to see the most in churches is people loving each other without fighting, and people forgiving each other when someone makes mistakes. The Church should love, forgive, and cover the weaknesses of others. The Church should let things flow like running water instead of nitpicking every error.

Do not stir the muddy water to make it clean, but let it sit. When you let water flow for about 10 minutes, the water will become clean again. It's the same when there are scandals in the church. Don't gossip about it. Let's say someone had an "accident" on the church carpet. What good will it do to discuss who did what and when did it happen while the "accident" is still fresh? Whoever saw the problem first must clean it up. It's as simple as that.

If churches stop evangelizing people, they will begin to rot. But when they do evangelize, they will become alive again. This was very evident when we first started our church. After introducing an assistant pastor from an island known as Eodo in the *Light and Salt* magazine, the entire church went there for an evangelistic rally. We divided ourselves into several teams and evangelized and invited the island residents to an evening rally. Sunday school children prepared performances and adults prepared food. In the evening, we showed a movie. The quiet island village became festive for the first time in many years. We didn't stop serving even after a week, and we decided to serve that village until a church was established.

After that week, three staff members of the evangelism team and other church members took turns visiting Eodo Island and worshipped there. Every Saturday, 10 to 15 sisters and brothers packed their bags and left for Eodo. In the evenings as they arrived, they held evangelistic rallies. On Sundays, they held children's Sunday school, middle and high school services, and adult services. Also, a dental team, ob-gyn team, and oriental medicine team provided several services and medicines. Sometimes, we also provided haircuts and perms and went around the town disinfecting several areas.

During those two months, the Holy Spirit worked with us, and almost 100 percent of the elementary school students came to the children's services. Middle to high school students and grownups also flocked to the temporary church building. Finally, island villagers who believed in shamans and mountain spirits came back to Jesus. The shock and joy spread throughout Eodo.

What was more moving than the changes in the island residents were the changes in our own members. At that time, the members of our church used to joke around and say, "We'll get slipped disks on the way and have them fixed on the way back," pertaining to the bumpy and unpaved road they had to travel to and from the island. Everyone who heard the joke laughed their lungs out. The road was rough, and their beds were uncomfortable. However, after the trip, the faces of the members who returned from the visit were shining brightly.

After that, little by little, our members started to become more alive. Their eyes beamed. They became full of life. They felt proud to share life. I saw old and formal ways being peeled off. The Holy Spirit made a deep impression upon the people, and they came together. Teamwork was developed. They formed a clear identity and understanding that Jesus' vision will be accomplished through the Church and themselves. Then, the church was transformed.

Some members heard about poor people in a small church in Bongcheong-dong who had to skip meals. These church members told me that they would visit Bongcheong-dong to give these people rice and clothes. There was a greater joy and excitement in the church that could not be compared with the feeling of regret our church members felt because they had to miss their church services.

Evangelism is about serving other souls with the grace we have received. When we evangelize, the Church of the Lord will come alive again.

Jesus came to seek the lost.

"For the Son of Man came to seek and to save the lost" (Luke 19:10). All around us, there are many people like Zacchaeus who want to climb a sycamore tree to meet Jesus. These people are rich but lonely; they have power but don't know how to live; they seem strong on the outside but weak on the inside. Jesus met and understood such people, yet others hated them passionately.

Maybe this is how we are today. We choose people with whom we want to interact. To protect the pride of the church, we avoid meeting certain kinds of people. However, Jesus wasn't like this. People criticized Jesus, but he still visited their homes, saying, "I came to seek and to save the lost. I must stay at your house today." Churches should speak the way Jesus spoke.

Don't we have many lost and forgotten people in the church? It is important to evangelize an unbeliever, but it is more important to find those who has come to the church and left. We must find the people who have been hurt or disappointed by the Church and Christians.

Every church is the same. Even if we don't evangelize outside, new people will consistently come to the church. The problem is that churches cannot hold on to these people for long, and another problem is that churches do not seek after them when they leave.

We should realize that when people leave the church, they have pretty good reasons, which may involve the sermons, someone they grew to dislike, or something they were unhappy about at church. We should face these situations honestly and then repent and correct the problems for each disheartened soul.

I once heard this story at Willow Creek Church. A woman told the story of how she was finally able to drag her unbelieving husband to church after persuading him for a long time. Her husband barely participated in the service and went home. The next Sunday, the woman asked him to come to church again, but this time her husband searched for excuses not to go. At first, he said he would not go because the men's room was dirty. What the woman did in response was to clean the restroom so he couldn't make that excuse again. Then, the husband said he would not go because the church had too much trash. So she cleaned the entire church. Finally, her husband could not come up with any new excuses and went to church. The determination exemplified by the wife shows the passion that holds on to a lost soul and does not lose it.

Jesus came to give us a full life.

"I have come that they may have life, and have it to the full" (John 10:10). This is nurturing. How can I feed green grass to those

I have brought to church? This is something that Christians should be concerned about. In short, the Bible is about the Father's heart. If you aren't able find the heart of a father in the Bible, you haven't found anything. The father's heart is to wait for a son who has left home. The real prodigal son is the one who doesn't know his father's heart. Although the father is heartbroken, he leaves the door open and waits for his son throughout the night, and yet the eldest son's heart remains icy cold. The elder son says, "Father, forget about him. He took all your money. Can such a bad man still be your son?"

Should the father agree with his older son? Would the father be happy if his older son bought him expensive clothes and delicious food to comfort him?

The real prodigal son is not the younger child who left, but the older one. If the older son truly understood his father's heart, what could he have done to console his own father? He should have looked for his younger brother, even if it meant selling the house or the entire property. That should have been his response to show how much he loved his father.

Sometimes, it seems as though Korean churches are like the older son who has a cold heart. It is hard to find a church that is still reviving when it's 50 years old or older. They are all busy keeping their traditions. People who have worshipped together for generations gather together to worship God, but since they do not like to break their tradition and change the atmosphere of their church, there are times when they seem unhappy to have newcomers. How can such congregations be considered true churches? We must know the heart of a father, who is patiently waiting for his son who left home.

The value of 99 sheep in the pen is equal to the value of one lost sheep. One is of the same worth as the 99. God does not look at the numbers but sees a soul. Do we have tears, sorrow, and a desperate heart for a soul? Are we willing to take a risk to save a soul? Pastor Bill Hybels at Willow Creek Church normally would keep his eyes wide open, but whenever he heard the phrase "the souls that do not believe in Jesus," his eyes would soon fill with tears.

I looked at him and wondered how many pastors would tear up like him when thinking of an unbelieving soul. Some may lecture about not evangelizing or shout and chant, "Let's evangelize!" but there aren't many pastors who would shed tears because their hearts are torn for a lost soul. A heart that cries for souls is truly a father's heart.

Churches today need such tears. Tears for lost souls; tears for dying souls who have gone astray, souls who are devasted, and souls who take their own lives because they don't know Christ! Hearts that will say in tears, "If only I told him about Jesus, he would not have lived like that!" or "If our church did not cause him to stumble, he would not have been like that!" Even Jesus said, "It would be better for him to be thrown into the sea with a millstone tied around his neck than for him to cause one of these little ones to sin" (Luke 17:2).

When we went to Willow Creek Church in 1996, we heard this touching story. The church was celebrating its 20th anniversary, and 20,000 members gathered in a large gymnasium. Everyone held a light bulb in their hands. After all the events and programs, the gymnasium lights were turned off, and the moderator said,

"Everyone who has met Christ and became a Christian for the first time upon coming to Willow Creek Church, please light up your light bulb." Soon, 85 percent of the light bulbs were turned on, illuminating the entire venue. The members of the church were so touched. They hugged and cried with each other, realizing that 85 percent of them met Christ in the church!

Willow Creek Church has been saying, "Christians can go to other churches. Only those who don't believe in Jesus, come to this church! We will do ministry for them! We will offer programs for them! We will prepare Bible studies for them!" Because this church made such a decision and put it into action, it possesses an overwhelming joy that many of today's churches have lost.

We should pay attention to seekers.

Churches should pay attention to seekers and unbelievers. Unbelievers are people who do not believe in Christ at all, while seekers are those who are interested in Jesus but do not know him well. Seekers may not know how to believe in Jesus, or they may have negative prejudices against churches, saying, "Churches only emphasize offerings," or "Churches always say 'be blessed.'" Some of them might have been hurt by churches before. Churches should pay attention to this group of people. When believers change their attitude and language, gradually caring for seekers, when the sermons are slightly altered, and when the church is changed a tiny bit, these people will be more than willing to come to church. How can we preach so that they will accept Jesus? Churches should think about this.

There are churches that focus entirely on evangelism because they recognize that the essence of the Church is that it "exists for the lost souls, dying souls, and sinners." In such churches, the evangelism team is not just one of many ministries because these churches bring all their resources to evangelizing people. A perfect example is the Seeker's Service of Saddleback Church or Willow Creek Church. These churches have changed their entire stage and programs for the sake of seekers. They focus on having seekers so that they will come, believe in Christ, be saved, and receive grace.

Seeker's Service helps people who have not yet received Jesus in their heart to come to church without feeling any resistance. Seeker's Service uses the bass guitar and drums instead of the pipe organ since it aims to encourage seekers to come to church consistently by offering comfortable music and comfortable programs and allowing people to come wearing comfortable clothes. They come and hear the story of Jesus.

Following such a pastoral philosophy, in the mid- to late 1990s, Onnuri Community Church also started to offer Open Worship, which is similar to the Seeker's Service. Open Worship is now a well-established program, and our members proudly invite new believers to worship together with them there.

However, in the beginning, it wasn't easy to establish Open Worship. At first, we made the sermons short and included a number of Christian artists, performances, and testimonies, and yet our Open Worship didn't grow. After several years, our pastoral team finally realized that even if it was a service for seekers, the service should center around God's message. The seekers came to the service to know the truth, not to watch a performance. We needed to present the Gospel more clearly. I hope that other churches will not forget this fact.

Three ways to evangelize

Evangelism can be categorized into mass evangelism and personal evangelism. Reverend Billy Graham and Pastor Seon-ju Gil of South Korea are those who did mass evangelism through TV shows, rallies, and Bible seminars.

Today's generation values action over words and has a strong negative prejudice against churches, which is why, although mass evangelism and television evangelism are good, personal evangelism is more effective.

Personal evangelism can be divided into instantaneous evangelism and contagious evangelism. The advantage of instantaneous evangelism is that you share the essence of the Gospel and lead the person to church right away. I perform instantaneous evangelism a lot and have experienced great blessings from God as I share the Gospel. I have met many people, including some who were on the verge of committing suicide. Like the thief who was crucified at the right side of Jesus and was saved at the last minute when Jesus said, "I tell you the truth, today you will be with me in paradise," sometimes there are people who need to hear the Gospel urgently. A sample evangelism program that implements personal evangelism is "Evangelism Explosion," created by James Kennedy, but one problem with such a program is that people will leave easily after they have come once to church because it is hard for churches to keep up with these people. They may have accepted Christ because they were excited, but if churches don't take care of them well, the newcomers tend to leave the church soon after.

Contagious evangelism is a relational type of evangelism. Pastor Bill Hybels' next door neighbor was a Korean, and to evangelize him, Pastor Hybels built a relationship with him for two years. The pastor did not specifically evangelize him or ask him to come to church. He just got to know his neighbor very well. When the pastor was finally invited to lunch at his Korean neighbor's house, he was so happy, like a child. For two years, pastor Bill Hybels made a good impression and developed a good relationship to share the Gospel with one person. Since the leading pastor set this example, other pastors and members of Willow Creek Church were also doing contagious evangelism. This is amazing.

Contagious evangelism, which is based on established relationships, has a high rate of new believers staying in a church. Today, we need to practice contagious evangelism. Pastors have a responsibility to nurture members so that the Word will naturally come out of their lives and so that they can practice contagious evangelism.

Customized evangelism: To share the Gospel at the eye level of a targeted unbeliever

Our church has been trying a new evangelism method for several years, and it has been fruitful beyond our imagination. It is called "customized evangelism." Customized evangelism is to share the Gospel at the level of the targeted unbeliever. In other words, it is about accurately identifying the crossing point between the need of the targeted unbeliever and the Gospel, and sharing the Good News using everyday language. "Customized" means sharing the Gospel at the level of the unbeliever, just like how Jesus became a man to meet us at our level. "Evangelism" means relational evangelism. Customized evangelism is a method in which the church and the person who wants to evangelize work together to share the Gospel to the same person.

In fact, several business companies have been using such customized strategies for a long time. Companies practice Customer Relationship Management, which is a marketing strategy that recognizes the strong relationship between the consumer and the company as being the key factor in product purchases, not price or performance. To this end, companies select targets and specialize and differentiate themselves to approach consumers more comprehensively. Customer centers collect consumer complaints and needs in a database, and the data is applied to production and sales.

Also, some companies do network marketing. In this strategy, companies sell products to specific targets by establishing a human network, unlike the traditional method of selling products to unspecified masses through mass media. This strategy is also based on relationships between individuals.

Companies value interactive communication. Gone are the days when companies simply had to create products to sell to consumers. Since consumers have more options to choose from nowadays, companies now actively integrate consumer requests into their products. The opinion of consumers has become important because companies need to manufacture products that consumers want, not what companies want.

In some ways, such business management methods were already shown in Jesus' evangelism strategies. The incarnation of Jesus is customized business management, and he practiced customized evangelism many times. Jesus valued relationships, he met others' needs first, and shared the Gospel at people's eye level.

Jesus used different methods of sharing the Gospel, depending on the level or need of the person. For Nicodemus, he used concepts like rebirth and God's kingdom. For the Samaritan woman, he explained the Gospel using "water" as a metaphor. To a rich and religious official, he asked the man to sell all his possessions. And to Zacchaeus, who had been greedy in making money, he first became a friend.

The characteristic of Jesus' evangelism is that he lowered himself to the cultural and social level of the person he approached. Jesus identified the needs of an individual and used that knowledge to share the Gospel with that person. Jesus showed that the content of the Gospel does not change at all, but how you present it can change, depending on the evangelism target. We need to adopt the approach exemplified by Jesus Himself.

Customized evangelism is a strategy centered around the person you want to evangelize. It is to introduce the Gospel by finding the point of contact between God's message and the person's culture, language, and needs. When the plan of salvation is presented in this way, the person will come personally into the power of the Gospel even though no one pushes him or her.

To do customized evangelism, you must prioritize the two following considerations.

First, you need to find the appropriate method to communicate with the person you want to evangelize. The communication method will change depending on gender, age, education, and culture. When you want to approach a person culturally, establishing common ground is important. When you communicate based on a common ground, the recipients of evangelism will be moved. When are people moved? People are moved when their emotions are touched, not after logical reasoning. To customize sharing the Gospel to your targeted evangelism recipients, it is important to operate using gifts-based ministries.

Second, take the responses of your targeted evangelism recipients seriously. In customized evangelism, how well and clearly the person understood and responded to the Gospel is more important than how well you shared God's message of salvation. Evangelism recipients want to hear the Gospel in ordinary, everyday language. Therefore, the person who is sharing the Good News should clearly understand the worldview and practical needs of the person and use the appropriate language.

However, unfortunately, today's churches have lost plain language. As the Bible played a huge role in Martin Luther's Reformation when it was translated into German that could be read by ordinary people, we need to use the "language that is alive" when evangelizing. We need to use the language that the evangelism recipients can feel, understand, and identify themselves with.

The five steps of a customized evangelism event

To hold a customized evangelism event, we will go through a five-step process.

First step: Target segmentation

We segment the target group and select the target group for evangelism. This step is critical in identifying the target's culture and needs and in ensuring consistency of the program and message.

There are three ways to segment a target group.

First, a church can select people that need to be evangelized first, depending on the church's situation.

Second, a church can select a target group by age. In this case, it is appropriate to segment the target by 10-year age differences (at least in light of South Korea's present situation).

Third, a church can select a group by occupation. In this case, the target group has a strong common ground in terms of occupation. In special circumstances, people with disabilities, military service people, and the socially marginalized can be target groups as well.

Second step: Needs and contact point analysis

To identify the needs of your target groups for evangelism, you can use either of these two research methods - the questionnaire or interview method. Using research results, you can analyze the needs, personalities, and life patterns of your targeted individuals and find the contact points between them and the Gospel. To discover contact points, ask questions such as: "What kind of era do we live in?" "Why do you reject the Gospel?" "What do you think about the church?" "What do you want to accomplish?" and "What issues trouble you?"

Third step: Promotion and invitation

Promotion can be done in two ways - promoting members to recruit evangelism targets and promoting evangelism targets. To achieve these, we produce promotional videos and form an intercessory team.

When promoting to your targeted evangelism recipients, minimize the use of religious elements and highlight relatable items such as a concert to encourage nonbelievers to come to church without being pressured. Also, don't forget to make a database of your target groups and the members who invited them. This will be an important resource for the following year when you hold another customized evangelism event.

Fourth step: Planning and execution of the event

When planning for a customized evangelism event, you should divide the event into three equal parts, corresponding to each of these three elements - fun, meaning, and a message that leads to a conviction. Usually, a customized evangelism event consists of a meal, performances, a message, and an altar call.

When preparing meals, the style should differ depending on who is invited to the event. People in their 20s or 30s are used to eating buffet style, but those in their 60s and over prefer a plate of food and a sitdown style of service. Also, you should put name cards of guests on their assigned seats in advance so that they will feel that they were treated with courtesy.

Performances should be consistent with the theme of the event. Above all, you should study the cultural tastes of the people you invited and prepare performances that they can relate to. When you use popular music, you may make them think differently about the church and reduce their prejudices against it.

Regarding sermons, a positive sermon that encourages the audience and recognizes their hard work is better than ethical and coercive guilt-trip preaching. Find a contact point between the Gospel and the needs of the people invited. These people may be exhausted in life, and you can help them gain new strength in the church.

Respecting the culture of your guests is important. Rather than pushing the people to show their conviction, it is better to use more subtle methods, such as giving flowers or signing a conviction card to help them take the first step of faith.

Fifth step: Follow-up

Our church started a "Nurturing School" to nurture those who have been evangelized through customized evangelism events and to help them get rooted in the church. The goal is to follow up with them. The Nurturing School is a seven-week program using a dedicated group of volunteers, who aim to build relationships, let the targeted recipients experience God's love more deeply, and encourage them to register at church to become members. The new Christians entering the Nurturing School will undergo five steps, namely, forming relationships, introducing the Gospel, nurturing, accepting Christ, and becoming registered members of the church. After completing these steps, they will be connected to the next nurturing program.

Develop new evangelism methods.

Customized evangelism restored the confidence of our church members in sharing the Gospel with people. According to Hanmijun & Korea Gallup 1988, 84 percent of the people evangelized revealed that they had negative feelings when the Gospel was shared with them. Another survey conducted in 2005 showed a similar result.

Customized evangelism was initiated in the midst of such a climate of stagnant evangelism activities. After some customized evangelism events, members said, "It's so great to work with the church," "Our small group can also hold an event," and "I'd like to move the hearts of the those we hope to evangelize," while some even asked, "When is the next event?" Such statements proved that our members' confidence in evangelism had been restored.

Also, through customized evangelism, we saw our church grow not because Christians from other churches moved to our congregation, but because non-believers accepted Christ and came to our church. Many people participated in each of our events and accepted Christ.

In the beginning, we started customized evangelism events by age. We held an event with the theme "Emergency Exit" for men in their 40s. We then organized other customized evangelism events for different age groups. Later, we expanded and held events by occupation. The events have evolved again, and today we hold community customized evangelism events for 100 to 200 people and small group customized evangelism events for 10 to 20 people. While the customized evangelism events by age or occupation were held in our church, the community customized evangelism events took place in other venues. Recently, church members invited their parents on the Korean holiday of Parents' Day to a customized evangelism event called "The most precious gift of my life," held at the Sheraton Grand Walkerhill Hotel.

Also, small group customized evangelism events are sometimes held in homes. We are taking such events further and bringing the events closer to where our evangelism targets may be found, including the army base, facilities for the disabled, and people's workplaces, such as the office for Korean Air.

The meaning of "customized" has now expanded from simply pertaining to people's cultures to including the spaces and places where they live. This is because we want to be more faithful to the spirit of the incarnation of Jesus, "who being in very nature God, did not consider equality with God something to be grasped" (Philippians 2:6). We are expecting to bear more fruit as we hold customized evangelism events not only in South Korea but also on the mission field. As our church develops customized evangelism, I would like to encourage other churches to explore various ways to spread the Good News to more people.

God does not look at the numbers but sees a soul. Do we have tears, sorrow, and a desperate heart for a soul?

Missions is not something grand. It is about sharing the amazing message of salvation as in the Scripture, "Believe in the Lord Jesus, and you will be saved--you and your household (Acts 16:31)," and "Yet to all who received him, to those who believed in His name, He gave the right to become children of God (John 1:12)." It is about sharing the message to those who live with "sin-amnesia" or "God-amnesia." It is the ultimate and greatest command for Christians.

7. Missions

Incubating the vision of missions

When I planted Onnuri Community Church, I prayed, "God, give me 2,000 young adults! Give me 300 soldiers who can destroy the power of the devil! Then, I will bring the world to you." At that time, we only had around 12 families, and around 100 people gathered at the most. How absurd was my prayer! However, God did not forget the desire of my heart, and He answered it. Within seven years of starting the church, we had 2,000 young adults. Fourteen years after, amazingly, we had 10,000 young adults, and in 2007, after 23 years, we have 20,000 young men and women.

This is a vision. The Bible says in Hebrews 11:11 that faith is being sure of what we hope for and certain of what we do not see.

Twenty-three years ago, we did not have a church building, land, money, resources, or people - where did they all come from? They all came from God. If we continue to follow God, we will be able to see something amazing that we could not see otherwise, and do something marvelous that we could not do otherwise.

God gave Onnuri Community Church a tremendous vision, which is "to send 2,000 missionaries to foreign mission fields and 10,000 lay ministers all across the country." We call this the "2,000/10,000 Vision." I think it was in 1994 when this vision became clearer in a practical way. The state of our church at that time played a more important role than the year itself in forming the vision. When our church started to pursue holiness and purity, the 2,000/10,000 Vision became more apparent. It was born when our church set our goals on holiness and purity and raced toward them after the Holy Spirit ministry.

When we tried to go back to the essence of the Church and accepted the Holy Spirit ministry, our blurred vision became crystal clear before our eyes, as if the focus of a camera lens were being adjusted. As the vision became apparent, I was no longer troubled with questions like: "How should I live?" "How should I preach?" and "How should I lead my church?"

So, we started taking stock. We counted the number of one-to-one discipleship mentors, praise and worship leaders, culture ministry leaders, and Quiet Time leaders. We had approximately 80 communities, and that meant that we had 80 ministry leaders. Also, each community had an intercessory team that focused on one ministry.

Our church is praying and preparing to send 2,000 missionaries. This is the vision God gave to us personally. I don't think God gave us the 2,000/10,000 Vision because we were a large church. When we first received the vision, we had less than 10,000 church members, but even then, we still nurtured the vision within us.

We asked God for church growth because we needed members to support 2,000 missionaries and 10,000 lay ministers. In some ways, the number may not have been that important. Differing opinions about when the vision would be fulfilled, whether sometime after 2000 or by 2010, were not that important either.

But surprisingly, in another way, the numbers 2,000 and 10,000 were important. It was important that we proclaimed the vision. Whenever I think about what Onnuri Community Church would be doing right now if we hadn't had that vision, my heart sinks. We could have probably ended up being content simply because "We built our church building well," or "We have many members," or "We became a large church." But if we hadn't had the vision, our church would not have grown to the size it is now. Our church probably would have succumbed to the aging phenomenon that other traditional churches experience. I am grateful that our church had a vision appropriate for our church's size.

I think the reason that Onnuri Community Church is able to do ministries actively even as its communities grow in size is that our church members are passionate about God's Kingdom and about seeing a soul undergo revival. That is why we get ourselves up even when we are sick and in pain.

The Cornerstone of Onnuri Community Church
"Therefore go and make disciples of all nations, baptizing them

in the name of the Father and of the Son and of the Holy Spirit, and teaching them to obey everything I have commanded you. And surely I am with you always, to the very end of the age" (Matthew 28:19-20).

This Scripture is engraved on the cornerstone of Onnuri Community Church. When we take a closer look at how the four Gospels end, we will notice that all of them conclude with a command.

> Matthew 28:19 Go and make disciples of all nations.
> Mark 16:15 Go into all the world and preach the good news to all creation.
> Luke 24:48 You are witnesses of these things.
> John 21:16-18 Take care of my sheep… Feed my sheep.

Moreover, how does the book of Acts begin? It says, "But you will receive power when the Holy Spirit comes on you; and you will be my witnesses in Jerusalem, and in all Judea and Samaria, and to the ends of the earth" (Acts 1:8). The Bible repeatedly emphasizes the importance of missions.

When someone asks me, "What is the Church?" my answer is, "It is a place where there are tears for the souls who do not believe in Jesus."

If you believe in Jesus, you should follow the noble command to go and lay down your life for the people who do not have Jesus. Christians who cherish this command evangelize the people around them and bring them to church. Gradually, their dream for evangelism grows, and they go beyond cultural and language differences; they reach out to other tribes that have never heard of the Gospel of Jesus Christ or who live in communities where the Gospel is not accessible. This is the mission.

There is an important thing to note. Before Jesus commanded his disciples to share the Gospel towards the end of Matthew, he said, "All authority in heaven and on earth has been given to me" (Matthew 28:18). The Lord Jesus proclaimed that He has all authority in heaven and on earth. This is extremely important. Until then, Jesus dominated the power of the earth, but after He was resurrected, He proclaimed that He not only has the power of the earth but also all the authority in heaven.

All commandments in Christianity are given by the one who has all authority in heaven and on earth. If we can accomplish God's missional command, we will fulfill His will. In this sense, this truly is a very important command. It could, in fact, summarize the entire Bible. That is why we call it the Great Commandment.

The interesting thing is that Jesus gave this amazing commandment to people who doubted him. In other words, it was given to imperfect people: to 11 disciples who were cowardly, moody, boastful, and acted differently when nobody was looking. It is a miracle that Jesus gave the command of evangelizing the world to these 11 people and then left. And today, Jesus gives the command to us.

Doing missions is not something grand. "Believe in the Lord Jesus, and you will be saved - you and your household" (Acts 16:31); "Yet to all who received him, to those who believed in his name, he gave the right to become children of God" (John 1:12). Missions is simply proclaiming this amazing message of salvation. It is sharing the message with all people who suffer "sin amnesia" and have forgotten the name of God. It is the ultimate and greatest commandment.

God will accomplish the mission.

Why does the church exist? What is the purpose for Christians on earth? Apostle Paul said that he wished he could die earlier because then, he would be able to be with Christ. But the reason he was still on this earth was to share the Gospel (see Philippians 1:23-26).

Yes. The only reason we are still alive in this world is to testify for Jesus Christ.

Many people want longevity, but that is not the correct mindset. Since we are already saved, there are no reasons for us to live long in this world. In fact, it would be better for us to die. However, God still left us here so we could accomplish his Great Commandment.

This commandment is beyond our capacity and that of the church. It is a command that can only be fulfilled by the one who has authority over heaven and earth. We should remember that Jesus promised us that He would give us the power to achieve this command: "But you will receive power when the Holy Spirit comes on you; and you will be my witnesses in Jerusalem, and in all Judea and Samaria, and to the ends of the earth" (Acts 1:8).

God will accomplish the mission. Through whom does God work? He himself will spread the Gospel through us and through our obedience. God said that if we lay down our faith and obedience before Him, He will use us, who are so little, to change the world. God wants to change this world through believers. It is the Great Commandment and a supreme order. As we are sure of our death, the purpose the mission that we must carry on until our last breath is clear. It is to go and make disciples of all nations (Matthew 28:19), rule over every living creature that moves on the ground (Genesis 1:28), and love one another (John 13:34). We all exist for missions, whether we are sick or healthy, wealthy or poor, powerful or powerless.

Missions: The secret to church revival

As I lead the church, I have experienced that focusing on mission work drives the church to grow.

Some people are skeptical about sending missionaries abroad. I would ask these people, "If no missionaries came to barren and poverty-stricken countries such as Korea a century ago, would there be Christians like us today?" You may have failed to evangelize your family, yet if we remember the grace we received, we cannot help but go. Missions are about having the faith to go to a mission field for the souls who have never heard of the Gospel, even if it means you have to leave unbelieving parents behind.

A church can become a real church when its purpose is to share the Gospel. Moreover, the Church should race to places where there are people who have never heard of the Gospel, to places that are physically and spiritually poor, and to places where there are people who are suppressed by misguided religions. It is in these places that we should share the Gospel with our lives. We should not "nest" in our churches and build a kingdom. Settling down is not a church's true calling.

A large budget doesn't guarantee successful missions work. A devoted heart and attitude are much more important than money or other material things. The secret to church revival is to obey

God's greatest commission - to challenge yourself more than you can bear; not to be calculating and complacent or to be confined by a budget, but to go overboard when it comes to missions work.

Untapping missions for the unreached tribes

On Onnuri Community Church's 11th Anniversary Sunday, we adopted eight unreached tribes. I preached the following message that day:

> God gave us a specific vision. It is to change the world, the people of South Korea, and the churches of South Korea. God gave us the power to do this. In this sense, Onnuri Community Church is not a church that belongs to a denomination, a region, or a country. Our church is God's church that stretches out to the world. God called us for that reason and allowed us to experience unprecedented growth in the history of Korean churches. However, He did not do it for us.
>
> As it is said in Acts 1:8, "But you will receive power when the Holy Spirit comes on you; and you will be my witnesses in Jerusalem, and in all Judea and Samaria, and to the ends of the earth," we are called to go all around the world.
>
> We want to train 10,000 leaders and send them to the world, their families, and workplaces home and abroad. Onnuri Community Church was planted to proclaim to the army, school campuses, and all regions that Jesus Christ is the ruler, the master and the king of everything. God gave us a holy burden of sending 2,000 missionaries worldwide to transform the world.
>
> Today, we adopted eight unreached tribes. I believe that this is a

7. Missions

significant blessing similar to the miracle of the five loaves of bread and two fish. I am blessed to see the people who devote themselves as missionaries for unreached tribes among elementary students, middle and high school students, college students, young adults, and adults who are here today. It is because the world will change through them.

A century ago, a handful of missionaries came to Korea. Some were martyred, while some built hospitals and schools. They developed a variety of welfare facilities and raised the banner of the Gospel in the land that was covered in darkness.

That is how it all got started, and today, God has made South Korea a nation that is unlike any in Christian history. Some of you may go to serve the Iban tribes, some to the Hanis and Azerbaijanis, while others to the Buryats, Uzbeks, Veddas, and many other tribes.

Just as Korea was changed a century after the missionaries came and gave their lives to a land of darkness, death, and oppression, I believe the tribes you will reach out to will be blessed after 50, 60 and 100 years. This is the special mission God has given to Onnuri Community Church.

From now on, we shouldn't just pray for our church but also for all the churches in Korea. I believe we should not stop praying for Onnuri Community Church but pray for the entire nation, North Korea, rural areas, and the world as well.

We don't exist for ourselves. Jesus did not come to earth to live long. He did not come to live happily ever after. He also did not come to get married and educate his children. Rather, he came to die on the cross.

> Onnuri Community Church does not exist to build the Onnuri Kingdom. We do not exist to expand the power of our church. We exist to die. We are here to sacrifice. We exist to march on.

We adopted eight unreached tribes that day, and since then we have adopted seven more tribes, totaling 15 tribes so far. Whoever confesses with his mouth and believes in his heart, he will be saved, whether he is a Jew or a Gentile. The way to salvation is the same for unreached tribes, Israel, foreigners, and Koreans.

Some Christians have gone all around the world to people with different languages, cultures, and races to share this Good News in spite of danger, pain, loneliness, and poverty. Some Christians have left their loving countries, families, and stable careers, and raced to meet with foreigners who do not know the Gospel of Jesus Christ.

We call them missionaries. Some missionaries are pastors, and some are ordinary Christians.

I am always reminded of a missionary whose name is Jae-hwan Lee. I cannot forget the letters he wrote while on the mission field, particularly one story. Once, his foot got swollen, and when he squeezed out the pus, a bug came out. He had to climb in and out of bed gently because his house was always covered in dirt, no matter how well he cleaned. When his wife was pregnant, he felt so sorry because his family didn't have much to eat.

Why did he continue to share the Gospel despite such suffering? Why and for what did he do these things?

I believe that his feet deserve to be called "beautiful" (see Isaiah 52:7). Churches should constantly send people who will share the Gospel, and we should support them. We should support them practically with $300 or $800 a month, or by building a hospital, farm, or language school. This is missions.

Proclaim the Acts 29 Vision.

The more our church has led in missions work, the more I have learned about one thing. Missions work is not just about building schools and hospitals. Missions must be done through churches.

Indeed, it has been our dream to become a model of nurturing and changing churches since our church was established. It has been our dream to become an Acts-like church. However, it was only when we proclaimed the Acts 29 Vision that we were able to mobilize all of our capacities to fulfill the vision. I would like to share the sermon I preached when we proclaimed the Acts 29 Vision. It will show how our vision for missions materialized.

> I had no idea that Onnuri Community Church would grow this big when I planted the church. I never dreamed of a large church or ministered to one, but we became one.
>
> Frankly, I do not know how this church should move forward. Still, we made it here today. The only thing that is in my heart is God's dream and vision. We made it here by just nurturing the vision and dream of becoming an Acts-like church and an ideal church that Jesus desires and by obeying God's leading.
>
> As I minister to Onnuri Community Church, I witnessed how the dream and vision from God came to be further materialized. Why didn't God send me to the mission field? Why did he lead me here when I had to drag my unhealthy body with me? I do not know myself. Why did God lead me this way?

Actually, I need to take a rest and take care of my health, but I cannot rest and cannot help it. God keeps on doing new things. Why did God lead us to intervene during the Handong Global University[17] incident? Why did our church have to offer two million won for the school? Dear members of the church, do you remember the three years our church was fiercely attacked? It was in those years when we were growing the most, most pure and holy. In fact, the offering we gave was more than we can give. As a result, Handong Global University survived. Although the president of the university had to go to jail and the school faced many challenges, in the end, God won the victory. The beautiful university of God was established. The 2,000/10,000 Vision was given to us through the inspiration of the Holy Spirit. The vision was proclaimed in Onnuri Community Church, and the vision drives us even today. Our church started the Holy Spirit ministry in the 1990s. God led many people to flock to our church, and we saw a great revival. Within a short period of time, he raised pure and holy leaders in the church. He sent many people who interceded, gave offerings, and were really devoted. In a sense, our church witnessed a growth that would go down in the history of Korean churches. Whenever I think about it, my heart is moved.

However, today, I have something I would like to share with you. The revival God allowed us to have is like the one in the Book of Acts. After the Holy Spirit had come during Pentecost, 3,000 people gathered to hear Peter preach (Acts 2:41). Five thousand men, not counting the women and children, gathered (Acts

---

17 A Christian private university in Pohang, South Korea.

4:4). If we add women and children, the number of Christians in the Early Church could have been around 20,000. At that time, wonderful, unbelievable, and moving miracles occurred one after another, including a crippled man walking. The church grew in numbers, miracles happened, and people were blessed. This is the church in Acts.

But then, from Acts chapters 5 and 6, the church was challenged. Sufferings and persecution began. In chapter 7, Stephen was martyred. In chapter 8, Phillip was introduced. He went to the wilderness of Samaria and shared the Gospel to an Ethiopian eunuch. The Jews persecuted the church fiercely, and the leaders of the church had to scatter. Why did God allow that?

In chapter 9, Paul appeared, and in chapter 10, Cornelius appeared. In chapter 12, James was martyred, and eventually, the Jerusalem church of 20,000 members had to split into small churches.

Starting from the liver cancer operation I had three years ago and the recent fourth surgery, God led me to meditate on my surgeries in relation to the sufferings that the Early Church had to experience in the Book of Acts.

I thought, "Oh, if Onnuri Community Church does not scatter, then we might face persecution!"

Dear beloved leaders of Onnuri Community Church, we should not be complacent with the growth and blessings God has given us.

Is there a problem in our church today? Maybe my ears are too small to hear things, but I have not heard of stories about any bitter relationship between our pastors and elders, or power struggles among them. We are a large church, but did we have incidents when we were mad at each other? No. Are we financially insufficient? No. Do we lack a building? No. Do we lack people, organization, and tools? No. We have abundance. We are rich. In fact, we have too much.

Why is God giving us new visions again and again? Why is God leading me to one surgery after another? When looking at the Book of Acts, the conclusion is rather simple. It is about time for us to scatter.

God gave us numerous blessings in many areas including evangelism, discipleship training, mission work, the Holy Spirit, the worship service, the praise songs, the community, one-to-one discipleship, and Quiet Time. What other churches have received as many of the blessings as our church has?

Some churches are big but lack resources. Some churches have the resources but lack power. Yet, God gave Onnuri Community Church the power, resources, and human resources all at the same time. The issue is how are we going to share them.

The revival and blessings that God poured onto our church are not for us to enjoy for ourselves. Whether with 30 churches or 300 churches, it is all good. In any form, we must share the blessings we have to the mission fields and churches in Korea. We cannot be an Acts-like church if we don't share. We should all devote and sacrifice ourselves.

From the beginning, I asked members to leave the church when they reached the seventh year here. Our members, however, did not leave, saying they wanted to go but there was no place to go. So, let's create places for them to go. Go to Suwon, Bucheon, Tokyo, or L.A. Let's stop flocking within Onnuri Community Church and start scattering around. Let's build Vision Churches to spread. Let's plant a church with a devoted heart.

When I think about it, I think God wants me to spend the rest of my life serving small churches. I would like to devote myself to that ministry. I think God will use me to build houses for small churches, preach and raise people in small churches. Now, the leaders of Onnuri Community Church should spread out in this sense as well. Don't worry about it, just leave.

I know the Holy Spirit led us, but Onnuri Community Church became a large church without our intention. Large churches have many limitations. Strength comes with size, but many weaknesses also follow. To win a battle, we need a large aircraft carrier, but we also need small destroyers. The world can be changed by small- and medium-sized churches because these churches can move the society around them. Presently, Onnuri Community Church does not follow the model of small- and medium-sized churches.

I never thought about it until I started to deliberate on the Acts 29 Vision. Our church proclaimed that we would send 2,000 missionaries and 10,000 lay leaders, but the question is, what will they do on the mission field? Of course, they will share the Gospel and teach the Bible. They will provide internal healing, one-to-one discipleship, and Quiet Time. They will also help the poor and build hospitals. But, these will end after several years. The only thing that does not go away until the Lord comes is churches. In reality, sending 2,000 missionaries is like planting 2,000 churches.

Do you know the only secret to sharing the Gospel in modern society? Old and traditional churches do not evangelize, but when you plant a church, you evangelize at least 10 people to survive.

New churches should spring up to change the rigid churches that have fallen into traditions and have refused to change. We must plant churches constantly. We should plant in the mission fields, in Seoul, Japan, and the United States. It is something we should continue to do until the Lord comes again.

Large churches are something you cannot build on purpose. There are only a few in one generation. That is why large megachurches are not a good model to follow. We must create a healthy model of small- and medium-sized churches or change the existing small- and medium-sized churches. I would like our church to take on this task.

And so, perhaps later, the members of Onnuri Community Church who want to leave after seven years will have a place to go. Water that is stagnant will go rotten. If you stay in one place for too long, nothing will change. We must plant a church and plant again. This is how God works. I hope that Onnuri Community Church doesn't become stagnant water. Our human and financial resources and great programs should be shared with others. We should build and serve small churches.

The signal for this task is Acts 29. We will devote ourselves and go as churches to places wherever we are needed throughout this nation and the world, and so change the world. We need prayers. We need offerings. We need to make up our minds. This is the secret behind creating an Acts-like church.

Dear Onnuri members, Antioch church heard the voice of the Holy Spirit urging them to send Paul and Barnabas. You need to send me. I don't know when but you need to send us. You should let me go on the first, second and third missionary journeys. This is Acts.

If we establish the Onnuri kingdom here, we will all die. As Jesus gave all of himself, we must lay down all of ourselves. We must become a sacrifice. God will show amazing miracles and grace. This is Onnuri Community Church, Acts and the vision we are sharing today.

Keep this vision in your hearts and plant a church. If each member of our church plants one church, we will see 20,000 new churches. Those churches will change the world, and beautifully expand God's Kingdom. The world will overflow with love instead of hate, peace instead of war, hope instead of despair, and joy instead of depression.

To be a kernel of wheat

Just like a coin has two sides, faithful mission also has two sides.

The first is the mission work of raising the banner of victory and singing a triumphal song. Faithful mission brings miracles, makes the impossible possible, and creates something out of nothing. Many people will gain eternal life through Jesus Christ and experience amazing miracles of faith. But this is not all.

The second is the opposite of the first one. Instead of getting everything, you get everything taken away and lose everything. In a sense, you may be defeated and face death in the end.

In other words, the spirit of martyrdom is a part of missions. Martyrdom may seem like a failure, but death gives rise to miracles of love and forgiveness, and ultimately, victorious resurrection. The mission work that reveals the truth that martyrdom is resurrection is the climax of missions. Before a church develops a faith of martyrdom, its people are not real Christians. Faith to heal one's illness and to make one's business prosperous is not real faith.

The faith of martyrdom is about not being obsessed with reality and death. If we are confident that we will live again after we die, we will be able to die with joy. This is the basis of the faith of martyrs.

On the first day of 2000, we woke up to the news of our church's first martyr. The late missionary Seung-chul Park, who was sent to China to share the Gospel through a school and bakery business, passed away. He worked under the name "Moses" and was killed in an unexpected car accident. The sudden death shocked his family and the church because we experienced martyrdom firsthand; something that we understood vaguely before.

Then, on February 21, 2004, we were stunned by another act of martyrdom. The late pastor Samuel Kim followed the path of Missionary Park. During Missionary Park's funeral service, it was Missionary Kim who said, "Farewell, Brother Park. See you soon." On September 18, 2003, Missionary Kim went to Iraq to build churches in this war-torn land. On October 10 of the same year, he planted the Iraq Korean United Church. He stayed in the church and took care of Koreans and locals there. Then, one day, he felt a pain in his back, and his health started to deteriorate rapidly. In December of that year, he came back to South Korea, had a medical examination and was diagnosed with hematological cancer. He underwent surgery at Georgetown University Hospital in the US. While battling with cancer, he saw a vision of God protecting Baghdad. Until his last breath, he thought about the church in Baghdad and closed his eyes.

7. Missions

"I eagerly expect and hope that I will in no way be ashamed, but will have sufficient courage so that now as always Christ will be exalted in my body, whether by life or by death. For to me, to live is Christ and to die is gain" (Philippians 1:20).

Before passing away, the late missionary Kim asked us to hold a funeral service based on the above Scripture. Missionary Kim's passion for missions inspired Onnuri Community Church and other missionaries all around the world including Japan, Iraq, and China.

In June 2005, the late missionary to China, Somang Kwon passed away in a traffic accident. In the army hospital corridor where she was being treated, three services were held every day. Some local Chinese heard the music being played during the services and followed it. They came, heard the Gospel, and accepted Christ.

In the same month, the first missionary dispatched by the Korea Association for Creation Research and also a missionary of Onnuri Community Church, the late Gwang-ho Chun passed away. He was doing missionary work in national universities in Indonesia, and he breathed his last breath when he came back to South Korea to treat a chronic disease. He was originally a researcher at the US National Institute of Health. When the Korea Association for Creation Research told him that Indonesia needed missionaries, he left his comfortable life behind and went to Indonesia.

In October 2006, the late missionary to Uzbekistan, Mi-ok Choi passed away of colon cancer, leaving two little children behind. She would raise her hands to praise God in the hospital bed and longed for heaven during the extensive chemotherapy. She gave hope to many Christians in the church and inspired them to hope for heaven.

Unless a kernel of wheat falls to the ground and dies, it won't bear fruit. Just like that, the death of these missionaries became kernels of wheat that bore much fruit. I hope that the precious blood of faith will flow in our souls as well.

God gave us a holy burden of sending out 2,000 missionaries to the world and changing the world. We will continue to march forward until the day the Lord returns!

The 2,000/10,000 Vision was given to us through the inspiration of the Holy Spirit. The vision was proclaimed in Onnuri Community Church, and the vision drives us even today.

Team Ministries: The Driver of Church Revival
Leadership That Achieves God's Dream

PART 5:

TEAM MINISTRIES AND LEADERSHIP

The church is like a living organism. It is the body of Christ. Therefore, its members should work together as a team. Each member should play its role, closely connect and communicate with the others. In order for the members to work as a team, the leadership needs to be alive.

1. Team Ministries: The Driver of Church Revival

Teamwork is crucial.

When the Israelites were building the tabernacle, the Levites divided themselves into three functional groups and served God's tabernacle. This is teamwork. We must develop team leadership to become the beautiful church that Jesus wants because the pastor alone cannot lead a church.

Even if a pastor changes, his church may not change. Also, the congregation may change, but it doesn't mean that the church will also change. We must change together. When it is only the pastor who changes, there will be conflict in the church. When it is only the members who change, the pastor will be frustrated because he will think his members are arrogant. If you want the church to change, the pastors, elders, and members should have the same vision and mindset. To accomplish something, everyone who is working together needs to change altogether. That is why teamwork is so crucial. If there is a good seminar or a good training program, it is beneficial for pastors and members to go and learn together.

Churches should promote teamwork and build the church by complementing each other. Leaders are not masters of all. In a sense, they are masters of one. In other areas, they need help from others. If leaders are gifted in leadership, they can work by partnering with and receiving help from other people with various other gifts.

One thing I learned from our church is that because I am lacking in so many areas, God has sent many incredible people to supplement my shortcomings. If you are loyal to God and you love God, God will send the people you need. Do not moan over what you don't have but pray for a partner who can complement your weakness. Then, God will send you co-workers. When you partner with them, the church will grow beautifully.

The beauty of team ministries

Moses and Aaron had different gifts. One couldn't speak well, while the other was an eloquent speaker. If we focus only on the gifts that we have and completely ignore the fact that other people have different talents, it is easy for us to criticize others with different gifts. We should remember that as my gift can complement other people's gifts, we can create beautiful team work.

Even husbands and wives are different. Each spouse has weaknesses, and because of their weaknesses, they complement each other. You don't show your weakness so that your spouse can criticize it. If your spouse is sick, don't say, "Why are you always sick?" Instead say, "Because you are sick, God made me healthy. God paired me up with you so I can help you." When you do so, you will experience peace and joy in your family. You will never stop fighting with your spouse if you say, "You're always sick, day and night."

If you find a weakness in a brother, remember that God didn't show it so that you can criticize him. Instead, God wants you to complement his weaknesses. It means that you should help. We should be grateful that we are different. In fact, we should be different because only then can God bring harmony and write a beautiful history, and we can see this through the story of Aaron and Moses.

One of the characteristics of our church is that we exercise team leadership instead of having one leader in one area for a long time. One person should not dominate one ministry. That is why we need to rotate locations, roles, and ministries. Three people are better than one, and ten are better than three. We should make sure that everyone's gifts work in harmony, we should support one another, and we should make preparations so that others can work. We are not working individually for ourselves, but all are working together for our Lord. We are not doing personal work but the work of God's kingdom together. The ministries and communities of our church dream together of such a beautiful vision.

In our church, the pastors serving Vision Churches abroad return to South Korea, and the pastors serving in South Korea go to Vision Churches abroad or to mission fields. I can't say how beautiful this practice is. Our church is run by a collaborative partnership, as the church in Acts was run.

Indeed, when pastors rotate, the members feel the pain of separation. It is painful when a pastor leaves right when his members are about to forge a relationship with him or when the pastor finally remembers all of his church members' names. But on the other hand, by rotating the pastors, we learn to rely on Jesus alone, not on people.

The biggest problem facing South Korean churches is appointing a successor. It is causing a problem because we lack the spirit of partnership. We must recognize how important this is. Let's say a pastor can help a church grow this much. Who then can take over and help the church grow to the next level? In any area of life, people tend to eliminate individuals who are better than they are and who could potentially be better successors. On the other hand, people tend to work with others who are not better than themselves and who cannot rise above them. With such thinking, societies and organizations cannot truly develop. People at the bottom try and struggle to climb up the corporate ladder, while those on top press other people down, and this wastes everyone's energy. This is how the secular world works. Sadly, such a phenomenon is quite apparent in churches as well, because the collaborative spirit is weak. We can bring God's kingdom to this earth and set a mature model for churches when we work in harmony, respecting each other's functions and talents.

The matrix model: The essence of team ministry

The churches in Acts operated according to a matrix. Churches were located in different areas, and the members were composed of diverse races and cultures. However, they were one because they all had the same Holy Spirit. But this doesn't mean they looked the same.

Each church was unique. The Jerusalem and Antioch churches were different. Likewise, the Antioch and Corinth churches were different, as the Corinth and Philippi churches were different. Also, the Philippi and Ephesus churches were different. But still, they were all connected. The ministers went to each other's churches; the churches sent ministers, and they partnered with one another. Whenever needed, they fellowshipped with each other. The distance could not stop them. The cultural differences could not deter them. Their ministers did not hold on to their churches, but instead, they were ready to leave whenever needed. They formed a matrix structure.

A matrix structure does not just focus on one factor, such as function or location. In a matrix system, all factors are woven together and operate harmoniously. For example, let's say a person is serving in the praise and worship team on a Seoul campus. Most of the time, that person will only work in Seoul, and that's it. Let's say there is another person who is serving in the praise and worship team in the Busan campus. Since they serve in the same ministry, they may meet once in a while, but there are no close exchanges or partnership. These two praise and worship ministers may work well with their respective team members, but it is impossible for them to collaborate beyond their campuses. In a strict sense, team ministry does not happen.

A matrix system allows teams to overcome this one-dimensional structure and work by function or location without being tied to one location. When needed, each team can work in each other's location. A system like this is called a matrix. The essence of team ministry is the matrix.

The important concept in a matrix: Sharing

The most important concept in a matrix system is sharing. People should let go of their obsessions of "mine" and share human resources, equipment, buildings, and other resources with one another. In this sense, the churches in Acts are a great model of the matrix system.

When the church of Antioch had issues, the church of Jerusalem sent people to help. When the church of Jerusalem needed help, the churches in Achaia collected offerings and sent them to the Jerusalem church. Such a matrix system can work well when the members of churches understand that their churches don't belong to them, but to the Lord.

Seven benefits of the matrix system:

1. Everyone can experience high-quality ministries.
2. People who are tired or exhausted can take a break.
3. When a church faces problems, other churches can help prevent the church from falling apart.
4. Each church can encourage and stimulate the others to grow.
5. Churches can be freed from the misconception that churches belong to them.

6. Churches can truly become one.

7. Churches can save money by sharing equipment and facilities.

Three elements enabling a dynamic matrix system

First: Clarity
The matrix structure should be simple and clear. When positions and roles are ambiguous and complex, functions can become conflicting, and people may wander around without having clear roles.

Second: Trust and Communication
Communication between churches should be smooth, and there should be strong trust among team members.

Third: Same Vision and Purpose
Each church can be unique. Churches may have different roles to play and be located in different areas, but their vision and purpose should be the same, so they are able to be one. They should be able to work as one team, even if they haven't met for a whole year.

Multi-site Church
Onnuri Community Church aims to become a multi-site church. We are not just in one area, but in different areas, including other countries. In South Korea alone, Onnuri churches are found in eight areas, namely Seobingo, Yangjae, Suwon, Bucheon, Daejeon, Namyangju, Pyeongtaek, and Incheon. We call them "campuses." We share human resources and church finances among

campuses. Ministers operate based on a matrix system. Outside South Korea, there are 24 Onnuri churches in several countries, including the U.S., Japan, and China. We call them "Onnuri Vision Churches."

Regarding Vision Churches, we share human resources, including the lead pastors and administrative workers, but our finances are operated independently. When needed, we share ministers and finances and work together with them. These campuses and Vision Churches are not bound together by religious bodies or denominations. It is the Acts 29 Vision that binds them. We continue to write chapter 29 of Acts until the day Jesus returns.

Network

Onnuri Community Church operates based on a matrix system. At the same time, it networks with various organizations. Horizontally, we share content, and vertically, we share structure.

When we cooperate with other churches that are not Vision Churches, we call them "partner churches." We also partner with CGNTV, whose ministry shares the Gospel around the world through satellite broadcasting, and Duranno, whose ministry is to build up churches through Christian publications, foreign missions, and Bible College seminars. We also work with universities that raise the next generation with faith, including Hangdong Global University, Jeonju University, Torch Trinity Graduate School of Theology, and with missions organizations like All Nations Worship and Praise Ministries. These organizations foster close relationships like a family, and we work together as one beautiful team in God.

One thing I learned from our church is that because I am lacking in so many areas, God has sent many incredible people to supplement my shortcomings. If you are loyal to God and you love God, God will send the people you need.

A true leader has a vision. A leader is not created through circumstances or hardwork. Leaders are appointed by God. Even if a person is incapable or weak, he could become a leader if God chooses him. Leaders are people who fulfill God's vision. True leadership is not about power but influence. We honor our leaders. Leaders can change the fate of a country, a society, or a family.

2. Leadership That Achieves God's Dream

Emphasizing vision and leadership

To become a 21st-century church, we must emphasize vision and leadership. There is one surprising thing that I learned during a Vision and Leadership Rally at our church. We discovered that upper-class families send their elementary school children to institutions that teach vision and leadership. A leadership school seems a bit too much for elementary students, but it still makes the point that knowing vision and leadership early in life is crucial.

With this thinking, we named our children's ministry "The Land Where Dreams Grow" instead of "Sunday School" because we wanted it to be a school of vision. When we changed the name, children started to dream and show leadership. Simply changing names can have great impact.

The same goes for middle and high school students and college ministries. Our college ministry is not a ministry where college students simply gather. It is where college students reach out to each college campus, which is why we put more emphasis on the meetings at universities than the ones at church. College students at Onnuri Community Church consider universities around the world as their parish. Many young adults stay and serve in the ministry even after they graduate from their university. Our goal is to take over colleges around the world. Our goal for middle and high school students is also for them to conquer the middle and high schools in South Korea and become intercessors for their schools. When students pray to bring the Gospel to their school with two to three parents, they are not just the students of Onnuri youth ministry, but also people who intercede for their school and change the world.

A leader: A man of vision

When I was returning to Seoul from London, my wife and I briefly traveled to some parts of Europe, taking advantage of low-peak season deals. We took a train to the top of Jungfrau Mountain in Switzerland and passed by icebergs. We almost reached the top, and from there, our eyes were captivated by a breathtaking view of spectacular ice-capped mountains, unimaginable from below. No words could fully explain the scenery! On our climb up, my wife struggled and had a hard time breathing. If we had decided to give up and stop climbing halfway, we would have greatly regretted not seeing the awesome view. Seeing the snowy scenery up in the high valley of Jungfrau in person and simply hearing about it are two very different things.

A vision is to see a new world. A person who has never seen a new world cannot do a new work. An unbelieving person who accepts Jesus and receives salvation is like someone seeing a new world or seeing heaven, when all that he experienced before was earth. So those who are saved and born again are those who have witnessed the new world. They are people who dream of a new heaven and new earth.

A person who thinks 10 years forward and an individual who thinks a century ahead talk and walk differently. "The gull sees farthest who flies highest."[18] People without vision only see the present, and those who lack vision have only today. However, those who have seen the new world have tomorrow. They have things they want to do and create. They have vast thoughts and dreams.

A true leader is a man of vision. Leaders are those who fulfill God's vision. Leaders are not created by the surrounding environment or hard work, but by God's appointment. Even if they may be incompetent and weak, when God appoints them, they become leaders. True leadership is about influence, not control. When a visionary leader is raised, a country in crisis can rise again, and a faltering church can become alive once more. When one man changes, the whole church can change. We should not forget that.

I believe that pastors are entirely responsible for a church. When a pastor bets his life on the church, I am confident that there is nothing he cannot do, because it is God who will work, not man.

---

18 From *Jonathan Livingston Seagull* by Richard Bach.

I am not a healthy man. But not once was I unable to do what I had to do because I was too weak. I have had a number of surgeries and am still not healthy, but I work harder than healthy people. I sleep less to work more hours. What drives me to do such things? It is the dream from the Lord that is in me. People who have received vision cannot sit still because they want to see it fulfilled.

A leader: A man who listens to God's voice

There are many leaders in this world, including secular leaders and godly men. Secular leaders think and act according to the secular principles and ways, based on worldly ideas such as philosophy, psychology, and sociology. However, spiritual leaders do not base their leadership on secular ideas.

Men of God root themselves in the Word of God and work as ambassadors or agents of God. They do God's work, not theirs. They strive to accomplish God's mission, not theirs, and fulfill God's dream, not theirs. This is the unique characteristic of the leaders of God. I want the leaders of Onnuri Community Church to be people founded on God's Word.

Vision starts by listening to God's voice. Vision is totally different from secular ideas, values, and philosophy. Biblically speaking, listening to the voice of God is "vision." True vision comes from God, and this vision creates leaders and leadership.

Leadership is not confined to pastors alone. Elders and female leaders also need leadership. Leadership doesn't just exist in churches. There are various kinds of leadership in every field and all walks of life.

Perhaps the essence of spiritual influence, which is a fruit of

2. Leadership That Achieves God's Dream

biblical leadership, is the anointing of the Holy Spirit. The anointing of the Holy Spirit is a secret that the world cannot find or understand. A person may not be famous, or maybe his name will never be heard of or be at the center of attention, but if the Holy Spirit anoints that person, he can demonstrate amazing spiritual influence and power.

The salvation of people today rests on leaders who will be used by God. The desire for today's generation is to meet a leader who has a dream of God. I mentioned that a true leader of God is the one who builds God's kingdom and fulfills God's dream. A true leader is a person who clearly recognizes God's vision, and not his own. He clearly sees, listens, and fulfills God's dream, hopes, thoughts, and plans.

The spiritual leaders who have changed and influenced the world in the past were all ethical people who were like Jesus Christ, who is the leader of all humanity. Such leaders followed the path of Jesus, saw the vision, listened to God's voice, foresaw the future, and then led the people accordingly.

If someone were to ask me what my dream is, I would not hesitate to say that it is to complete the Church of God as it is. It is my dream, and I am fulfilling this dream at Onnuri Community Church. It has been 23 years since I planted our church, but I am still in love with it. I am in awe of the things happening in our church day after day. In fact, I think we have so far achieved only barely a millionth of God's intended and ideal church. I look forward to where our church being led to where God wants us to go, where we can perform what God wants us to do.

Moses and Joshua dreamed of Canaan, the land of milk and

honey. Although they had to pay the price, suffer pain, and put up with resentments and complaints, they faithfully pursued God's dream and made it come true. I want all the leaders of our church to have the same vision and dream for the church.

In the past, people with dreams did not live glamorous or pleasurable lives. Most of them lived with the bleak despair of not knowing how to survive another day, and they were frustrated because nothing was happening the way they had hoped for and wanted. They were thrown into a furnace or a lion's den, as Daniel experienced, and had to wander around the desert for 40 years. No one welcomed or praised them; no one understood them.

All throughout the three years of his public life, Jesus was not understood. Even the disciples who said they would follow him with their lives could not understand Jesus. When you read the Bible, the people who met God were incredibly joyful, but they had to fight with utter solitude, loneliness, and pain until they fulfilled the dream. This is the path for leaders and a lonely life for people with a dream. However, if you are walking the path with a dream, you should never say that you are lonely or in solitude because that is normal. Leaders do not have the right to complain or be resentful.

A leader needs to be anointed by the Holy Spirit.

Reverend Jim Graham has been visiting our church to preach for several years now. He is an intellectual and a Baptist pastor with an excellent sense of balanced faith. Once, Rev. Graham told me this story.

After I was ordained, I led my ministry pretty well. Many people gathered. I was into the 12th year when one day, I met a young pastor. I can't put it into words, but his face had power. He didn't get exhausted or tired at all. There was something about his face that I didn't have. I was troubled, thinking, "What is it? Why don't I have it?" I felt empty.

As I continued to contemplate on it, I prepared for a sermon alone in the study. Suddenly, I burst into tears and started to repent. Later, I realized that what was missing with me was the anointing of the Holy Spirit. That realization was a glorious experience for me, one of heavenly joy coming inside me. After I was anointed by the Holy Spirit, my church was transformed. The circumstances surrounding our church didn't change, but everything else changed. The members started to be engulfed by the Holy Spirit.

A pastor with 12 years of experience, I felt the presence of the Holy Spirit for the first time. Rev. Graham testified that after that, his ministry changed, and his church saw miracles and wonders.

Meanwhile, Pastor Keith Intrator is another pastor who frequently visits our church. He is a Jewish Christian and an intellectual, a graduate of Harvard University. He shared that he received the anointing of the Holy Spirit through a person he disrespected. In fact, Pastor Intrator completely disliked this person. One day, this man, who Pastor Intrator used to think was an odd person, came to him and yelled at him to receive the Holy Spirit. Pastor Intrator returned home feeling uncomfortable. But that night, he was baptized by the Holy Spirit. For three consecutive days, he read the Bible without sleeping, and the Bible started to make sense to him. He said that "the work of the Holy Spirit in you can be fulfilled even through someone you don't like." He also added that he was dramatically different before and after the baptism of the Holy Spirit.

True leaders are people who have been baptized by the Holy Spirit and have experienced the presence and fullness of the Holy Spirit. The anointing of the Holy Spirit means that the Holy Spirit gives various gifts and powers to a person. It also means that the individual has been sealed. It means that the person is captivated by the Holy Spirit and does what God wants him to do, and is where God wants him to be. That is the person of God.

It is different from doing God's work using the knowledge and specialty we have studied in seminaries. Leaders must have the anointing of God. I want all the leaders of our church to be baptized by the Holy Spirit.

When the Holy Spirit is present in us, we feel optimistic, as though we can do anything. "If the Spirit of him who raised Jesus from the dead is living in you, he who raised Christ from the dead" (Romans 8:11), we will feel empowered. It doesn't matter whether you are doing small or big things. We shouldn't nitpick the size of the task. No matter who you are and whatever the circumstances, when the Holy Spirit comes, the spirit of resurrection will reside in you and you will no longer be fearful, worried, or troubled. You will feel assured, and an incomprehensible spiritual peace will rule over you. I always pray that such peace will be in all the leaders of our church.

When the Holy Spirit anoints you, you feel that your business will go well, your family will be happy, and your church will prosper. As you see and pray with such perspective, things will unfold that way. It is not just about having an active or positive mindset.

The Holy Spirit within me renews me, gives me power and new ideas every day. How can we explain this with words?

God's leaders change the world.

A person who has a vision and has received a word from God can change the world. As I talk about Christian leaders, church leadership, and leadership that changes the world, I would like to raise a question.

"Why is it that nothing is happening to us?"

Although I'm a pastor, nothing is happening. What good are leadership and vision when we can't change the world? This is the tragic reality of Korean churches today.

There are many churches, pastors, and Christians, but the world is not changing. Rather, economic crises are looming, and unspeakable seeds of tragedy are being sown. Facing such stark realities, we cannot help but ask the fundamental question:

"Can having many people and pastors in churches really change the world?"

"If we have many churches and Christians, will the world change?"

Let's look at Genesis chapter 18 when the angel of God visited Abraham. When the angel of God prophesied to Abraham that Sodom and Gomorrah would perish, Abraham began to negotiate with God.[19]

He approached God and argued: "It is fair for the people who

---

19 Genesis 18:16-33.

deserve to be destroyed, to be destroyed. But if there are righteous people inside, wouldn't it be unfair for the righteous? It is not right to treat the righteous and the wicked alike. If you find righteous people in the city of Sodom, will you still destroy them with the wicked?" His argument was, in fact, compelling. God agreed with Abraham. Unfortunately, there were not 50 righteous people in the two cities.

When Abraham realized this, he started to negotiate with God further: "God, how about 45 righteous men? How about 40? How about 30? What about 20? Although I'm unworthy like dirt, please allow me to plead with you once more. Will you destroy the cities if there were 10 righteous men?" Abraham asked for 10, but still, God could not find 10 righteous people.

What does this mean? It means that Sodom and Gomorrah were destroyed because they did not have 10 righteous people. Apply this to our present situation. Isn't South Korea suffering because it doesn't have 10 righteous churches? Isn't our generation troubled because we don't have 10 pastors, including me, that God recognizes and uses? Thinking about this, I reflected on myself.

No matter how closely a fake resembles the real thing, it's still a fake. It's useless no matter how many fakes you have. Something that is fake cannot become real. There is a world of difference between people with vision and those without vision. At a glance, they may seem similar, but in reality, they are extremely different. If we have a leader who listens to the voice of God, embraces God's vision, clings to the vision in spite of humiliation, hardships, and tribulations, our world will be different. The world will be saved, and the churches will be reformed and transformed. This is also the goal of our church.

Leadership is not about titles, but influence.

When you have a vision, you will see a new world. The Apostle Paul, after meeting Jesus, said that he was called to be the apostle for the Gentiles. When you believe in Jesus, you will change. "Therefore, if anyone is in Christ, he is a new creation; the old has gone, the new has come!" (2 Corinthians 5:17)

I believe that the jobs and workplaces of church members and the ministries of pastors should be renewed. It doesn't mean that ministry is more important than secular work. It is an idea of the devil's that pastors are more important than laypeople. Everyone is the same. We don't have ranks.

We have different roles to play, and we function differently. Biblical leadership is not about ranks. You don't exert leadership because you are in a high-ranking position. Christian leadership is not about ranks, but relationships. We are privileged people because of our relationship with God, a father-and-son relationship. Such privilege is not given to us because we are pastors or elders. We are people who build the kingdom of God together. Whether you are an employee, a housewife, or a pastor, you should do your best where you are planted.

Whether we live or die, we do it for the Lord, whether we eat or starve, we do it for the Lord, and whether we are healthy or sick, we live for the Lord. When we commit our whole life to God like this, the world will change. We don't need to yell "Change!" at the world. We just need to change.

When leaders have dreams, churches will change, and the world will be transformed. Buildings are not important. It's okay even if buildings break down 10 or 20 times. I believe that churches should be like convenience stores that are open 24 hours a day, seven days a week. They shouldn't skip being open even for one day. Churches are where people come to pray, cry, receive training, and sleep. Churches should be alive. How can churches close their doors after the Sunday or Wednesday services? Can you spare the church buildings and bring them to heaven?

It doesn't matter if you knock down the church building and rebuild it over and over. What is important are the people and the manifestation of the Holy Spirit. We cannot be saved by holding onto traditions. Instead, we should cling to Jesus.

There is something I tell the members of our church. I say that they should not just stay in our church, but that they must leave. I tell them that we met in order to be apart. I encourage them to go wherever it may be when Jesus calls them to share the Gospel. Only then will the world change. Jesus told his followers, "Therefore go and make disciples of all nations" (Matthew 28:19). He didn't tell secular people to come to church to be changed. It is us, Christians, who must go. We should willingly go to poor areas, rural areas, Japan, and other places that call us, and unsparingly share the Gospel of Christ. This is the kind of leadership we need. When we do that, the world will change.

I want the Lord to use us to transform the world. I hope that through my job, sermons, families, and children, God will change the world.

2. Leadership That Achieves God's Dream

Leaders should possess the leadership of Jesus.

Our everlasting leader is Jesus Christ. As I grow older, we want to be more like him. I want to resemble His influence, life, and character. I hope that His image will be completed in us every day. How much of the Lord's work I have done, how much fruit I have borne in my ministries, and how hard I have worked for the Lord are not as important as how much I have grown into the image of Christ and how much I loved him through the process.

Jesus Christ, the eternal leader of humankind, his own influence and power were stronger when He gave up His life than when He was still alive on earth. In Jesus' leadership, there are three traits.

First trait: A serving servant. A leader is not a master, but a servant. He serves and obeys instead of ruling, commanding, or giving orders. Our Lord Jesus was like that. I hope that the leaders of our church carry the beautiful aroma of being like Jesus.

How wonderful would it be if going to lowly places didn't hurt our pride? How great would it be if we weren't upset even when people looked down on us? If someone did not get offended when people pretended that he was not there and completely ignored his opinions, that person would be Jesus. I also want to be like that.

Jesus did not come to be served but to serve. He came to this earth to give his life as a ransom for many. How can we feel God in this world? How can we experience him? We can feel the presence of Jesus when we serve others. We can feel him when we put a towel around our waist and serve people who are sick, dirty, smelly and abandoned (and that person you are serving could be Jesus Christ himself!)

On the other hand, it will be difficult to find Jesus in places that are fancy, glamorous, and sophisticated, where people normally love to go. When we are served, when we are soaked in fame, surrounded by loud applause, when we are used to people's praises, we won't be able to feel Jesus.

One day, at one of our Vision and Leadership Festivals, Pastor Nagayoshi from Japan came and shared this testimony.

"When I first came to this church, many people would stand along the stairs and the restrooms to welcome people. At first, it seemed strange, but at some point, I realized that they were like Jesus. I felt as if Jesus was waiting for me even in the restrooms."

I was surprised to hear this. I thought it was our duty to welcome and serve the people visiting our church with respect and kindness, but I hadn't thought that far. I quietly contemplated on what he said and realized that, in fact, what he was saying was true. We meet the Lord everywhere from the church parking lot to the restrooms. It is because the place we serve is where Jesus is.

I want the leaders of our church to stand in those places. True leadership is not about filling oneself up with something, but about emptying oneself. The Bible said, "Blessed are the poor in spirit" (Matthew 5:3). Possessions are not a blessing. Rather, it is a blessing when you can let things go.

Second trait: A good shepherd. The trait of a true leader that we can find in Jesus is to be a good shepherd. Shepherds lead their sheep to lie down in green pastures and by quiet waters. Sheep follow the shepherd saying, "The LORD is my shepherd, I shall not be in want" (Psalms 23:1). What does it mean to lack nothing in life? It means that you are happy.

Happiness is not a state of possessing many things. Rather, it is the state of not lacking anything. What happens if you ask a person who is full to eat with you? He would say, "No, thanks." When you're full, you don't want to eat anymore, even if offered the most delicious delicacies, and even if you became stuffed just from eating cheap noodles. Likewise, a person who is satisfied with God won't have desire for more materials, popularity, or higher positions.

The reason why we are obsessed with status, wealth, fame, and recognition is that our thirst and desire in life hasn't been satisfied. When we read old Korean folk tales, we always find stories of something eating up something else - a tiger ate something up, or some beast or another gobbled something up. They are stories about something preying on something else because it is hungry. In reality, hunger is not just about having an empty stomach. Even if your stomach is full, you can still feel hungry psychologically.

When I see people going on picnics, they always pack a lot of food. When visiting a friend at a hospital, we don't bring flowers, but a large gift box of juice. When something good happens to someone, Koreans start to clamor that they'll treat the person for a meal to congratulate him. We observe these things perhaps because Koreans often starved in the old days. But in contrast, those who are always full don't carry much food with them. They may bring a roll of *gimbap*[20] or a sandwich as a snack, but nothing more.

Likewise, a person who is spiritually content doesn't struggle when his other desires are not satisfied, even if it means his "life"

---

20 *Gimbap* is Korean-style rice roll made with dried seaweed. They are served in bite sizes. Unlike the Japanese sushi roll, gimbap doesn't use raw ingredients.

will be taken away. When that person faces death because of a deadly disease, he will be happy because he will soon see the Lord.

Good shepherds feed their sheep and lead them to green pastures and quiet waters. When an enemy comes, the shepherd uses his stick to protect his flock. When a sheep is lost, the shepherd uses his staff to guide it back. When a sheep is sick or in danger, a hired hand will run away, but the good shepherd will protect his sheep even if he has to give up his life. From the example of a good shepherd, we find Jesus Christ and the true leadership of our Lord.

A false leader takes advantage of the people who follow him. He treats them as the means to accumulate wealth, increase the number of followers, and achieve success. He uses them only when he needs them for something, but when the need is met, he kicks them out. The Bible calls such leaders "hired hand" shepherds.

In contrast, Jesus loves us, his flock, to the end. Whatever damage, crisis, and misunderstanding He may have to face, Jesus will not abandon us and will continue to love us until the very end. I want all the leaders in our church to become leaders resembling Jesus, who leads His sheep to good paths and feeds them well.

Third Trait: A loyal steward. A steward should remember that he is not the owner, but a manager. We are custodians. The sheep is the Lord's, not ours. A church does not belong to the pastor or the elders. It belongs to Jesus Christ. The head and the master of a church is Jesus, and we are stewards called to serve his church.

Stewards should be loyal and unwavering. They should be willing to obey Jesus' command and press on until they have completed the command, no matter what they might need to sacrifice.

Stewards need to be genuine. They should not lie, cheat, or cover up. They should be loyal to their master, rain or shine. We should become stewards like this and carry out the job God has given us according to our gifts, and serve others. Those who are carrying out their duties in the church should loyally serve Him as custodians and stewards of God's church.

Overseers should be good shepherds, pastors should be good shepherds, and elders should be good shepherds. All Christians should live like stewards, but pastors, elders, and overseers who lead churches should live as good and genuine stewards.

I want all the leaders of our church to be loyal and genuine.

Leaders must pay the price.

The ways of a leader and of a disciple have something in common. The way of a disciple eventually leads a person to glory, but to get there, the journey is neither comfortable nor pleasant. It is a way of suffering. There is no way to maturity without going through suffering. Have you seen a baby who can walk well without falling at the first try? For a baby to walk, it has to go through the process of falling numerous times and having its knees scratched.

The way to accomplishing a vision is the same. Vision from God grows when fed with food called "affliction." There is a blessing that comes with suffering. One of them is that suffering purifies us. When you continue to eat "suffering," all the impurities and imperfections disappear.

When you hear the voice of God and see His vision, you will have a goal and sense of direction. Then, what you need is the passion to fulfill that vision. Also, you need to receive the power and fire of the Holy Spirit. You need to have holiness and purity, as well.

The path a leader has to walk is a thorny path. He must deny himself and pay the price for others. What lies in front of God's leaders is a way that is far from wide and glamorous. Although God's leaders may seem insignificant and even foolish at times, they are the ones who faithfully walk the path without complaint. They do not reject the cross but take on the cross! People who are like that are the leaders of the kingdom of God.

Truly sincere Christians have faced swords, thieves, and the dangers of rivers and the wilderness; they have been starved, beaten, and killed since the days of the Early Church, and in fact, even back in Old Testament times. Look at the people of faith in Acts, Corinthians, and Hebrews. In contrast, what are Christians today like?

We say that we are good Christians, but how much have we suffered for Christ? Have you endured sufferings, gotten sick, or became lost because of Jesus? Honestly, we haven't suffered that much. Have we bragged about small challenges and minor pains, perhaps exaggerating about being sick with a cold as if it were like having cancer? We should reflect and check ourselves and see whether we have inflated our minor troubles as if they were cosmic-shaking events.

Think of the many sufferings that the members of the Early Church or other men and women of God have had to go through. They were torn apart by lions or crucified on crosses to protect their faith! This was real. This was the norm.

How could there be salvation if Jesus didn't die on the cross?

If Jesus did not suffer on the cross, how could there be salvation for any of us? When we believe in Jesus, we will be blessed. But more fundamentally, we will suffer, sacrifice, and bleed. This is the essence of Christianity.

How good a church is, is related to how much suffering it has gone through. The righteousness of a pastor does not depend on how well he preaches and counsels or how many members the church has, but on how much sacrifice he has made. I believe that the more a pastor suffers loss, is despised, and is insulted, the better the pastor becomes. If we haven't experienced sufferings in our lives, we may not be doing anything right now. If you're a leader, you should ask yourself, "Have I been insulted, suffered a loss, felt pain, or been mistreated for Jesus? Have I experienced sufferings because of Jesus, not because of myself?" Fixing your eyes on Jesus and living honorably even when you don't receive compensation and no one recognizes you is how godly people should live.

Our church tries to live like this, or at least imitate this. When South Korea was hit by the IMF crisis in 1997, it was hard to send missions offerings, due to the high value of the US dollar. As the number of dispatched missionaries grew, at times, it was difficult to support them with special missions offerings and 30 percent of the regular offering. However, we never gave up.

Also, our church supported Handong Global University. Thanks to our church's prompt support, Handong Global University survived. Of course, we did not support the university because we had a lot of money, and we did not provide 100 percent of the university's budget. Since 30 percent of our offerings were going to the 2,000/10,000 missionaries, we always lacked money. At the same time, we could not ask our members to give a special offering to help the school. We may have asked them if the church size back then was similar to today, but at that time, our church was much smaller. The question then is, Where could the money have come from all of a sudden? No rich businessperson gave money. It had to come from our pockets. We borrowed money from a bank to help the university. Since then we have supported the university with over 20 billion won.

Dr. Young-gil Kim, the university president, said that he prayed while crying in an apartment overlooking the East Sea in front of Handong Global University. His vision moved all the members of Onnuri Community Church. When you pray, the vision will be transmitted to other people. When our church followed the vision of the university, God expanded our faith to meet the needed funds. Through that experience, my heart and our church's heart were enlarged. As huge as the sufferings were that we went through, our hearts became bigger. If we had not helped the university at that time, we felt we would not be able to look directly into Jesus' face in heaven.

Leaders must exercise balanced leadership.

We can find a lot of leaders who have a well-rounded exterior. They're extremely capable and popular, and have many followers. They are influential leaders. However, for some of them, their inner world is in shambles. They may look amazing and perfect on the outside, but some have serious problems at home.

Some of them have unique personalities, strong personalities, odd personalities - all are different. A leader may seem charming or able to carry out a task because of his somewhat strange and odd character, but in the end, his character could lead to his demise. We often see people who are recognized for their abilities but have distorted personalities. That is why we should be cautious of famous people and also be wary of becoming one of them. The most important qualification of a leader is not external, but internal, and that is the leader's morality. The first thing that is required of the president of the United States is morality. I believe that South Korea should observe the same standard. Morality should be the first thing that is required of the president, lawmakers, and others who work in public office.

It is more important for a pastor to have personality and morality so that he can refrain from lying, recognize mistakes he has made, and accept his weaknesses than to have eloquent speaking and preaching skills. People with such characters are gentle. They do not get angry easily or treat others roughly. They are not afraid of people, yet they do not look down on others. They love and respect others and treat others with politeness. They are sexually innocent and do not have complicated financial or relational problems. They are always genuine and honest in front of God.

However, internal strength is not enough. Leaders must have well-rounded internal and external capabilities. Leaders that God uses possess good character and external leadership at the same time. If a person has inner strength but lacks external abilities, he might be able to guard his faith but could find it difficult to lead others.

Joseph and Daniel were well-developed leaders inside and out. They are great role models that Christians should follow. They demonstrated the kind of leadership that is required in churches today. They had inner and external strengths, served God, and led the world. I hope that all the leaders of our church will become magnificent leaders of God who can transform the world.

Ten commandments for true leadership

I believe that true leaders are those that observe these 10 commandments, and I would like to encourage everyone to cultivate these qualities.

First, guard your inner life with holiness and purity. The position you hold at the moment and what your business card says about you are not important. What is more important is the honesty of your heart. A person who possesses a blameless heart and guards himself with holiness and purity is a true leader.

Second, ask God if your vision is from him. Always evaluate whether your dream is a vision from God or a mere personal ambition. If you think it is just an ambition, stop now and turn back from where you are, no matter how much you have progressed already. Do not hesitate to leave the place where you are if God does not want you to be there in the first place.

Third, put people ahead of work, and put God ahead of people. Leaders always think about heaven. Those who can think of heaven can also think of earth. People who look at the big picture can understand parts of it as well. However, those who only see the parts cannot understand the whole picture.

Fourth, learn how to deal with crises and turn a crisis into an opportunity. Welcome conflicts. Accept sufferings as blessings, as indeed, sufferings can turn into blessings. If Moses had not stood before the Red Sea, how could he have seen the Red Sea divide in two? The reason that God makes us stand before a crisis is to show us how he will overcome that crisis. Therefore, do not be afraid of crisises. Neither doubt nor worry.

Fifth, work also with people who have problems. We will always have people with problems around us, so we should learn to work with problematic people. One qualification of true leaders that they have learned how to work with people who oppose them. Don't just choose the easy way out.

Sixth, identify your gift and work according to it. We shouldn't imitate others or do something because we are jealous of others. Working according to our gifts is important. God gave everyone the gift that he or she needs.

Seventh, work with others, even if you can do it alone. Even when you can do something on your own, work with other people. And when you do so, make sure they feel that they are truly doing the work as well. One of the things that makes a leader happy is when other people are talking about an issue that the leader himself is talking about, in other words, when others are thinking what their leader is thinking.

Eighth, choose a way that might incur a loss. Suffering loss can happen to you at any time. Leaders are people who can endure losses at times. When there are places you want to visit and places you want to avoid, try choosing the place you don't want to go.

Ninth, be joyful always, pray continually, and give thanks in all circumstances. In whatever you do, check if you have the following three qualities: "Be joyful always; pray continually; give thanks in all circumstances" (1 Thessalonians 5:16-18). Do not ask God, "Shall I live in Seoul or the United States?" God's will for us is to be joyful always, pray continually, and give thanks in all circumstances. If you possess such qualities, you are in God's perfect will. But no matter how great a place you are in, if you are not joyful, if you do not pray, and if you do not give thanks, you are not in God's will.

Tenth, clothe yourselves with humility, and be filled with the Holy Spirit. Humility is God's way of completing everything. Being filled with the Holy Spirit brings forth the power of God. Humility and being filled with the Holy Spirit are the principles of leadership.

Always keep in mind the 10 commandments for true leadership. Then, your leadership approach will be one step closer to that of Jesus.

A true leader is a man of vision. Leaders are those who fulfill God's vision. Leaders are not created by the surrounding environment or hard work, but by God's appointment.

God's Love Story for Japan: Love Sonata

PART 6:

SINGING THE LOVE SONATA

In 2007, Onnuri Community Church started an outreach called Love Sonata, a cultural evangelism rally for Japan. We wanted to sing God's love song for Japan. Love Sonata is the fruit of important methodologies, rooted in Onnuri Community Church's pastoral philosophy. The Love Sonata event is a gift from God for Onnuri Community Church.

1. God's Love Story for Japan: Love Sonata

Incubating the vision of Love Sonata

At the end of last year, while I was sick, I received a vision from God. I was told that we should take everything that Onnuri Community Church has and go to Japan. The year 2007 was the centennial anniversary of the revival of Korean churches. It was a year when we could reflect on the churches' new growth and vision. But instead of taking part in the celebrations and focusing on Korea, God told me to go to Japan.

In 2007, South Korea was filled with many problems. The presidential election was held, the two Koreas were in a very delicate situation due to the North Korean nuclear issue, labor union protests shrunk economic activities, the number of people unemployed grew, churches were severely criticized by the society, and internet users carried out an anti-Christianity movement. With all these things going on, I was confused when God said, "Leave in my hands what is going on here and go to Japan."

When a situation is difficult and challenging, the first thing I do is pray. Responding to the vision I received from God, I started early morning prayer meetings with our church members for 40 days. That's how we started Love Sonata, a cultural evangelistic rally that would run from Okinawa all the way to Sapporo. Love Sonata is God's love song for Japan. I shared God's love through a sermon titled, "The Wave of Love," which I delivered during the Love Sonata rally in Saitama, Tokyo.

> "For God so loved the world that he gave his one and only Son, that whoever believes in him shall not perish but have eternal life" (John 3:16).
>
> There are two great powers in this world. First is the power of hate and anger, and second is the power of love and forgiveness. Hate and anger lead to destruction, violence, and murder, but love and forgiveness bring reconciliation, restoration, and peace.
>
> Someone once said, "Satan attempts to turn this world into hell by planting hatred and anger in us. But God tries to create heaven on earth by planting love and forgiveness."
>
> Tokyo Love Sonata being held at the Saitama Super Arena today is the story of love and forgiveness of God for Japan. God loves us dearly. All the languages of man and people's imaginations cannot fully explain God's love.
>
> One day, God told me to embrace Japan. He asked me to love,

1. God's Love Story for Japan: Love Sonata

pray for, and be devoted to Japan.

Truth be told, I am not healthy enough to love other people. I have suffered from diabetes and hypertension for 30 years. I had six liver cancer surgeries and cardiac surgery. I am currently undergoing dialysis three times a week. As you can see, it is hard to keep my body as it is. So when God told me to preach his love and forgiveness in Japan, I was confused and afraid.

However, once I realized that God's love for Japan would not stop, my thinking changed. God told me to "overcome the walls of conflict and pain, but first, reach out with hands of reconciliation, and then create a wave of love!"

When something impossible arises, I begin praying. I challenged the church to engage in a 40-day series of early morning prayer meetings from January this year. I told our church members that those who were weaker than me physically did not need to come.

Every morning at 5:00 a.m., over 8,000 people gathered together and started to shout, cry, and pray. We prayed that we could love Japan with the heart of God. On the last day of the early morning prayer meetings, we borrowed a stadium, and to my surprise, 28,000 people gathered. They started to gather as early as 3:00 a.m.

The power of prayer is fiercely strong. It is like a typhoon or an earthquake. The Holy Spirit responded to our prayers immediately. God rebuked our ungodly ideas and attitudes, including spiritual arrogance, and taught us to repent. God spoke to us that Japan was not the problem but we were. He said that the past wrongs Japan committed against Korea were not the problem. He pointed out that the important issue and the real problem was that we harbored anger and ungodly feelings towards Japan for the atrocities it had committed upon us in the past. God revealed to us how much He loves Japan. God's heart is beyond words.

We could not help but weep. We cried out, "God! Do you really love Japan that much?" We could no longer make an excuse for not loving Japan as much as God does. We cried further, "God, forgive us that we could not love Japan. How can we keep ourselves from loving that country when you love it so much?" We held Japanese flags in our hands and prayed for Japan saying, "God, bless Japan. If your love is great, help us all to understand your heart."

Love brings miracles. As we prayed, 5,000 brothers and sisters decided to join Tokyo Love Sonata to bless Japan. The greatest act one can perform is prayer. When we pray, we can love. When we pray, people will change. When we pray, history will change, and God will move.

So far, we have held Love Sonata, in Okinawa, Fukuoka, and Osaka. When we went to Okinawa, we had to fly out in a chartered plane because there were not enough seats. The 5,000 Christians from Onnuri Community Church who are here today are not here on vacation. They came because they sincerely want to reconcile and partner with Japan and serve Asia and the world together as ambassadors of peace. We came here to repent of our ungodly feelings. We came to share the love of God.

The peace in Asia and the world is in our hands. When we love and serve one another, the world will change. We can shock the world by showing everyone that we have been reconciled and united. South Korea and Japan should love and serve each other

1. God's Love Story for Japan: Love Sonata

and be one. When we criticize, compete, and fight with each other, we will all perish.

What do people need the most in today's world? It is love, not money, power, or honor. Love is the only answer. Genuine love, everlasting love, eternal love, sacrificial love, and unconditional love can change a prodigal son and bring him back home. Because of love, God gave His one and only son, Jesus Christ, to the world and to die on the cross.

Love is death, giving up, and sacrifice.

The Bible says, "Everyone who calls on the name of the Lord will be saved" (Romans 10:13), and "Yet to all who received him, to those who believed in his name, he gave the right to become children of God" (John 1:12). Jesus said, "I am the way and the truth and the life" (John 14:6).

What is God's love story? It is the story of His son, Jesus Christ, being crucified on the cross to die. Love is completed in death. I pray that the story of Jesus who loved us until death will touch the heart of the Japanese and send a wave of love throughout the islands of Japan.

Do you want to know the true purpose of life? Do you want real peace in your heart? Do you want to experience the power of love and forgiveness? Then, come before the love of God!

Let go of material things, idols, pleasures, power, and wealth, which you have idolized for so long. Stop hating, accusing, and killing each other. Stop being mad at each other. People fall into despair, become frustrated, get divorced, and commit suicide. People without God are standing at the edge of a cliff. There is no way out.

Now, listen to the voice of God.

Take heed of the loving voice of God who is crying out continuously and steadfastly.

His love does not give up.

His love never changes.

His love is persistent and earnest.

He gives His life for the people He loves.

His love saves us from death and destruction.

His love heals hurts, pains, and sufferings.

His love lifts us from poverty, condemnation, and sickness.

My dear brothers and sisters in Japan, won't you come and kneel down before the love of God? Won't you look at Jesus who died on the cross for the sins of humankind 2,000 years ago? Jesus broke the power of sin and death, and rose again from the grave.

"Come to me, all you who are weary and burdened, and I will give you rest" (Matthew 11:28). "'Come now, let us reason together,' says the LORD. 'Though your sins are like scarlet, they shall be as white as snow; though they are red as crimson, they shall be like wool'"(Isaiah 1:18). "Believe in the Lord Jesus, and you will be saved - you and your household" (Acts 16:31).

Dear loving brothers and sisters, let's ride the wave of God's love. When Japan changes, Asia will change. When Asia changes, the world will change. Japan is in many ways the number one country in the world. It has everything except Jesus. When the Japanese people accept the love of God and become apostles of God's love, you will send shockwaves of love across the world. When South Korea and Japan love, reconcile, and cooperate with each other, the door of North Korea, which is tightly closed, will open. China will change. India, Africa, and Muslim countries will change. Let's ride the wave of God's amazing vision and love.

Please lay your hands on your heart and pray with me.

"God! I am a sinner. I rejected you. I was indifferent and pretended I didn't know you. Sometimes I thought I could live well without you. God, please forgive me. I loved the world instead of you. I pursued earthly materials, pleasure, and success. There were times when I thought that living without God was courageous and wise. I repent and come before you now. I open my heart to the love and forgiveness of you and that you give to us freely. Please accept me as I raise my two hands and approach you. I have criticized for no reason those who go to church or believe in God. Please change me and accept me at this moment. Change my family and my country, Japan. I pray in Jesus' name. Amen."

We will pray one last time.

"The living God. I have relied on my strength. Forgive me that I lived relying on my strength alone. Today, I have decided to believe in you and depend on you. I would like to invite Jesus Christ to come into my heart. From now on, I will go to church, read the Bible, and pray. Please help me. I pray in Jesus' name. Amen."

When the Christians of South Korea and Japan reconcile and are united, the historical conflict between the two countries will be resolved. The conflict between regions, countries, and people will be done away. Those who do not believe in Jesus say that it is impossible for South Korea and Japan to reconcile. However, I believe that it can come true, because reconciliation is God's plan for world peace.

We want to move quietly and constantly towards Japan. In the past, Pastor Billy Graham and Pastor Franklin Graham held a public evangelistic rally in a large arena in Japan that attracted many people. Also, Pastor Yonggi Cho and Pastor Benny Hinn held a Holy Spirit rally where people saw many miracles. These rallies were for Christians in Japan. However, non-Christian Japanese did not show much interest in them.

What then can we do to attract Japanese who do not know Jesus? There are two ways through which we can invite them to come to such rallies.

The first way is by using culture. I thought that if we invited Korean celebrities who are popular and influential in Japan, many Japanese would show interest. Many Japanese who do not know Jesus may very well be interested in the Korean Wave,[21] and many Korean celebrities are Christians. The second way is by evangelizing the next generation, sharing the Gospel with the youth who will lead Japan into the future. To do so, we could hold concerts involving Korean singers and actors who are famous among Japanese youth.

Love Sonata is an evangelistic rally that was designed and based on these two above-mentioned methodologies. Love Sonata is a cultural evangelistic rally that partnered with CGNTV and Duranno. Nowadays, the internet and television are top forms of media that could be used to share the Gospel to young people. We

---

[21] Korean wave or *Hallyu* is a newly coined term used to refer to the popularity of South Korean entertainment and culture across Asia and other parts of the world.

1. God's Love Story for Japan: Love Sonata

used CGNTV to produce live broadcasts of Love Sonata around the world, while Duranno conducted the seminars. Churches and missionaries from other countries can definitely help in taking this rally further.

Love Sonata is not a one-time event. It will be held repeatedly just like the waves that hit the shore over and over. We would like to invite many Japanese to the rally.

Preparing Love Sonata through 40 days of early morning prayer

Love Sonata for Japan started in 2007 with 40 days of early morning prayer at Onnuri Community Church. At the end of 2006, God gave me a heart to launch 40 days of early morning prayer meetings. When I thought about my health at that time, it seemed impossible to go through such an ordeal. But by faith, I declared that we would start the prayer meetings. I told our church that everyone who was healthier than I was (as someone who was on dialysis) should come to the prayer meetings.

The result was phenomenal. From the first day, people flocked to church. Almost 10,000 members rushed to church every morning. They were filled with passion. The morning prayer started at 5:00 a.m., but the main sanctuary was packed with people by 4:00 a.m. At 5:00 a.m., Duranno Hall, Handong Hall, and Vision Hall, where the service was broadcasted live, were filled as well. The passion was so intense that it did not seem to decline after one or two days. Moreover, people started to gather at the main sanctuary earlier and earlier as the days went by.

Amazing miracles started to take place during the meetings.

Members shared their testimonies on the internet, and I read those at every meeting. As people listened to the miracles performed by our living God, the same miracles began to happen with other members as well.

Two meetings were held at the Olympic Gymnastic Arena instead of our main sanctuary. The thrill of that day still resonates in my heart today. On the second meeting that was held in the arena, more than 28,000 people gathered. We praised God until we lost our voices, waving the flags of the nations. We projected a laser light display and celebrated. No matter how I look at it, that momentous event was not made possible by the power of man.

For the entire 40 days, the enthusiasm never cooled down, and we went forward like a speeding train. The special early morning prayer meetings were held under the anointing of the Holy Spirit until the last day. It was the grace of God.

Why did God pour out such grace to our church? There are probably many reasons, but one thing I believe for sure is Love Sonata. God poured out His grace upon us in advance so He could do what He wants us to do. He prepared us and empowered us in advance. He made us one.

Love Sonata started with prayer and was prepared with prayer. Many people interceded for Love Sonata during the process, and we continued to prepare everything with desperate and passionate prayer.

Love Sonata begins.

On March 29, 2007, Love Sonata finally began in Okinawa. Japanese people started to line up at the entrance of the Conven-

1. God's Love Story for Japan: Love Sonata

tion Hall an hour before the event started. Over 2,800 people filled the venue. On that day, 97 non-believers decided to accept Jesus, and 98 non-believers expressed interest in knowing more about the Savior.

The next day, Love Sonata was held in Fukuoka. Some people began to line up as early as 11:00 a.m. to participate in the evening event. My heart was touched. At the event, 97 non-believers decided to become Christian, and 95 people showed interest in Jesus. God gave us courage through the first Love Sonata held in Okinawa. He reminded us that it is neither a foolhardy challenge nor an impossible task. At the leadership reception that was held before Love Sonata, Pastor Kuniyoshi Mamoru of Naha Baptist Church shared that "Korea and Japan are close but distant countries. We have had past hurts, but because Korean Christians first forgave and loved us, we were able to host Love Sonata. I am confident that this event will shock both believers and non-believers. I am sure that an amazing thing will happen in Okinawa."

The next day, for the first time in nearly 10 years, the churches in Fukuoka joined hands and partnered with each other. This initiated unity and harmony among Christians. The cooperation between South Korean churches and Japanese churches inspired the Christians in both countries.

The wave of reconciliation and forgiveness also spread among Korean Christians who came to serve at Love Sonata. Over 450 Christians worked tirelessly from dawn until evening to help out with this event. They interceded for the salvation of the Japanese people outside the venue. During the time of blessing, the visiting Korean Christians opened their hands wide and poured God's blessing onto the Japanese. They sang the blessing song until the last Japanese in attendance had left the venue. The Christians of South Korea and Japan who had interceded for the event hugged each other as tears rolled down their cheeks. They said, "We hated each other before, but now we forgive and love each other."

Blossoming team ministries

Another amazing result from organizing Love Sonata was that team ministries flourished. Onnuri Community Church's local campuses in Seobinggo, Yangjae, Suwon, Bucheon, Daejeon, Hamyangju, Pyeongtaek, and Incheon worked together and formed several teams for Love Sonata. The leaders of Onnuri Community Church in Tokyo, Osaka, Ueda, Yokohama, Yachio, and Nagoya actively participated as well, and their members also helped out according to their gifts. CGNTV and Duranno also established a solid network with our church.

Before Love Sonata, these entities had work together and functioned well according to their strengths and roles, but through Love Sonata, they were able to form perfect teamwork, truly belonging to one body.

Likewise, Handong Global University and the Shingdonga Educational Foundation, which is made up of Jeonju University, Vision College of Jeonju, Youngsaeng High School, and Ongoul Female High School, caught the vision and participated in Love Sonata. Teamwork for teamwork's sake has no power, but teamwork that is forged to achieve God's vision has power.

If Onnuri Community Church had worked alone for Love Sonata, the event would not have had the same dynamic that it

1. God's Love Story for Japan: Love Sonata

has now. We had power because all these partnering organizations cooperated.

CGNTV Japan was established in October 2006, and I believe that CGNTV is a gift from God to spread the Gospel effectively in the country. At first, we planned to broadcast for only 12 hours. However, without thinking, I declared that we would broadcast in Japanese 24 hours a day, and to keep that promise, we started broadcasting in Japanese for 24 hours. Many Japanese trusted us and began tuning into the program.

Duranno also started translating their major books into Japanese to enhance the effectiveness of sharing God's Word through Love Sonata. They translated the Bible and books for the next generation and are still translating more books.

Vision Church members in China and the United States also participated in Tokyo Love Sonata.

Love Sonata should not end as a one-off rally. Follow-up programs should be offered continuously, and so we are planning to provide programs like one-to-one discipleship training, Quiet Time, and evangelism training in Japan.

Duranno and CGNTV will spearhead this task. Duranno will translate and offer resources and hold seminars so that churches in Japan can be firmly established. CGNTV, on the other hand, is aiming to broadcast Japanese programs to provide training. Through Love Sonata, we will see even more beautiful teamwork between South Korean and Japanese churches.

Love Sonata must go on. I hope that Japanese churches will take a more active and leading role in the future. Japanese and South Korean churches should be more actively involved in team ministries.

Lay leadership showed their worth.

Lay leaders proved their worth through Love Sonata. Elders, deaconesses, and members who were receiving training at the Elders Training Academy as chosen elders participated in Love Sonata by forming an intercessory team that prayed continuously during the event. Also, lay leaders wore white clothes and light blue scarves as they served as ushers and handled registration.

During Osaka Love Sonata held in May, it was the lay leaders who gave the lecture at seminars that were held during the day. Elder Nam-sik Lee, the president of Jeonju University, gave a lecture on "Laity Revolution." He explained that many laypeople are passive in their faith life and think that going to church on Sundays is enough. He added that if a pastor is a coach, laypeople are the athletes, whose mission is to evangelize. He emphasized that laypeople should enthusiastically make known the will of God at their workplaces, with their families, and around the world. Also, Ms. Ae-ran Moon, a deaconess and an advertising expert who worked in the area for over 30 years, lectured on "Declaring the Gospel at the Center of the World." Finally, Jang-soo Lee, a recognized movie and TV drama director, gave a lecture on "Eternal Protagonist, Jesus Christ."

These topics were difficult for pastors to take on, but these laypersons tackled them amazingly. Their lectures received very good responses from the audience and were more influential than the pastors' lectures. They were powerful and effective because these three laypersons commanded a positive influence in the world through their unique positions. Love Sonata served as a platform where the lay leaders truly proved their worth. We also held a forum where over 400 leaders from South Korea and over 300 leaders from Japan came together. They were ordinary Christians who were leaders in different fields - political, cultural, economic, and educational.

Love Sonata is not an event led by pastors but a place where ordinary Christians can blossom with their gifts. We will continue to send one-to-one discipleship and Open Worship trainers to help coach ministers of new believers.

Even today, many lay professionals are volunteering for Love Sonata. As Mary broke her alabaster jar and poured expensive perfume on Jesus' feet, these laypersons have offered their time, resources, and gifts to fulfill God's dream. Love Sonata is an opportunity for lay leaders to become warriors, not bystanders.

Customized Evangelism Rally

Love Sonata is a cultural evangelistic rally. To share the Gospel of Christ, Love Sonata actively utilizes cultural elements that are suitable for the Japanese. This evangelism rally was designed and carried out having the target in mind. The programs were not what we preferred or what was appropriate for us. Instead, we prepared programs that were suitable for the Japanese and what they would be interested in. We used all the know-how we gained by holding customized evangelism rallies and Open Service at Onnuri Community Church, and we believe that we were able to share the Gospel effectively by using cultural methods that suited our target audience.

South Korean celebrities, who are well-known in Japan and who love Japan, came forward. They testified clearly in their language. We also offered performances that the Japanese would appreciate, including gayageum[22], B-Boy, pop music, ballet, and piano performances. We did our best to create videos, too. During the time of blessing, we placed flower crowns on everyone (we made the crowns in advance in South Korea), congratulated one another, and threw paper planes that had our dreams written on them.

I kept the sermon strictly about the Gospel. Although we approached our Japanese audience using culture as a tool, what we really wanted to give to them was the Gospel, nothing else.

At Osaka Love Sonata, the pastor who was supposed to give the benediction prayer forgot about it because he was too busy throwing paper planes with everyone. Every time a session ended, the hearts of people opened, and their faces lit up. Famous South Korean actors and actresses, including Ryeo-won Jung, Yeon-soo Oh, and Ji-chang Son, shared their testimonies. Steve Yoo and Esther Park put on dance performances with the worship team. Also, Seul-ki Lee played the gayageum, a traditional Korean stringed instrument, Se-hun Jung gave a pop opera performance, and soprano opera singer Young-mi Kim rendered a beautiful solo performance. The Japanese audience cheered and was naturally absorbed in the event.

On the first day, I shared a message on "The Way, the Truth and the Life" and on the second day on "Faith, Hope, and Love." The first day's sermon went like this.

---

22 Zither-like Korean instrument with 12 strings

1. God's Love Story for Japan: Love Sonata

There are three things that people have lost today. The first is "the way," the goal of life; the second is "the truth," the center of life; and the third is "the life," the energy of life.

First, let's take a closer look at the way. The way pertains to one's purpose and the direction in life. It is the meaning of life. When people are lost or have gone astray, they are devasted and frustrated. They give up and take their own life.

What is death, in essence? Where are we from, what are we doing, and where are we headed? We eat and sleep, and the sun rises again the next day. Where did we come from and where are we going?

There is one thing I can predict for sure, and that is we will all die. We grow old day by day and one day, we will die. Sometimes, we feel like as though we are mere beasts. We're human beings, but we find ourselves living like animals. Also, sometimes, we feel like robots. Who are we, really?

There are two kinds of people. First, there are those who believe in their own strength. They are their own god. Believing in one's own power means they consider themselves their own god. People like this give up hope, feel desperate and lonely, go astray, and even commit suicide. Second are those who believe in God, and because they depend on God, they have hope. They have eternal life, faith, and hope. They create and build.

What kind of person are you? Do you believe in God? More importantly, what kind of God do you believe in? There are two types of God. The gods created by man and the real God. Most of the gods people believe in are created by people. Ancestors, mountains, and trees can be gods. Some people believe that Mount Fuji is a god. But they are not the real God. Gods made by humans are false gods, and are called idols. You may be comforted by the gods, but when you die, the gods will betray you.

We must believe in the one true God. He is the creator, and we are his creation. How can creation understand the creator fully? The creator is the subject of our worship. We must worship him and believe in him.

If we are lost in life, it is because we have lost God. Jesus speaks to us today. He said, "Do not let your hearts be troubled. Trust in God; trust also in me" (John 14:1). I would like to encourage you to believe in the real God today. If you have believed in yourself, in false gods, or in a god you have created, I would like to encourage you to change your life today.

As we were conceived by our parents, there is one who created all human beings. He is the creator, God. He sent His son because He loves us. His son is Jesus Christ. He was crucified on the cross and died for us. The savior must be both God and man at the same time. The one who can save human beings must die for human beings. And not just die, but He must rise again from the dead. If He did not rise again, He could not be our savior. Jesus Christ is risen and is here now with us. He said, "I am the way and the truth and the life. No one comes to the Father except through me" (John 14:6).

Jesus Christ is the way in life. He is not just one of the ways, but He is the only way and the absolute way. People think that they can be saved if they live morally. But living a moral and good life doesn't save us. People say it's important to live sincerely, but sincerity does not save us.

1. God's Love Story for Japan: Love Sonata

Salvation is like swimming in water. An Olympic gold medalist swimmer, for instance, could easily cross the Han River and maybe even the Korean Straits. However, no matter how well he swims, he cannot swim across the Pacific Ocean. To do that, he must fly in a plane. Just as with religions made by man, the swimmer can only swim a certain distance, but to make it all the way through, just like taking a plane, you must choose Jesus Christ to be saved.

Some say that there are many ways, such as through Buddhism, Confucianism, and Islam, but that is not the case. There is only one way to heaven. We can go to heaven only when we believe that Jesus Christ, the son of God, came to this world and gave His life on the cross for us.

We have lost the truth in our lives. At the center of our life, there should be truth, shining our path like a bright lamp. Having a way is not enough. There must be light guiding the way. If the path is in darkness, it will be very difficult to reach our destination. We need the bright light of truth.

Is having a way and light enough? No, those are not enough. There is one more important thing, and that is life. Without life, there is no strength to walk the bright path. What good is a great car if it doesn't have fuel? Cars must move. A person that does not move is probably dead. People today seem to be living in graves. Why is that? It's because they don't have life. Why does a tree not bear fruit? It doesn't bear fruit when it doesn't have life. When does a plant not have flowers? Again, when it doesn't have life.

There are many fake flowers in the world. Artificial flowers do not have fragrance and cannot bear fruit. People today are like fake flowers. They wear beautiful clothes and makeup, but they are like dead men.

Are you dead or alive? Is there sin, lust, jealousy, and envy in your heart? Is there an evil spirit in you? How can you fix this?

Jesus is life. Life is the opposite of death. People with life have no death. People with life have no unlawfulness or darkness. When you have life, there is joy, peace, purpose in life, and excitement. When death comes today, Christians can die with joy. Christians are not afraid of death, sickness, or failure.

I would like to introduce one person to you. He wants to be in you but will not force you to take Him in. He only comes in when you invite Him. He respects us. He will be the light of truth in your life. He will give life to those who have gone astray in death and sin.

Don't you want to meet God? It is very easy to meet Him. He doesn't ask you to fast or give an offering. He doesn't ask you to work hard. He only asks of you one thing, and that is to say, "I will accept Jesus."

Tokyo Love Sonata

The Tokyo Love Sonata was phenomenal because all the preparation and talents that Onnuri Community Church had accumulated were used for this rally. No words can explain the enthusiasm of the crowd that filled the Super Arena Hall in Saitama. Sisters and brothers from South Korea entered the venue as early as 9:00 a.m. They were full of excitement and exhilaration. On January 2007, over 5,000 Korean Christians prepared for the rally by praying in the early mornings and coming to Japan at their own expense. They came praying and dreaming. They dreamed of South Korea and Japan reconciling and becoming one.

1. God's Love Story for Japan: Love Sonata

The Love Sonata rally at the Super Arena was divided into four parts. The first part began at 2:00 p.m. and was for Koreans. It started with missionary Jae-chang Byun's preaching and pastor Jun-seok Ra's prayer.

It was followed by the second part, which was led by the Japanese churches. Japanese brothers and sisters started to enter the venue at 3:00 p.m., and by 5:00 p.m. the hall was packed with people. The choir was made up of 600 Japanese and 400 Korean singers. They sang "Hallelujah" and it was ecstatic, reminding us of heaven.

The third part was the highlight of Tokyo Love Sonata, and it was an amazing miracle. Over 20,000 people who filled the Saitama Super Arena laughed, cried, and clapped together upon hearing the special performances and preaching. After the message had been proclaimed, an altar call was given, followed by a special stage presentation from celebrities. Then, we asked all the Christians and those who decided to believe in Jesus to turn on a small light, and we lit up the arena, creating a splendid sight like that of the Milky Way. It was like a grand chorus of love and reconciliation. It was a touching and dramatic movie that only the Holy Spirit could direct. It was a special moment when people become one, beyond national boundaries, age, and culture.

The fourth part was for young people. After Pastor Gyu-dong Kim's message, young Koreans and Japanese jumped up and down and praised God together. They proclaimed the name of Jesus and prayed for the revival of Japan.

Tokyo Love Sonata was not a one-day festival. God was already at work at the Leadership Forum held at the Prince Park Tower

Hotel in Tokyo, the night before the rally. Over 900 political, economic, cultural, educational, and religious leaders from South Korea and Japan gathered at the forum. Leaders from Taiwan also came to the event. There was love and reconciliation, as the leaders read out a declaration for the peace and development of Asia. The Gospel of Jesus Christ was also declared. It was a night of hope and vision. It was a night of miracles performed by God.

Meanwhile, the Passion Rally, a rally for the youth at Yamato Calvary Church, was simultaneously held with the Ezra Rally, also for the young people at Yodobashi Church. Young people from South Korea and Japan became one in Jesus and sang about the love of God. Also for two days, we held a church revival seminar under the theme "The Gospel and Culture" at Yodobashi Church for Japanese church leaders. All these events served as waves of enthusiasm that were added together, creating a huge wave of love and the Gospel at Saitama Super Arena. God gave us a dream. When we obeyed his call and put it into practice, God moved us all and wrote a new history.

This Love Sonata made me feel like I was at Onnuri Community Church in Seoul, not in Tokyo. Korean Christians seemed like they were with us from the very beginning, not just at one point in time. I strongly felt that we were one. We were a community of Jesus' love.

The members of Onnuri Community Church embraced Japan with a humble, unselfish and serving heart. The women served Japan without sparing themselves. For the Japanese, it is our culture to feel the burden to repay after receiving so much, but there

1. God's Love Story for Japan: Love Sonata

is no way we can repay Onnuri Community Church. I believe we can only repay your church by keeping the love we received from you before God. The members of Yodobashi Church want to be awake all the time and learn the attitudes of Christians at Onnuri Community Church.

Although Japan's response to Love Sonata was not enough, when we look at Japanese churches today and those Christians who participated in Fukuoka Love Sonata, I believe that something amazing will happen through this amazing event in ministering to Japan. After Pastor Billy Graham's rally in Japan, churches here rarely came together in unity to hold a large event. We were losing confidence that we could do it.

However, as we invited people for the glory of God, we once again felt the heart of God in a mighty way. We saw a movement allowing Japanese churches to closely work among themselves and partner with each other, even beyond denominations. We are motivated into believing that we can do it and so we tell ourselves, "Let's do it. We can do it." In the history of Christianity in Japan, there has never been a time when these many churches gathered together for such a short period of time in Tokyo. It is truly an amazing and monumental event. It is a living testimony. I pray that God will protect Pastor Yong-jo Ha's health.

- Mineno, Yodobashi Church, Senior Pastor

The Holy Spirit is leading us! Since 1999, I traveled to Japan from the United States to do mission work. Three years ago, I moved to Japan and lived at the Matsuura Mission Center as a missionary. I have been doing "caravan evangelism" since I started doing mission work in Japan. Caravan evangelism is driving a caravan across Japan to distribute leaflets in areas the Gospel has not reached.

I stayed in churches in different regions for a week to 10 days and distributed leaflets. During the process, I witnessed the miserable reality of Japanese churches. Many churches only had a few members although they had been in ministry for several decades. Some churches did not have a pastor. Naturally, I was interested in the revival of small churches. I sent young Koreans to churches in Japan through Campus Crusade for Christ and tried to support those churches through short-term missions. However, this effort reached its limit. The programs prepared by the short-term mission teams were very similar and after awhile Japanese members were able to memorize them.

I was deeply moved by Pastor Ha's vision for missions to Japan. I could feel that the Holy Spirit was leading the work. The weekly prayer meeting with Japanese pastors while preparing for the rally was great. At first, the pastors in my group seemed a bit cold. Pastors from small churches grouped amongst themselves, and they seemed to have difficulty in interacting with the pastors of big churches. But through Love Sonata, the pastors became one and fellowshipped with one another. It was beautiful. I look forward to and pray for the revival of churches in Japan through a continuous partnership with Onnuri Community Church.

-Byung-myun Chung, Matsuura Mission Center, Missionary

Thank you for coming all the way from South Korea and serving us according to Onnuri Community Church's vision for

missions. We are praying for the event and doing our best to participate instead of just receiving the blessings. Usually, in a rally of about 2,000 people, around 1,500 are Christians, and only 500 are non-Christians. However, this rally is the other way around. More than 80 percent of the audience were unbelievers. I believe that this is unprecedented and it happened because of the hard work, service, and prayer of Onnuri Community Church.

I believe that the day Okinawa Love Sonata was held was the day the revival of Okinawa began. We pray that Korean churches and Japanese churches will become one and embrace the revival. Okinawa churches will run to the world with you. We look forward to having more fellowship and partnership.

-Kuniyoshi, Naha Baptist Church, Senior Pastor

Okinawa is thirsty. There was an overwhelming number of participants for Love Sonata. This is the time of harvest. We are praying for more people to receive salvation. Thank you for Onnuri Community Church's spirituality, prayers, and service. It is amazing that we can hold a rally beyond denominations.

-Kani, World Mission Church, Pastor

We are looking forward to the event. Japan is often called the "graveyard for missionaries." This country is like a monster that does not respond to any form of missions or evangelism. It has been 20 years since I came to Japan. I often thought and asked myself, "Could there be any other country that is thoroughly abandoned as Japan?" Most of the Japanese say that they have never seen the Bible, which is the world's best-selling book. Church chapels are treated as wedding venues, and Christmas is taken advantage of to boost sales at department stores. Every year, the number of churches declines. Pastor Ha said that he could not help but cry when thinking about Japan. I believe that what he felt about the situation in Japan was truly from his heart.

Fukuoka is one of the five major cities in Japan, but it has not seen any united body of churches. For over 10 years, churches here could not put together an event. Against such a backdrop, I heard about Love Sonata, and I thought it was a great way of sharing the Gospel in this country where the Korean Wave is booming. Since the churches here are small, organizing a big event is financially burdensome, which was why when Onnuri Community Church told us that it would provide financial support for the event, the pastors started to respond.

We fasted for 40 days and shared the Gospel during Love Sonata. On March 11, for the first time since our church was established, 19 new believers came. We were surprised and did not know how to deal with them. Many pastors became very interested in providing education to new believers and training in one-to-one discipleship that will be offered after Love Sonata.

We believe that the Onnuri Community Church's evangelism method that uses culture is effective in Japan because the Japanese will open their hearts to cultural things. I think we failed in using traditional evangelism methods because we did not understand the Japanese. Therefore, we have high hopes for Love Sonata.

-Il Kim, Full Gospel Fukuoka Church, Senior Pastor, the headquarter church of Fukuoka Love Sonata

1. God's Love Story for Japan: Love Sonata

Osaka Love Sonata was a festival filled with God's grace and joy. We witnessed the wind of the Holy Spirit that swept across the islands of Japan starting from Okinawa via Fukuoka to Osaka.

We were most blessed by Pastor Ha's words on life. His message was filled with God's love as the Lord seeks after lost souls in Japan. He revealed that he is receiving dialysis three times a week, and even had one before the rally. Yet, we couldn't see in him an image of a sick person because he enthusiastically preached God's Word for the salvation of one more soul. I am deeply moved by him as he preached the Gospel without fearing death.

Over 600 volunteers from Onnuri Community Church brightened Love Sonata. They paid for their own expenses to come to Japan. They ushered and served the participants at the entrance and various spots. They were like angels sent from heaven. Their service will become seeds of the Gospel, surrounded with love, and sowed in Japan.

The programs that were designed to lead the participants to Christ were amazing. Well-known Korean celebrities who were at the center of the Korean Wave shared their testimonies and gave a variety of performances. These were more than enough to open the hearts of Japanese and pique their interest in heaven. When we placed the flower garlands on the heads of Japanese and blessed them with the song, "You are Born to be Loved," Japan was no longer a distant country but a nation that became one in God.

I can clearly remember the last performance we did together. We all wrote our hopes on a paper plane and threw them to fly and float in the air. Participants wrote their dreams, hopes, and prayer requests, and released the paper planes as if they were little children. We all became one. With one heart, we wrote our visions and dreams for Love Sonata to bring revival to Japan and lifted them up to God.

In the morning before I returned to South Korea, I visited Osaka Onnuri Church, the first Onnuri Vision Church. I heard that the church was established by the late Pastor Samuel Kim, who planted the church in Japan where less than one percent of the population believed in Christ. I believe that because God loves Japan so much he used Pastor Kim's martyrdom to establish this church and prepare it ahead of time for today's Love Sonata. The church was God's seed for the Gospel in Japan. I pray that this church will become a spiritual generator in Japan that will reap much fruit.

During the event, two Korean-Japanese guides who escorted us around came to accept Jesus Christ. They said they became Christians because while they were guiding us around, they saw the faces of people and were impressed by their happy countenances as they were coming out of the event. After those two guides had said the prayer of acceptance, an elder gave them a CGNTV satellite reception antenna as a gift. So their joy was doubled.

-Woon-seob Jung, Christian CEO, Volunteer

I believe that this Osaka rally will empower the Japanese. Among the 1,000 staff members of Yodogawa Christian Hospital, 300 of them attended the morning service every day. The Japanese people have gone through years of difficulties in their faith because of Buddhism, which has a long history in Japan. From today's special seminar, the message that we should help a new believer have a dream touched my heart. The way I can put it is that the Spirit came upon me. It was a moving lecture that I accepted without resistance. As a pastor, I wondered how the pastor of Onnuri Community Church would preach, and as I heard him, I was so blessed. I would like to thank members of Onnuri Community Church for giving your time, prayer, and resources to bring salvation to Japanese souls.

-Tamura Hidenori,
Osaka Yodogawa Christian Hospital Church, Pastor

I would like to write Acts chapter 29 as well. I live in Japan now and want to share God to the people around me, but it has not been easy because of their ancestral religion. I lived in the United States for 18 years and participated in many Bible studies. But today, as I listened to Pastor Jun-seok Ra's sermon and lecture, I learned that we must act with our whole being and not just think with our head. I am happy to listen to the living word of God in Osaka. In the past, every time I came to Japan, I felt down, as if dark clouds overshadowed my heart, but yesterday, I arrived in Japan and felt that something was different. I believe that Love Sonata changed the atmosphere in Japan. Now, I have hope that even Japan can change.

-Gushi Kajue, Gakuenmae Seisho Church, Member

I hope that Love Sonata will bring revival to Japan. I am a pastor preparing to plant a church. I heard about Love Sonata from a sister in my denomination and I wanted to come. During the rally, I felt God's tremendous love for Japan. As Pastor Ha said, "I hope Japan will see revival." -Ono Hideyaki, Pastor

I felt loved. I came because my friend Aida invited me. It was my first time to attend a church event, and it was great. I felt the love from everyone's smiling faces, the warm welcomes, and the gifts the church prepared. I could feel the love in the rally and festive atmosphere. The programs were great, so I enjoyed the festival.

-Majuri Sachiko

It was an amazing festival. I was interested in Love Sonata because Japanese churches don't often have huge events like this. I look forward to new and amazing things happening because of Love Sonata. I think launching paper planes was amazing and I also felt the message was truly genuine. I experienced tremendous love from God's Word, the attitudes of the people, and the energy of the venue.

-Koyasu Junji, Kobe Ichibaku Church, Pastor

Vision is a mosaic.

When I first caught the vision of Love Sonata, I could only see Japan and thought only about the revival of churches in Japan. But as Love Sonata progressed, I started to see a glimpse of God's immense vision. I felt confident that we would be able to evangelize China as well when we held hands with Japan.

In the meantime, the leaders of several Taiwanese churches who had heard about Love Sonata asked us if we could hold a similarly large rally in Taiwan as well. Taiwanese church leaders had been participating in Onnuri Community Church's festivals, and we also held leadership and ministry seminars in Taiwan. They said we must do missions to China with Taiwan. I thought that as Korean and Japanese churches become one and if Taiwanese churches worked with us to do missions to China, we would be able to do missions work more powerfully.

I dreamed of Japan, South Korea, and Taiwan doing missions work in China, and also dreamed of Japan, South Korea, Taiwan, and China sharing the Gospel in India. Soon, the door to Muslim countries, which rejected the Gospel, will be wide open. I felt like what used to be scattered pieces of a vision were finally coming together.

Onnuri Community Church has been doing missions work in Israel. Also, we adopted unreached tribes to evangelize. When the Gospel is spread effectively in Muslim countries, Israel and the Muslim world will be united. This will also allow us to do missions work more effectively in unreached tribes that are dominated by Muslims.

As I was praying, I realized that this is the Acts 29 Vision. As the puzzle pieces of the vision came together one by one, the whole picture became clearer. Vision is like a mosaic. As you take a step forward, you see the vision only, but when you obey God and move forward, you start to see the bigger picture as pieces connect with each other.

Love Sonata was like that. When we obeyed and began the work, it became clear why God poured so many blessings to Onnuri Community Church, as if the puzzle pieces were being put together. God's visions for customized evangelism rally, open worship, CGNTV, Duranno, and overseas missions all became connected.

Moreover, the unity of churches in Japan and South Korea,

as well as churches in Taiwan and China through missions made sense. Then, these churches will strive to do missions together in India, Muslim countries, and Israel. Through this, Islam and the Middle East will become united, and unreached tribes will hear the Gospel. The most important piece of the puzzle is Love Sonata, and God gave us this very important piece in 2007.

Love Sonata is God's dream.

Love Sonata is God's love song for Japan. It is a cultural evangelistic rally filled with joy and God's Word. It is the dream of God. I would like to talk about five aspects of Love Sonata.

Love Sonata is a revival. We experienced an amazing revival in our country a century ago. Christians, who were only one percent of the population, became the hope of our nation and its people. As we commemorate the centennial of the great 1907 revival movement of Pyongyang, we share the blessings and the grace of revival that God gave South Korea with churches in Japan through Love Sonata.

Love Sonata is reconciliation. South Korea and Japan have deep historical hurts and conflicts. When we can overcome the conflicts, reconcile with each other, and become one, we will see miracles in the world. The United States and Iraq, Israel and Palestine, and South Korea and North Korea will become one. During Love Sonata, churches came together and sang together beyond denominations, historical conflicts, and national boarders, giving hope to the world.

1. God's Love Story for Japan: Love Sonata

Love Sonata is missions.

Japan is a country that has everything. After Japan changes, Asia will also change, and then the world will change. When Korean and Japanese churches hold hands and do missions work together, missions to Asia will take an incredible leap. When Korean, Japanese, and Taiwanese churches cooperate with each other, the tightly closed doors of China will open, and when China's doors open, the door to Islam will open as well. Love Sonata begins with changing Asia, beyond the Korean peninsula and Japan.

Love Sonata is culture. Love Sonata is testing the effectiveness of a cultural evangelistic rally. No matter how famous a pastor becomes, non-believers won't care. However, if a popular Korean Wave celebrity comes, thousands of people will gather at the airports. That means that without using culture, it is hard to gather and engage non-Christians. We are developing a new model by using the cultural code of the Korean Wave to reach out to non-believers.

Love Sonata is God's dream. God wants Love Sonata to also run from Okinawa to Hokkaido. I will do everything to accomplish God's dream.

Epilogue

When I think about the Church, I feel happy.

There seems to be no other time when churches have been more collectively criticized than today. Even in the past, churches were attacked and slandered by anti-Christian groups. However, the intensity seems to be growing more these days. Indeed, there are negative aspects within churches and Christianity, but they are mostly internal problems.

The most unfortunate problem is the division among us. Groups of people come in and out of churches like foxes ruining the vineyards (Song of Solomon 2:15) and degrade the church's beautiful image in a self-deprecating manner. Do not be deceived by those who think they are called prophets or reformists. Belittling God and the Church cannot be justified for any reason.

I once had negative thoughts about churches as well. In particular, my negativity about the church was at its worse when I was in a missions organization. Back then, to me, all churches seemed rotten and powerless, like empty shells and whitewashed tombs. It seemed as though churches were without life and did not evangelize people, did not hold Bible studies and did not conduct discipleship training. I was disappointed by the churches that lacked love and devotion, and that did not send missionaries. I couldn't find anything to be excited for or to be moved by in churches.

In contrast, when I went to a missions organization, I felt like I was in heaven. There was life, passion, and enthusiasm. The people around me prayed all night. They did Bible studies and evangelized. Everything was dynamic. I could sense the aroma of living believers. I believed that this was the true way to live as a follower of Jesus.

For this reason, I hesitated to go to seminary, because it seemed better to serve God by not becoming a pastor. It seemed much more appealing to do ministry outside the church. During those times, I was concerned about the many problems in churches. I wondered, "How should I view churches? Should I go to seminary?"

Then, when I got sick and suffered during my military service, God reminded me that churches are precious. When my misconceptions about church disappeared, I was able to feel the true church of Jesus in my heart. I began to realize that churches are precious and holy.

The Church of God is eternal. Churches cannot rot or be powerless. Also, missions organizations are not eternal. They were established because there was a need, and they will disappear when the need disappears.

The Church will exist on the earth forever until the day the Lord returns. Walk away from the misguided prejudices and ideas about the Church. The true church Jesus established is not about denominations, institutions, or buildings. The Church is the body and bride of Christ. Institutions can be criticized, and the buildings can be attacked, but the Lord's true Church is not to be the subject of criticism. We must protect the holiness and purity of churches with our lives.

Whenever I think about the Church, tears roll down my cheeks, my heart beats, and I feel overwhelmed. I think about the Lord's glorious churches standing at the center of the world and lifting high the banner of Jesus Christ.

It is my responsibility to come into a church to serve, change, and renew the church. It is my responsibility to create a glorious church, which is the body of Christ. We do not have the authority to criticize, but the responsibility to serve.

I feel most honored to be a pastor. If I could re-live my life, I would walk the same path, and not regret it even after death. "In the last days, God says, I will pour out my Spirit on all people. Your sons and daughters will prophesy, your young men will see visions, your old men will dream dreams" (Acts 2:17).

A church anointed by the Holy Spirit. A church that performs miracles. A church that revives people. A church that dreams and sees visions. A church that saves the world and builds God's kingdom. This church is Onnuri Community Church. I want to die for Onnuri Community Church. I want to die while I preach. I want to die while I pray. I want to die while I share the Gospel on the mission field.

Epilogue

There is one thing I regret as I serve Onnuri Community Church. It is that I did not take care of my family enough. My wife always missed me. My children always longed for me. I did not properly carry out my role as a husband and father.

How foolish it is that only now I try to take care of my wife and pour out my life for my children! When I see my wife grow weak, I feel so sorry and sad. Yet, I believe it is not too late, and I will still try. I now have the heart to take care of my family at the expense of other things. I must grow mature in my old age.

I will leave Onnuri Community Church one day. How can I minister forever? How long can I live, and how much more can I work? I will be able to preach only as long as God allows my health to hold me up. This is my golden time. Onnuri Community Church is my dream and my everything. I want to live without regrets and with crazy passion. I don't want to be calculating. I want to live without finding fault in everything. I love the Church. I love the Church of the Lord. I love Onnuri.